S0-BBG-647

The Mystery of
MORAL RE-ARMAMENT

Other Books by the Author

COLONNADE

THE BEST OF BOTH WORLDS

BEAVERBROOK: A STUDY IN POWER AND FRUSTRATION

GUY BURGESS: A PORTRAIT WITH BACKGROUND

THE MYSTERY OF MORAL RE-ARMAMENT

A Study of Frank Buchman and His Movement

TOM DRIBERG

LONDON

SECKER & WARBURG

First published in England 1964 by
Martin Secker & Warburg Limited
14 Carlisle Street, Soho Square, W.1

Printed in Great Britain by
The Camelot Press Ltd., London and Southampton

CONTENTS

LIST OF ILLUSTRATIONS

ACKNOWLEDGEMENTS

MY thanks, and those of the publishers, are due to a large number of persons from whom I have obtained information on the history and operations of Moral Re-Armament and on the life of the late Dr Frank Buchman. Some of these are named in the text of the book; some, for reputable reasons, would not wish to be named.

In particular, I am grateful to those in charge of the well-equipped libraries at Mount Airy Seminary, Philadelphia, and Muhlenberg College, Allentown, for readily making available to me much documentary material on Dr Buchman's early life; to the Director of the Franklin D. Roosevelt Library, Hyde Park, New York, for undertaking a thorough search of President Roosevelt's official and personal papers, the results of which provided data for Chapter 5 of this book; to the National Assembly of the Church of England for permission to quote from the Report on MRA of the Social and Industrial Council (CA 1129 1955) and the *Report of Proceedings*, Vol. 35, No. 1 (1955); to the Editors of the *Times*, the *Guardian*, the *Daily Telegraph*, *The Observer*, the *Sunday Citizen*, the *New Statesman*, the *Spectator*, *Tribune*, and the *Christian Century*, and Sir Alan P. Herbert, Mr Wayland Young, Mr John Herbert, Mr Ivan Yates, Miss Honor Tracy, Mr Bamber Gascoigne, and the Revd Russell Barbour for permission to quote from letters and articles published in those periodicals; to the Student Christian Movement Press and the Bishop of Woolwich for permission to quote a passage from *Honest to God*; to Miss Fearne E. Booker for permission to quote passages from *The Group Movement* by the late Dr H. Hensley Henson, sometime Bishop of Durham; to Mr Sidney L. Bernstein for permission to quote from the transcript of Granada Television's *World in*

Action programme on MRA; to the Editor of the *New York World-Telegram* and Mr William A. H. Birnie for permission to reprint the whole of the interview in which Dr Buchman expressed his views on Hitler and the Nazi régime; and to the Editors and Librarians of the *New York Times*, the *Philadelphia Inquirer*, the Allentown *Morning Call*, and the *New Yorker*, who generously opened to me their extensive files on MRA.

I owe a special debt of gratitude to Sir Alan Herbert for letting me use the documents and letters which he accumulated when, as Senior Burgess for Oxford University, he was repeatedly involved in controversy with the Oxford Group, as MRA was then called.

Thanks are due also to the United States Mission Berlin, Berlin Documents Center for a photostat of a report on the Oxford Group by the Central Security Office of the SS.

Miss Sara Barker, National Agent of the Labour Party, kindly made a number of enquiries. Valuable material on Caux was provided by Mr Robert L. Kroon and other Geneva journalists; on MRA activities in Scotland by Mrs Janey Buchan, of Glasgow, and others; and on events in a grammar school (described in Chapter 17) by Mrs J. L. Wilson, of Germoe, Penzance.

A number of personal friends have been kind enough to read all or part of this book, in typescript or in proof. In addition to the publishers and their diligent staff, these include Mr Handasyde Buchanan, the Ven E. F. Carpenter, Archdeacon of Westminster, the Revd Canon F. Hood, Chancellor of St Paul's Cathedral, Mr E. R. Radcliffe, Mr Gore Vidal, and my wife. I must also thank Mr W. G. Stewart for assistance in research. All of these have made helpful suggestions, but the responsibility for any errors of fact or of judgement is mine alone. I shall be grateful for any factual corrections that may be sent to me.

Finally, I must express my thanks to the large number of correspondents, known to me personally or strangers, who have written to me and contributed personal reminiscences and documentation. Some of these have been of great value and have been made use of: I only regret that I could not use them all, either because, in some cases, independent verification was impossible or because it was necessary, in order to keep this study within reasonable compass, to select those examples of varying aspects of the subject which seemed most typical.

T. D.

INTRODUCTION

MOST PEOPLE in Britain, the Commonwealth, Western Europe, and America must have heard of the movement called Moral Re-Armament, usually known as MRA; for, apart from any more direct contact, most people must have read or glanced at some of the full-page newspaper advertisements, sponsored by MRA, which have appeared from time to time in recent years in many countries; and lengthy obituaries were published when the movement's founder, Dr Frank Buchman, died in August, 1961.

Most people, however, seem to have only a vague idea of what the movement actually is and what it stands for: this may be partly because, in some respects, its character is nebulous; partly because its name has twice been changed and, over the years, its objects and strategy have seemed to vary; and partly because its spokesmen have consistently shunned public oral debate.

It is necessary, therefore, to start by stating, in the barest outline and without (at this point) comment, something of MRA's history, beliefs and practices. These are examined more fully—and, I confess, less objectively—in various chapters of this book.

Dr Buchman (born 1878) was a Lutheran minister in Pennsylvania. In 1908, after a personal crisis, he had a 'conversion experience' in a chapel at Keswick, England. The movement that he founded some years later, in consequence of this experience, was originally called A First Century Christian Fellowship. Later it became more widely known as the Oxford Group or Oxford Group Movement. In 1938 Dr Buchman proclaimed the need for 'moral re-armament'; and this phrase became the movement's name. In the post-war years MRA has widened the scope of its activities, claiming to provide 'an ideology for democracy' in the struggle against Communism.

The ethical content of MRA's teaching is summed up in four absolutes: Absolute Honesty, Absolute Purity, Absolute Unselfishness, and Absolute Love. The two most important of its techniques are Sharing and Guidance: Sharing is the confession of sins, either privately to another member of the Group or semi-publicly in a Group meeting or 'house-party'; Guidance is believed to be obtained direct from God, especially during the morning 'quiet time' observed by all Buchmanites, when they lie on their beds or sit in silent groups, with pencil and paper, noting down the thoughts that come to them. If two Groupers, on checking, find that they have received conflicting guidance, their Guidance is cross-checked by that of the leader of the Group (and ultimately, if the contradiction is not resolved, at MRA headquarters). Converts to MRA are said to have been 'changed'; evangelists are 'life-changers'.

MRA stages World Assemblies, usually at one or other of its main centres. One of these is at Caux, in Switzerland, where, in the immediate post-war years, sympathisers acquired several large hotels and equipped them for the use of MRA. There is a $5-million 'training' (i.e., indoctrination) centre at Mackinac Island, off the coast of Michigan, USA; here 1,200 people at a time can be accommodated in some fifty buildings (including America's second largest television film studio). There is the relatively modest centre in Mayfair, London, consisting of several houses in which full-time workers and visiting VIPs are lodged: the latter are also entertained at Dr Buchman's old home in Berkeley Square (bought before the war, as a sixtieth birthday present to him, for £35,000 and now probably worth £200,000); there are offices and a bookshop round the corner, in Hays Mews. Newest major centre—'a power-house for Asia'—is at Odawara, near Tokyo.

There are also offices in Fifth Avenue, New York, and other American cities. MRA's many properties include the Westminster Theatre, London (owned, technically, by 'a distinct and separate' body, The Westminster Memorial Trust), where propaganda plays are presented; and its plays, films, and 'task-forces' are constantly touring the world. Further information on properties and benefactors will be found in Chapter 8.

Since Dr Buchman's death, there has been no appointment of a new Leader. (MRA's obituary hand-out on Buchman stated categorically: 'There will be no formal leader.') There may have been an attempt, in Britain, to establish 'collective leadership' through the Council of Management. Since MRA has no membership, in the strict sense of the word, this Council is not elected. It is presumably, therefore, self-appointed (or, originally, appointed, under Guidance, by Dr Buchman) and self-perpetuating.

Two leading veterans of MRA in Britain are Mr Loudon Hamilton, in whose rooms at Christ Church, Oxford, in 1921, it may be said that the movement first took shape decisively, and Mr Roger Hicks. In so far as any one man may be described as Buchman's successor, he is Mr Peter Howard—the movement's most prolific propagandist since his conversion from Beaverbrook journalism in 1941: he does not specifically claim the title of Leader, but states that he (not 'we') is responsible for the work of MRA. The national secretary is Mr Roland Wilson.

As I suggest towards the end of this book, speculations on the future of MRA, being necessarily based on guesswork, have little value. One point, however, relevant to the movement's present and future development, may be mentioned here, since it seems to have escaped general notice and may usefully be borne in mind in connection with the account given in several chapters of MRA's change of emphasis and 'image', from Christian evangelism to political ideology.

This point was made, concisely and exactly in the House of Commons on 7th October, 1941, when the Oxford Group was seeking exemption from military service for some of its lay evangelists, by Sir Robert Aske, Liberal National MP for Newcastle-upon-Tyne, East. Sir Robert, referring to the Memorandum of Association deposited by the Group when it obtained official recognition in 1939, quoted from it 'the real purposes' of the Group. These were defined in the Memorandum as 'the advancement of the Christian religion and, in particular, by the means and in accordance with the principles of the Oxford Group founded in or about the year 1921 by Frank Buchman.'

Sir Robert added 'The Group has no power to do anything outside the objects as stated in this Memorandum. If it set about secular objects, it would be doing something *ultra vires* and illegal.'

I

THE EARLY DAYS

Buchman: a first encounter—Childhood and youth—Doctrine of the Inner Light—Theocracy and God-control—College days—A hospice down town

One of the best descriptions of the physical presence of Dr Buchman, as seen by hundreds of thousands—perhaps millions—of people when he was at the height of his powers, is that given by an early disciple, Harold Begbie: 'tall, upright, stoutish, clean-shaven, spectacled, with that mien of scrupulous, shampooed, and almost medical cleanliness or freshness, which is so characteristic of the hygienic American'. He would then have been in his forties.

In old age his back was bent, his fingers twisted by arthritis, and the rather owl-like beakiness of his face became more pronounced; but his eyes retained their penetrating glint and, until within a year or two of his death, his memory remained keen; and his clothes were always impeccably tailored and pressed.

When I first met him, in 1928, at a Group house-party held, during a vacation, at one of the Oxford women's colleges, he fitted Begbie's description well. (He was then fifty.) I cannot now remember much about the other people I met there, except that Cuthbert Bardsley (now Bishop of Coventry) and Austin Reed, the men's outfitter, were among them, and that they all seemed friendly and pleasant enough to talk to. We waited on a sunlit lawn for Dr Buchman (whom, even then, they all called 'Frank') to join us. He came striding briskly across the grass, accompanied by two or three young men. He seemed to have that invaluable politician's or pastor's gift of instantly recognising people, for he hailed several by name as he passed them. 'Hi there, Mr Austin Reed!', he cried jovially. 'How's that lift-boy of yours coming along?' (I recall thinking at the time that it was considerate, or clever, of him to use the English 'lift' rather than the American 'elevator'.)

Later he took me to his room for a private talk. I asked some of the questions that people were already beginning to ask—why the Group's accounts were not published, where the money came from, and so on. 'Why', he cried with the utmost geniality, 'who'd be interested in our little accounts?' He pointed to a handsome overcoat hanging near the door: a friend had been 'guided' to give him that. Another friend—he drew me by the arm to the window—had been guided to provide the luxurious car that awaited him outside. It was the gentlest possible brush-off of questions that he gave no sign of finding at all awkward.

I did not succumb to his theories, or find his charm overwhelming, but his company was not disagreeable; certainly I did not feel what some others felt on meeting him, as I later read in a *New Yorker* profile by Alva Johnston—that he was apt to make 'an unfortunate first impression: the stranger is repelled by a sudden rush of ingratiating holiness'.

Though this was my first encounter with Dr Buchman, I had discovered the Buchmanites a few months earlier. 'Discovered' is not out of place; for I was then a reporter newly employed by the *Daily Express*; I had heard something from Oxford friends of this strange new religious group that was beginning to be talked about there; I had gone there at the news-editor's bidding—and because I was interested in such things, anyway—to see if there was a story in it; and the first report that I sent from Oxford was published on the front page of the *Express* and was, I believe, the first account of the Buchman Group to appear in Britain in a popular national newspaper. 'Follow-up' stories appeared on three succeeding days.

Since they provided me—an inexperienced journalist—with my first scoop, I might have been expected to be well-disposed to the Buchmanites. I mention this unimportant personal point merely because they have, since then, accused me of pursuing a 'vendetta' against them. Re-reading these *Express* reports now, I am relieved to find them reasonably well-balanced and objective. I attended and described a Sunday evening meeting of the Group in a private lounge at the Randolph Hotel: 'fully a hundred and twenty-five men were present, almost all undergraduates'. I interviewed Canon B. H. Streeter, of the Queen's College, who spoke well of the Group; Dr A. E. J. Rawlinson of Christ Church (later Bishop of Derby), who thought some of the Buchmanite manifestations 'extremely peculiar—one might almost say, grim'; the head of a college, who denounced the movement as 'a morbid sensualism masquerading under the guise of religion'; and Fr Ronald Knox, then chaplain to Roman Catholic undergraduates, who said (interestingly, in view of the theme of the book, *Enthusiasm*, which he was to publish twenty-two years later): 'I have been thinking that a revival of specifically "enthusiastic" religion was about due. These revivals usually come in cycles of about a century. . . .'

I also interviewed a number of undergraduates, and a senior member of the University who thought that Buchmanism presented 'every appearance of a schismatical body in embryo'; and the Vice-Chancellor himself, who made it clear that no immediate official action against the Group was contemplated.

By any standards, including 'worldly' ones, the career of Frank Nathan Daniel Buchman was remarkable. He was born on 4th June, 1878, in modest circumstances, in the small town of Pennsburg, Pennsylvania. In his youth he showed no special qualities of mind or spirit. At the age of thirty (like Mahomet) he felt that he was finished: professional failure was followed by acute nervous depression. In his early forties—though he had regained his faith and his zest and had begun his roving ministry—he was still unknown to the world at large. Yet by the time he died, aged eighty-three, the movement that he had created was known throughout the world and he had been photographed with and decorated by more monarchs, statesmen, and other potentates than any other religious leader except, possibly, the Pope.

To some extent—to a greater extent, perhaps, than most Americans today—Frank Buchman must have been conditioned by hereditary influences and childhood background; for he belonged to an ethnic and cultural minority that preserved jealously, almost fiercely, traditional values and ancestral ways of thought and speech. Pennsburg is in the heart of the 'Pennsylvania-Dutch' country; Buchman's forefathers had migrated to Pennsylvania from a German-speaking canton of Switzerland, and throughout his life he showed a special affection both for his native state—especially for his home town, Allentown, to which his parents moved when he was fifteen—and for the land and people of Germany. It was at Freudenstadt in the Black Forest, where he died, that, treading the soft carpet of pine-needles, he had first been inspired to coin the phrase 'moral re-armament' (which in 1950, consequently, he called 'a German product'); and of all the post-war European statesmen whose support he canvassed so assiduously, Dr Adenauer was probably the one who responded most wholeheartedly. Earlier, he may even have been attracted to the Nazi leaders more by the fact that they were German than by their political notions (for he had no such links, so far as I know, with Mussolini or Franco).

A study of Buchman's life by E. W. Hocker, published in the Philadelphia *Evening Bulletin* on 13th February, 1929, refers to his 'conservative Pennsylvania-German antecedents'. Pennsburg is in the upper Perkiomen region. 'In his youth', says Mr Hocker, 'scarcely a word of English was heard in that community.'

In 1939, when both of them were in their sixties, one[1] who

[1] E. S. Gerhard, of the Department of Languages, Northeast High School, Philadelphia, writing on 10th January, 1939, to Dr Ernst Pfatteicher, President of the Ministerium of Pennsylvania and Adjacent States.

had known Buchman as a boy described him thus, in a letter tinged inexplicably with resentment:

> I attended school (Private Co-ed)[1] with 'Frankie' Buchman way back in the early '90s when Frankie still wore knee-breeches. . . . Frankie's father was a butcher at the time.[2]
>
> . . . Later his father conducted a tavern in the village, and I as a young man was on the ice-wagon at the time; I put many a chunk of ice on the copper coil behind the bar to keep the beer cool. . . .
>
> I still see him at school enjoying nothing more than loitering around with the girls indulging in silly, gossipy, trifling talk. . . . *Gossip* is the core of his whole movement.

This correspondent (who failed to recall that, though Buchman's father sold liquor, there were only soft drinks on the family dinner-table) went on to tell what he had witnessed, more recently, at a Buchmanite evening-dress party at an hotel: a man, in the presence of his wife, 'owned up that he had had improper relations with another man's wife'. A minister, shocked by this unseemly disclosure, walked out. The letter continues:

> I have wished I could get back of his YMCA work at Penn State, it seems 'fishy', but no-one seems to know the facts.

The 'YMCA work' was to come later. Before that, Frank Buchman went on from school to Muhlenberg College at Allentown—a substantial and respected institution, founded in 1848 and affiliated to the United Lutheran Church in America—and to Mount Airy, the Lutheran theological

[1] Perkiomen Seminary, a small church school.

[2] Franklin Buchman senior married Sarah Greenwald in 1875, and settled on her father's farm. Their first son, John William, died in infancy. At the time of Frank's birth his father was running a grocery business.

seminary in the suburbs of Philadelphia at which he was trained for the ministry.[1]

In his youth, therefore, he seems rarely to have left his native State, and the influences and atmosphere of home, college, and seminary alike would have helped to preserve undiluted the Pennsylvania-Dutch traditions of his forbears. Some of these traditions he never lost. On his seventy-fifth birthday the Allentown *Morning Call* published a special supplement in his honour. An article in this supplement, by Fred McCready, praised him for 'those strong traits that made his ancestors leave their homes . . . seeking religious freedom'. Mr McCready recalled that Buchman would say to his friends, if their 'Pennsylvania-German dialect' was ridiculed: 'Never be ashamed of your mother-tongue.'

Buchman shared one habit with an otherwise utterly different country lad who rose to even greater fame—Nikita Khrushchov: just as Mr Khrushchov enlivens his speeches and conversation with the proverbial lore of the Ukrainian peasantry, so Buchman, throughout his life, would drive home his points with homely sayings and illustrations that could almost certainly be traced back to his childhood in a small country town. 'Don't put the hay so high the mule can't reach it', he used to say; and 'If a man's got eye-trouble, it's no use throwing eye-medicine at him from a second-storey window'; and (of a sinner on the brink of Changing) 'Don't forget that a hooked fish jumps, kicks, and runs.' So, too, his *Morning Call* eulogist asked: 'Who but a Pennsylvania-German could describe religion as he did in a recent interview: "It's like a nice, thick, juicy steak with onions and French fries—you just can't help but like it"?' (Who would use just this simile, one might add, but one whose earliest memories were of a butcher's skilled selection of the finest cuts?)

[1] I can find no confirmation of a statement attributed to Buchman in Mr Peter Howard's contribution to *Three Views of Christianity* (Gollancz, 1962): 'Although I went to one of the best schools in France, the only words I can remember are *mauvais garçon*.' It is improbable that his parents would have sent him so far in boyhood. Perhaps he was simply pointing up his joke about his poor French.

More important in the formation of his thought must have been the ethical and theological concepts that he learned in his youth. When I asked a Lutheran scholar—Dr Theodore G. Tappert, of the Department of Church History at Mount Airy Seminary—about the antecedents of Buchmanism, he said that it represented 'a combination of pietism and the YMCA movement'. He added that 'the emphasis on a sharp conversion experience' was 'typical of the Lutheran pietism of the eighteenth century'.

But there was one such influence of a more unusual kind. It happened that Frank Buchman was introduced, very early in life, to a small, mystical German sect—originally, in the sixteenth century, a schism derived from Luther's own following (via the Anabaptists) by Caspar von Schwenkfeld. This sect had many members in Silesia and Swabia, and in the eighteenth century some of them went to settle in America, where, few as they were, they earned the respect of their neighbours. Thus, in 1938, when *Time* magazine was rebuked in the *Philadelphia Inquirer* for applying to Pennsburg a brash *Time*style adjective —'unswank'—the *Inquirer* had no doubt about the chief claim to cultural fame of 'classic Pennsburg': this was that it had 'America's No. 1 library in literature pertaining to what the learned Governor S. W. Pennypacker declared was the highest-type group of emigrants who ever came from Europe to this continent. He meant, of course, the Schwenkfeldians.'

In Buchman's youth there were still several thousand of the Schwenkfelders (as they were usually called)[1]; and the 'private co-ed' school that he was sent to—the Perkiomen Seminary—was run by them. This early contact may have influenced him more deeply than was realised at the time; for it is, surely, of great significance—in view of the technique of Guidance which is still of central importance in MRA—that a distinctive doctrine of Schwenkfeld and his followers was the doctrine that God communicated himself directly to every individual believer. This is what is sometimes called the doctrine of the Inner Light. It is a doctrine characteristic also of the Quakers,

[1] The *World Almanac* for 1963 records their number in 1961 as 2,500.

but its pedigree is traced further back by Monsignor Knox in *Enthusiasm.* According to him, the Quaker George Fox was a spiritual heir of Schwenkfeld—and he, in turn, not only of the Anabaptists but of such medieval heretics as the Waldensians and the Albigensians. Together with this belief in the Inner Light, the Anabaptists in particular held one doctrine, and cherished one hope, that seem highly relevant to the study of Buchmanism: they were anti-institutional, they rejected Church and State alike—because 'all the time' (as Monsignor Knox puts it) their 'dreams were of a theocracy'. Moreover:

> The true enthusiast can only be at home under a theocracy, with an accredited prophet as its invisible head; any other form of government . . . is not merely inadequate, but evil. . . . A full-blooded theocracy demands the presence of a divinely inspired leader or leaders, to whom government belongs by right of mystical illumination.

Such a vision was, in the strict sense of the word, eccentric: it was as remote from the main stream of Protestantism—from Luther, Calvin, and John Knox alike—as it was from Catholicism; but it is not remote from the ideas which, in his middle age, Frank Buchman began to spread round the world. One of MRA's main watchwords, 'God-control', is almost precisely synonymous with the word 'theocracy'; and it is confidently asserted in MRA propaganda that when the key men—the rulers—of any nation are Changed and submit to God-control, their whole nation changes; and in consequence that, when enough 'top people' are Changed, the world will be controlled by God, almost automatically or as though by some exercise in mass-suggestion.

It is sufficient at this point to quote two warnings from Christian sources: one, again, from Monsignor Knox, who writes that 'when once a theocratic state is set up, under a "perfect" ruler, . . . there is danger that he will be not less but more bloodthirsty than is the common wont of "psychic" men'; the other, from a report[1] by the Social and Industrial

[1] *Moral Re-Armament.* Church Information Board, 1955.

Council of the National Assembly of the Church of England (known as the Church Assembly), which observes:

> There have been many Christians who have thought that moral men, or specially religious men, would be able to govern society without such deficiency [infection by sin]—but history has proved them lamentably wrong.

One other aspect of Frank Buchman's youthful environment is worth mentioning. The *Evening Bulletin* article already quoted remarks that 'the Pennsylvania-Dutch were often religious innovators', and that 'even in colonial times travellers marvelled at the variety of religions among the German settlers of Pennsylvania': among their sects were the Amish, the Reformed Mennonites, and the Brethren in Christ (all resulting from Mennonite schisms), the Church of God, and the Seventh Day Brethren, who were 'an off-shoot of the Dunkers'. Modern American reference-books list more than a score of different Mennonite bodies, and show that the Dunkers, who may be Progressive Dunkers, Conservative Dunkers (the most numerous), or New Dunkers, are also known as German Baptist Brethren. Evidently the traditions of these conservative immigrants included a vigorous tradition of experimental dissent. From early youth Buchman must have been aware of this proliferation of sects around him; and, though he himself remained a Lutheran and may well have intended sincerely that his Group should not become a new sect, the mere fact of schism—in one or other variety of which, after all, many of his friends and neighbours were involved—can hardly have seemed quite so unthinkable to him as it would to some settled and orthodox Christian of the old world, to an Austrian Catholic peasant or an English country clergyman of moderate views.

There is nothing, however, to show that Frank Buchman in his youth was particularly interested in such matters: his was not an unduly early vocation. His parents would have been, by the standards of Pennsburg or Allentown, comfortably off. Even at the Perkiomen Seminary he showed, according to his mother, the taste for good clothes that he always retained, and 'did not like to get dirty'. The Principal of the school, the Revd Dr O. S. Kriebel, said of him many years later:

> Frank Buchman came to our school the day it opened. He was about fifteen[1] . . . well-behaved, and fond of such sports as we had, including croquet. He was a student of average ability, not outstanding in any respect. No one at that time would have ever predicted for him such a career as he has had.

Dr Kriebel said this in 1929, when the Oxford Group was still fairly new. He would have been astonished indeed if he had been able to see the full efflorescence of his 'student of average ability'.

At Muhlenberg College, where Buchman spent the last three years of the nineteenth century, one of his class-mates recalls that he 'soon fitted in, even though he was not of the he-man type'. In the college group photographs he does not look particularly prepossessing (but few of that period do): his face is pensive and peaky, his hair is combed straight across the right of his forehead, he wears a high stiff collar and looks, generally, ill at ease (except in a Bicycle Club group, in which his legs are nonchalantly crossed).

In the college year-book he is described as 'a noticeable man with large green eyes'. There is also a facetious (but now, alas, sadly unfunny) table in which a number of students are listed, with their supposed characteristics, now hopelessly obscure. Opposite 'Buchman' we see that he was 'better known as Kate', that his 'developed faculties' were 'eyes', that his 'byword' was 'Doctor, I don't understand that', and that his 'aim in life' was 'to be a friend of the professors'; while under

[1] It is not clear what education F.B. had already had; and, since his parents moved from Pennsburg to Allentown early in 1894, when he was fifteen, and the Perkiomen Seminary was at Pennsburg, Dr Kriebel may have slightly over-estimated his age. After the move he attended Allentown High School.

the heading 'always at' is an entry so mysterious that only a psychiatrist could interpret it—'using small slips of paper in class'.[1]

As at his preparatory school, so at college he does not seem to have been outstanding either academically or athletically; but the files of the college periodicals show that his interests were diverse. He was one of eighteen members *in collegio* of the Alpha Tau Omega fraternity, and soon belonged to the Sophronian Literary Society, the Augsburg Society, the Franklin Literary Association, and the Junior German Literary Society. He was also a business manager of a college paper, *The Muhlenberg*. Later he joined the Bicycle Club and the Skating Club. In 1898 he was on the committee of 'one of the most brilliant social events of the season'—his fraternity's 'progressive euchre'. He contributed thoughtful, if stilted, articles to various publications—e.g., one on 'The Importance of Cultivating a Proper Taste for Reading'—and showed a slight gift for drawing caricatures. He also had some talent as an actor: in a 'Herodotus play' (of which his mother was one of the patronesses) he appeared as 'Miss Terry', one of 'three Fem. Sen. girls'—'Fem. Sen.' being the local women's college. Then, one year, he won a prize of $10 awarded 'to the student excelling as to knowledge of subject and proficiency in physical culture'.

So it may be assumed that his record at Muhlenberg was sound, if not brilliant, and that he was fairly happy there. But the only hint that he may have had an intimation of future fame is in a sentence that he chose to include in his commencement oration when he graduated in 1899. It is a rich rhetorical fragment, and must have stirred ambition or speculation in the minds of some of those who heard the twenty-one-year-old Frank Buchman recite it in his brisk, resonant voice. It ran:

> When, in the twilight of the coming century, the roll will be called of those who figured prominently in the

[1] Mr Gore Vidal, a connoisseur of American academic *mores*, suggests, distressingly, that this is an allegation of persistent cheating.

moulding and guidance of our nation, may we hope that the names of some of us may appear thereon.

In those days, in Pennsylvania, the actual period of training for the Lutheran ministry seems to have been rather shorter than is normal in other denominations; or Frank Buchman's progress in theological learning and the spiritual life may have been more rapid than his friends in the Alpha Tau Omega fraternity at Muhlenberg would have expected. At any rate, only three years after he had left Muhlenberg, the Minutes of the Proceedings of the annual convention of the Evangelical Lutheran Ministerium of Pennsylvania and Adjacent States show that 'the Revd F. N. D. Buchman', having 'entered the ministry', had 'accepted a call to Overbrook, Pa., September 11th, 1902.' The years between were spent at Mount Airy Seminary; but he seems to have been able—perhaps with help from his father—to go abroad at least once during this period, and thus to indulge for the first time in his lifelong habit of foreign travel. Some editions of *Who's Who* state that he 'visited Europe for the purpose of making a special study of Inner Missions, 1902'; and it was presumably during this trip that (according to the Philadelphia *Evening Bulletin* article already quoted[1]) he was 'impressed by the monastic hospices for distressed travellers in Switzerland'.

The impression was sufficiently strong to inspire him to emulate, in the newly built-up Philadelphia suburb of Overbrook, the sanctified hospitality of the Augustinian Canons of St Bernard. Accordingly, he established there a modest hospice—without dogs, I suppose, and his guests were not snow-bound Alpinists but young men new to Philadelphia and, as an appeal in support of this work dramatically put it, 'drawn into the maelstrom of a large city's underlife'.

His cure of souls at Overbrook, which lasted for three years, was the only parochial charge that he undertook in the whole of his fifty-nine years' ministry. It must have become clear quite soon that his vocation was not to 'the trivial round, the

[1] See p. 18.

common task' of running an ordinary parish, but to something much more unusual and exciting, which his admirers were later to call 'soul-surgery': the provision of extraordinary pastoral care for individuals in special need. If he had stopped at that, he might have become a kind of Lutheran Curé d'Ars. But that saintly priest never saw himself as remaking the world.

A lifelong friend of Buchman's, the Revd Dr Gustavus Bechtold, who talked to me about him in Philadelphia in January 1962, thought that it was the 'settlements' such as Oxford House, in the East End of London, rather than the Swiss hospices, that had inspired the Overbrook experiment. 'It first began', Dr Bechtold told me, 'with a young man who was working as a servant in an erratic family. They chased him out at midnight. Frank took him in and found a bed for him. Then there was a young man from Buffalo: Frank took him in, too. Then he called me and said "Gus, I need a bed!" I told him to go to Wanamaker's and buy a bed and charge it to me. . . .

'He had a natural way of dealing with men—with people of every walk of life. He went into the humblest homes. . . .' (This testimony is important, because it conflicts so directly with one of the commonest charges against Buchman, that he cultivated especially the society of the wealthy and famous.)

Overbrook thus provided the first test and practice of his undoubted gift for dealing with the problems of individuals; and, since this gift was always manifested most happily when the individuals were young men, his rudimentary hospice was a valuable part of the experience.

Soon a more ambitious project was mooted. The Ministerium Minutes for 15th-21st June, 1905, contain an announcement which is not the less momentous for the prim and orderly language in which it is dressed:

> The Board of Managers of the Inner Mission Society has the pleasure of announcing that on the 1st of September it will open at the southeast corner of Twentieth and Race Streets, Philadelphia, a commodious and perfectly

equipped boarding house or hospice for Lutheran young men, capable of accommodating between forty and fifty, and in which comfortable rooms and good board will be furnished at the most moderate rates possible. . . .

More than a year ago, the Revd F. N. D. Buchman, impressed with the need of doing something for this class of young man, began a work along similar lines in connection with his parish at Overbrook, and soon had more applicants than he could accommodate. Here then was the small beginning; and when the Board of Managers of the Inner Mission Society began to move in the matter, it made overtures to Mr Buchman[1] for the transfer of his work to a more central location and to larger quarters. . . . To this he readily consented: and when the Board of Managers of the Inner Mission Society had effected the lease of the house . . ., it also extended a call to Mr Buchman to become the house-father of the new hospice, which call has been accepted by him. It is his and the Board's purpose to actualise as nearly as possible the Christian family life, with all its comforts, refinements and wholesome influences. An elderly lady of good education and fine Christian character will be the house-mother.

Though it is hoped to make the hospice self-sustaining, its very purpose might be defeated were an effort made to make it altogether so. . . . The deficit . . . will have to be covered from the treasury of the Society. A large quantity of furniture, bedding, etc., has already been contributed.

(Signed) J. F. Ohl,
Superintendent.

How many worthy enterprises have begun, in their 'glad, confident morning', with the assumption that it will always be easy enough to cover deficits on the running costs! Much later, Buchman was to have no difficulty at all in financing infinitely vaster projects; but the optimism of this announcement was

[1] Another account says that Buchman 'talked them into' the scheme; but there is no reason to doubt the accuracy of the Minutes.

not really in keeping with the frugal temper of the Pennsylvania Lutherans and, in particular, of Dr Ohl, Superintendent of the Board of the Inner Mission.

Next year an anxious note crept into his report on the hospice. It could accommodate forty-five men: the number sleeping there fluctuated between thirty-seven and forty-two. 'From a financial viewpoint it is very desirable that it should always remain filled to its utmost capacity'.

Then, in 1908, came a real snorter from the Ministerium's Finance Committee, typical of the reproofs submitted by finance committees everywhere. Two years earlier—i.e., just after the opening of the hospice—the Committee had expressed disapproval of 'the careless and improvident method pursued by the Ministerium in the management of its finances': it now reiterated that 'Synod must, like other corporations, confine its expenditure within its income, or certain financial embarrassment will be upon us'.

This was the background of the first major crisis in Frank Buchman's life. If it had not been for the rigidly prudent accountancy of the Finance Committee of the Ministerium of Pennsylvania, the Oxford Group and Moral Re-Armament might never have come into existence. It is at this point that what has hitherto been the record of an obscure life passes into the area of public myth; for the Buchmanite scriptures mostly take as their starting-point the dispute between Buchman and the committee under whose general oversight he had been running the hospice.

2

LIGHT AT KESWICK

The Ministerium of Pennsylvania—An emotional crisis—Buchman's 'poignant vision' at Keswick—Six unanswered letters—Dr Pfatteicher's testimony—'Hob-nobbing with nabobs'—The way to the top of the world

The Ministerium of Pennsylvania and Adjacent States met for a special convention in January, 1908, and for its annual convention in June. The down-town pastoral work among young men had expanded: there was now a settlement house (with 'many classes') as well as the original Lutheran Hospice. By June, however, the Board of the Inner Mission Society was able to answer with confidence the Finance Committee's sharp challenge. In Dr Ohl's report occurred these sentences:

> The Settlement is now well organised. Last fall the Board of the Society called the Rev Jos. S. Schantz, of Millersville, Pa., to become the house-father of the Hospice and the pastor of the Settlement House.

It was added that Mr Schantz had been installed on March 12th. Nothing was said about the founding-father of the hospice, who had been called to this work, with such high hopes, only three years before; there was not even a conventional word of thanks for all that he had done to get it going. The name of F. N. D. Buchman, indeed, still appeared in the Roll of the Ministerium, printed with the Minutes, but against

FRANK BUCHMAN IN YOUTH: these two group photographs were taken at Muhlenberg College, Allentown, Pennsylvania, in 1897-99. In the Bicycle Club group above, Buchman sits, with legs crossed, on the left; in the group below, of the Class of 1899, he stands on the extreme left at the back.

Dear Brother Ohl—

Am writing to tell you that I have harboured an unkind feeling toward you—at times I conquered it but it always came back. Our views may differ but as brothers we must love.
I write to ask your forgiveness and to assure that I love you and trust by God's grace I shall never more speak unkindly or disparagingly of you.
The lines of that hymn have been ringing in my ears—
When I survey the wondrous cross
On which the Prince of Glory died
My richest gain I count but loss
And pour contempt on all my pride.

With love
faithfully yours—
Frank N D Buchman

July 27—1908— See last page.

'DEAR BROTHER OHL': Facsimile of one of the six letters written by Buchman from Keswick in 1908.

it is the curt intimation 'No parish'. (In the previous year's Roll, his 'parish' had been given as 'Luther Hospice'.)

The Ministerium is a venerable body, dating from 1742. One rule strictly imposed on its members was that all of them must attend its conventions, or send satisfactory explanations of their absence. Nor was there, as in most committees, a mere perfunctory 'Apologies' item on the agenda. The Minutes contain a 'Report on Excuses', prepared by a special committee, from which it is evident that each absentee's letter had been scrutinised rigorously. One, for instance, had been in the ministry for forty years and was 'excused' on grounds of old age. Those working in the foreign mission field were 'excused'. There are lists of those who sent other satisfactory reasons for absence and those who 'failed to send valid excuses': the committee recommended that these should be, respectively, accepted and rejected.

But there is also a black list of those who 'neither reported their presence nor sent any excuse for their absence'; and in these cases 'we recommend that they be not excused'. In this list, both in January and in June, is the name F. N. D. Buchman.

The assurance in Dr Ohl's report that 'the Settlement is now well organised' is, of course, a fairly plain hint that things had been going wrong before. This—and the other items of negative evidence—suggest that the struggle between Frank Buchman and the ecclesiastical bureaucrats who employed him had been a fierce one.

This dispute has been described repeatedly in MRA propaganda literature. Details vary slightly, and the reference in the Ministerium Minutes to 'last fall' suggests that the incident may have been inadvertently post-dated; but the gist of the account is that the committeemen insisted on economising on the hospice food. ('Rations' is the word mostly used.) 'Sometimes the budget would not balance—when the young folk were numerous and hungry', is how Mr A. J. Russell puts it in *For Sinners Only*. (But, as we have already learned from Dr Ohl, the more numerous they were the easier it was to balance the budget.) Buchman resisted the threatened cuts. In the official biography, *Frank Buchman's Secret*, Mr Peter Howard writes, in his hammer-fist staccato: 'The boys were hungry. Buchman was angry. He was awake all night brooding in bitterness. . . . That day he resigned his job.'

An emotional crisis—indeed, what is usually called a nervous breakdown—followed: 'his feelings', says Mr Howard, 'were so deep that he fell ill'.

> He consulted a specialist who told him to take a hot and a cold bath each day and he would feel better. He took baths as suggested for six months. He became one of the cleanest men in the world outside, but felt no better inside. His organisation, which had seemed so successful, was thwarted. He was hurt. He hated. His health cracked under the strain of his bitterness.

There were several courses that Buchman could have taken. He could, presumably, have taken the constitutional course of appealing from the committee to the full Ministerium, where, if his work at the hospice was so vitally redemptive as it is said to have been—comparable, say, with Padre Borelli's rather similar work among the *scugnizzi* of Naples—he might well have been supported. Or, if food was so dear in down-town Philadelphia in the 1900s, he could have charged slightly more for meals. Or he could have gone out and begged for money for a special food fund. (One of the legends of this period relates how, when he was starting a hospice from scratch—presumably the one at Overbrook—he came home late one night with $17 in pennies, a mop, and a bucket.) Or he could simply have accepted the committee's ruling, as many hostel wardens have no doubt had to do in similar cases, and explained it as best he could to the boys. Instead, he took the one course completely lacking in common sense, in balance, in humility and in real consideration both for his fellow-ministers and for the boys and young men in his care: he fumed, collapsed, quit, and threw what seems to have been a prolonged fit of hysterical sulks.

There is no need to labour the folly and irresponsibility of this conduct, for Buchman himself constantly said, in later years, how wrong he had been. 'I was wrong in harbouring ill-will', he would say. Of course—but he was already an ordained minister of a Christian church, with some knowledge of right and wrong; and his talents had been sufficient to secure him two successive calls from the serious-minded Ministerium. When, therefore, we read of the dramatic conversion experience at Keswick which formed the unexpected climax of his breakdown, we are entitled to wonder how stable his mind and personality were (and indeed how authentic, and objectively real, the Keswick incident was).

Both parties to the dispute—Buchman with his tantrums and vapours and Dr Ohl and the committee, with their strangely ungenerous failure to pay, if only for the sake of appearances, even a formal tribute to his work—surely made a quite disproportionate fuss, if the dispute was only (as is always said) over the cost of catering at the hospice.

But was it? Since the subject-matter of human quarrels is so often not the same as their real causes, it is hard not to suspect that the argument about food was only a surface symptom of some deeper-seated difficulty. Considering, too, the extreme informality characteristic of Buchman's man-to-man evangelistic methods in later years, and his child-like faith, often justified, that any money needed would turn up somehow ('Isn't God a millionaire?' is one of his most-quoted sayings), one may surmise that there was a clash of personalities, a natural, unsurmountable, mutual antipathy between the staid Lutheran committeemen and the volatile young *patron* of the hospice.

In January, 1962, visiting Philadelphia and Allentown, I was able to talk with many men and women who had known Frank Buchman, including some of his contemporaries. Their views of him were curiously ambivalent: some admired him warmly and supported him, others (including some who shared his Lutheran faith) spoke of him with hostility, even with detestation; others, again, thought that he had done some good—*but* . . . (or that he had done a lot of harm—*but* . . .).

In particular, I was fortunate enough to find two of Buchman's contemporaries with an intimate knowledge, and clear recollections, of this hospice dispute. Their testimonies followed the usual pattern: one was anti-Buchman, one pro-Buchman.

The anti-Buchman witness was perhaps naturally so, for she was a close relative of Dr Ohl, the superintendent who fired Buchman, or accepted his resignation. (She stipulated that I should not publish her name, for she is old and not strong.) When I asked her what the trouble had been, she did not mention food. According to her, Buchman had run the hospice in a completely slipshod and inefficient way: 'Schantz found terrible chaos when he took over—*he* did a wonderful job.' She recalled two specific causes of complaint against Buchman. The first was that 'one of the things he insisted on was keeping a drunken cook—said he wanted to rehabilitate her'. (This cook was Mrs Mary Hemphill, and if she had been 'drunken', she was indeed rehabilitated; when she died in 1937, aged eighty, Buchman cabled a message to her funeral: 'A cook by the grace of God . . . a living link with the very beginning of the Oxford Group. She was one of the God-sent women to the fellowship. She fed the poor and lived by faith and prayer.')

The second complaint seems, at first sight, surprising, in that the conduct complained of is not what one would expect in a Lutheran minister brought up in the regular ways of a small American town in the nineteenth century: 'Dr Ohl was always on the job good and early, but when he used to call at the hospice, Dr Buchman was often still in bed—at ten or eleven in the morning! Of course he ought to have been around by then.' In the end, she said, 'not only Dr Ohl but the boys thought it better he should go'. She added: 'Our church was really fair to him—they decided in closed session not to strike him off the Roll.' (This, I think, refers to a later occasion.)

My pro-Buchman witness was Dr Bechtold, whom I have already quoted.[1] He put most of the blame on Buchman's

[1] See p. 27.

antagonists. 'Ohl', he said, 'was a difficult personality. He was a musician, a liturgical scholar, a student of social movements —but he couldn't get along with people.'

Without prompting from me, Dr Bechtold got on to the subject of Buchman's late rising. He seemed to think there was nothing in the complaint: why should the house-father get up early, since the boys would mostly be out at work in the morning and there wouldn't be anything for him to do? Moreover, 'Frank used to sit up half the night with those boys —he gave himself so thoroughly he was exhausted.'[1] Then, after one of these midnight bouts of soul-saving, 'Dr Ohl would come snooping round about eleven o'clock and Frank would still be in bed. It was no use: they were irreconcilable'.

Frank Buchman was to make one more attempt to be reconciled with the irreconcilable. After his breach with the hospice, the most galling aspect of which must have been the ingratitude of his charges—if it is indeed the case that 'the boys thought it better he should go'—he did not do what most people in his position would have done: take a short holiday and look for another job. He was still, after all, a minister of religion; and if he felt that his relations with the Ministerium of Pennsylvania were under too much of a strain, he could have moved to another area—with, no doubt, the excellent, if guarded, testimonial that even Dr Ohl might have been glad to give him. Instead, he went for a holiday tour in Europe—it is not known at whose expense: presumably his parents'. If, incidentally, they were sufficiently prosperous to afford this luxury for

[1] *Cf For Sinners Only*, by A. J. Russell, p. 118: 'Ken Twitchell now reappeared, and Frank . . . "shared" that he felt guided to say the three of us should dine together, and that later Ken and I should go on to Harley Street . . . Frank's reason for staying away himself was that he had an unfortunate to see whose need might keep him far into the night.' *Cf* also the case, cited by Harold Begbie in *Life Changers*, of a young soldier who went to see Buchman alone just before ten o'clock and did not leave until past two in the morning. Begbie met him next day, 'his pale face and suffering eyes lighted by a strange smile of boyish gladness and triumphant serenity, in spite of all the marks of a sleepless night and great spiritual strain which showed behind the brightness of his face like so many bruises'.

him, he might surely have persuaded them to make some modest regular contribution which would have eased the problem of catering for the hospice.

Then came the visit to England and to Keswick; and there in a chapel, during a sermon by a woman, Frank Buchman had 'a poignant vision of the Crucified', followed by 'a dazed sense of a great shaking-up'.

Whatever the full explanation of this experience, whether it was a genuinely paranormal manifestation or purely subjective —a return, in a less disagreeable form, of that hysteria latent during the crisis of the previous months—Buchman himself sincerely believed that his whole life had been changed in that moment; and he was to find, in the years that lay ahead, ample confirmation of this belief.

He said later: 'I returned to the house feeling a powerful urge to share my experience.' Obeying an impulse, he immediately wrote six letters, to the six committeemen with whom he had quarrelled. This is a favourite anecdote in MRA propaganda. The form of the letters, as given by Mr Howard, Mr Russell, and others, is as follows:

My dear Friend,

I have nursed ill-will against you. I am sorry. Forgive me?

Yours sincerely,

Frank

Coupled with this edifying gesture, almost invariably, is the statement that none of the six committeemen replied to the letters. Sometimes it is said that they 'did not bother' to reply. This detail even found its way into the *Times* obituary of Buchman. The reader naturally feels that such ungraciousness on the committeemen's part shows up the more radiantly, by contrast, the saintly whiteness of Frank's penitence.

So I, too, might think if I had not found, in the Krauth Memorial library at Mount Airy Seminary, one of these six letters—the original letter written by Buchman to Dr Ohl. The actual text is rather fuller than the version usually given (which is presumably a summary written from memory many years later). It is scribbled, rather illegibly, on cheap ruled paper. It runs:

Dear Brother Ohl—

Am writing to tell you that I have harboured an unkind feeling toward you—at times I conquered it but it always came back. Our views may differ but as brothers we *must* love.

I write to ask your forgiveness and to assure [*sic*] that I love you and trust by God's grace I shall never more speak unkindly or disparagingly of you. The lines of that hymn have been ringing in my ears—

When I survey the wondrous cross
On which the Prince of Glory died
My richest gain I count but loss
And pour contempt on all my pride.

With love
faithfully yours—
Frank N. D. Buchman

July 27—
1908

Handsome as the *démarche* is, there are some slight awkwardnesses in it: one might feel vaguely uncomfortable on receiving, from a colleague with whom one had quarrelled, an assurance that he hoped not to speak disparagingly of you in the future. But this would be no excuse for not replying to so forthcoming and humble a communication; rather the contrary.

Why, then, did the six committeemen not reply? The reason is surprisingly simple. Buchman, roaming the world, put no address on his letters!

On the back of the letter in the Mount Airy library is this note, written in pencil by Dr Ohl:

Fortunately I have found the letter . . . the like of which Mr B says he wrote to a number of others, and got no answer. But you will notice that he gives no address. Had he done so I surely would have written. As nearly as I can make out the post-mark the letter was mailed in England.

This letter is among the personal papers left to the library by the late Dr Ernest P. Pfatteicher. Dr Pfatteicher, who died in 1943, was at one time President of the Ministerium of Pennsylvania. He seems to have been an implacable opponent of Buchman. In 1934, as a Christmas present for his friends, he had printed privately a small volume of lectures, or 'Summer School soliloquies', entitled *The Man from Oxford*: to his Pennsylvania-Dutch colleagues there would be a hint of a sneer in this title, and the lecture devoted to Buchman is indeed a striking manifestation of the *odium theologicum*. It is worth quoting at some length both because it illustrates the strong antagonism that something in Buchman's personality and methods provoked throughout his life—balanced as this was, indeed, by the devotion of those who remained his intimates—and because it contains an early authentic account of an ill-judged attempt by Buchman to promote, if only vicariously, the practice of Sharing.

Pfatteicher (then about sixty years of age) wrote: 'I know Frank Buchman and know him rather well'. He added:

> Pastoral activity in a limited mission field irked him. The call to become the pastor and house-father of our hospice for young men and of a settlement house for down-and-outs appealed to him. He had gifts along this line. However, it was not long before this task proved trying. The glorified story of his restraint and discontent which I have read in more than one book reminds me of the statement attributed to the Queen of Sheba to the effect [that] 'the half has not been told'. Frank Buchman, genuinely interested in individuals in need of help, was of a roving disposition. . . . As long as I have known Frank Buchman he has always had three passions, one to help the down [-and-out] and up-and-out individual, another to hobnob with those in positions of social prestige, and a third, the 'wanderlust'.

Pfatteicher wrote ironically (but, was the irony spiced, just faintly, with envy?) about Buchman's sense of vocation at

Pennsylvania State College, where he had found a job that satisfied him, for a time at least, as YMCA Secretary. This was in 1909, the year after the trouble at the hospice and the spiritual upheaval at Keswick. He stayed there until 1915.

> Even in those days he knew a riding habit from a dress suit and could wear both with equal composure. . . . It has been said that Mott discovered Buchman at Pennsylvania State College and sent him to China and elsewhere. I am under the impression that it was Buchman who quite legitimately at the time forced Mott to recognise him.

Apart from these personal digs, which by the time they were in print Buchman could afford to ignore, Pfatteicher was mainly concerned, as a loyal and devout Lutheran, to show that Buchman had *not* experienced some great new revelation as Keswick: he had 'learned to know Jesus Christ through his home and his church. His visit to England after "his work had been seriously hampered by a difference of opinion with a governing committee" did not in my opinion cause him to catch a new "vision of a Christ-led world untrammeled by sin".[1] It led him to a reappraisement of the faith which was his and gave him the needed opportunity to come to grips with himself.'

Some may feel that the distinction between these two definitions of what happened at Keswick is a slight one. It is, in any case, hardly possible for anybody to presume to contradict another's account of an experience which must have been, in part at least, subjective. Nor is there much substance in the sour complaint that the technique of the house-party 'is no more original to Buchmanism than it was when as a pastor I invited some of my fellow-pastors to join me at Wernersville for a discussion of spiritual problems. There have always been house-parties.' More serious is an opinion quoted by Pfatteicher from Professor Wilson of the University of Western Ontario, writing in *The Christian Century*: 'I know of no minister who has achieved signal success as a result of the Group who was not

[1] These are quotations from a Buchmanite hagiography which must have seemed to Pfatteicher over-euphemistic.

formerly serving effectively.' This is a general criticism that was to pursue Buchman throughout his life. There is evidence both to support and to rebut it: of its nature, it cannot be proved conclusively either way. Pfatteicher endorsed it heartily —but he had clearly mistrusted Buchman ever since a curious incident at Pennsylvania State College, his description of which tells us something about both men:

> How well I remember an intimate conversation between us late on a Saturday night at State College. I told him of a class-mate of mine . . . whom I was compelled to escort to his room on more than one occasion because of his inability to navigate his own boat and who had turned out to be a big man both in the business world and in the church. The following day while I was talking to several hundred Freshmen I was amazed to hear Frank say as he was seated back of me: 'tell them about Smith'. I feigned a lack of hearing when the request was repeated in a louder tone, the actual name of the man being used. I turned and said as quietly as I could: 'I can't do that.' To me this was repulsive and contrary to my thought of Christian courtesy or even of Christ-like propriety. To him it was a necessary step in the spiritual education of Freshmen. It was sharing.

Buchman was obviously at fault here. His behaviour was pushing, impertinent and indiscreet. But it may also occur to the impartial observer that Pfatteicher, even in 'an intimate conversation . . . late on a Saturday night', while he might well have recounted the story of the reformed drunk, should not have mentioned his name, especially to one of whose unconventional methods and propensity to gossip he must already have been aware.

It was, however, the Group's exploitation of those unanswered letters that Pfatteicher found most galling; and the passage in *The Man from Oxford* that deals with this contains also what may be a clue to Buchman's main offence:

> Did the prodigal son . . . send a letter home or did he

> return? Has the writer of these letters in his many visits to Philadelphia ever called on those to whom he wrote?... Surely there must be at least one or two real Christians among the number. I have known these men and believe them to have been Christians. The majority of them can no longer speak for themselves. Here Frank makes a saint of himself and sinners of others.

The last few words convey succinctly an aspect of Buchmanism—its self-congratulatory sanctimoniousness—which others besides Dr Pfatteicher have found distasteful.

The clue contained in this passage is amplified thus:

> As President of the Synod to which my friend Frank Buchman still nominally belongs, I am asking him to share with me and others what worship in a congregation ... means to him.... In other words, Frank, is there a place in your life for the visible Christian Church?

And the lecture ends with an appeal to pastors who are friends of Buchman 'not to introduce Oxford groups or circles into their congregations, the sure germ of ultimate schism ...'.

Apart from the risk of schism, it seems possible that (whether this was consciously admitted or not) Buchman's main offence, in the minds of Pfatteicher and other orthodox Pennsylvanian pastors, was his perennial absenteeism. Here were they, quietly attending to their humdrum parochial duties: there was he, always globe-trotting, publicised, fêted, 'hobnobbing with nabobs' (as Dr W. C. Schaeffer, Pastor of St John's Evangelical Lutheran Church in Buchman's own home-town, Allentown, put it in a letter to Pfatteicher), and yet, year after year, anxiously insistent on retaining his membership of the Ministerium of Pennsylvania and—maddeningly!—never, in later years, forgetting to send a letter of explanation and apology sufficiently plausible to satisfy the exacting committee responsible for the Report on Excuses.

Scrutiny of some of these letters suggests that Buchman was not free from one common human weakness: he really did seem to enjoy his 'hobnobbing with nabobs'. There is a note of exultation in his reports of the world-wide demands for his presence and of the tributes to his work from the great and famous. He is careful, however, not to take personal credit for the success of his efforts, and to suggest, sometimes in a way verging on vulgar flattery, that his success is, so to speak, one up for the Ministerium of Pennsylvania—a thought that can rarely have occurred to his supporters in Oxford or Scandinavia or New York. The letters are drafted with care: it may be that the hostility of Pfatteicher and some others was aggravated rather than assuaged by their tone and content, but Buchman knew his fellow-ministers and calculated—correctly, as it turned out—that the reactions of most of them would be favourable. They could hardly, for instance, fail to excuse him in the summer of 1940, when he wrote:

> The City of San Francisco is celebrating my sixty-second birthday with a week's program in which the Mayor, the Board of Supervisors and six hundred citizens are co-operating. There will be three broadcasts reaching the corners of the earth. So I trust you will present my excuses to the Ministerium for not being able to be present at this year's meeting. Surely it must be heartening to the Ministerium to find that such a world-wide spirit, fostered by a Lutheran, is abroad in the world today, and it would naturally expect me to be on the front line of advance.

None the less, the criticisms kept on cropping up. One member of the Ministerium, Dr Edward T. Horn III,[1] recalls a Synod at which there was a real risk that Buchman would be 'unfrocked', at the instance of the then President (probably Pfatteicher). 'Buchman was a brilliant man', Horn told me, 'and very well able to defend himself.' Buchman was present and asked that the charges against him should be specified: 'the President was unable to answer'. Or, as Dr Bechtold put

[1] Pastor of Trinity Lutheran Church, Germantown, Pa.

it, 'they never had the courage to charge him with syncretism'[1] —partly, perhaps, because of the assurance given by Buchman (repeatedly in conversation with Dr Bechtold, for one) that 'the only doctrine' he 'ever taught' was 'that set forth in Luther's small catechism'—an assurance that would be surprising to some of MRA's Asian converts today.

Buchman's critics seem to have been busy in 1936, and in February Pfatteicher wrote telling him that his absences were resented and asking for an early meeting. The Mount Airy library contains no fewer than four letters from Buchman which are, in effect, replies to this challenge. In the first of these, dated 5th March, he said:

> . . . There is no one who would be more eager than I to attend the meetings of the Ministerium of Pennsylvania had it been at all possible. . . . I have been careful always to keep the Offices of the Ministerium informed and to present my excuses. I should think the Ministerium of Pennsylvania would be proud to have part in the work of a spiritual awakening of growing national and international importance. . . . Had I been present at the meeting of the Ministerium last year, I am sure the Dean of Copenhagen would not have been able to say in Oxford, as he is quoted in the London *Times* as saying, that they had seen in Denmark during the past year 'a mighty spiritual awakening which is an answer to the menace of materialism'. One of the older members of the German-speaking section of the Ministerium said a little time ago, 'My, this is not only Inner Mission work, but real Foreign Mission work of the highest order'. Then he emphasised the importance of the missionary opportunity presented by a luncheon like the one given by Dr Beneš, President of the League Assembly, to the statesmen of Europe and to which the *Journal de Genève* devoted a special supplement. If these facts were presented to the Ministerium, I am sure

[1] 'Attempt to sink differences and effect union between sects or philosophic schools' (*Concise Oxford Dictionary*).

they would agree heart and soul that there can be no question whatever about whether, as God wills, I am present or absent, they are partakers in the beginning of what so many leaders feel is our instant necessity—that the crucified Christ should once more become the centre of our modern life.

By now the Buchmanite habit of name-dropping (the Dean of Copenhagen, Dr Beneš) was fully developed; and with the same letter he enclosed one from Professor Runestam, 'son-in-law of the late Archbishop Söderblom', urging him to come to Sweden.[1] 'If my answer is "Yes" ', he told Pfatteicher, 'I may have to leave for Europe on the 19th March'; and he mentioned 'several important engagements' before his departure—adding, to stress the weighty character of the Swedish invitation:

> The invitation, which came six months ago from Stockholm, is signed by 80% of the Lutheran clergy of Stockholm, and by the laity, and the Primarius is to preside at the opening meeting.

The next letter, dated 11th March, drops several more names and contains further evidence of Buchman's incessant mobility:

> My dear Dr Pfatteicher,
>
> It seems likely that I sail next Wednesday unless the present tense European situation may make it unwise. I have appointments in Washington which are being made for me, but I would now tentatively suggest either Monday

1 Uppsala, Febr 11th, 1936.

Dear Frank Buchman.

You ought not to wait any longer. You *have* to go to Sweden. Have you not got guidance for that?—Excuse me, I am anxious to get you here. I do not know any longer to handle the work. And I am afraid it will turn out very badly, if you do not take care of it. I am not the man to do it. And nobody here. And our Norwegian friends won't come without your guidance and assistance. What to do?

Yours very faithfully

or Tuesday at such time as would be convenient to you. . . .

I have been giving your letter considerable thought. You say, 'to me there is a very real tragedy in the confession of churchmen, whether they be of the Church of England or of the Scandinavian Church, who say that it took Buchmanism to arouse them out of a certain stupor'. Taking it for granted that the witness of these men is correct, then it would seem to me a worth while service if the Holy Spirit can use a clergyman of the Ministerium of Pennsylvania to bring about such a renaissance. . . .

I am enclosing a page from the London *Times* which tells of the happenings in Oxford, as well as a programme of a meeting in London, which gives the names of people who have come from various countries to these meetings. Most of these men have come into power during the past year.

A letter will reach me at Mrs Harry Blair's, 4567 Indian Lane, Washington DC. . . .

I had an interesting visit in Nassau this week-end, seeing Church conditions there. The Bishop of Croydon asked me to see the Bishop of Nassau and the Dean of the Cathedral who knows the work from a House Party in England. The work is gaining a foothold in Florida. I had a good hour this morning with the Governor and Mrs Sholtz.

I hope to put in your hands a book, which has just appeared by the Canon of Hertford[1] Cathedral, on Group Movements in relationship to the Oxford Group Movement. Of course, it never crosses the mind of a scholar like that, who has followed the progress of the work, that this is a sect.

Looking forward to our fellowship,

Believe me,
Faithfully,
Frank N. D. Buchman

Soon Buchman was in Miami, Florida—whence he wrote, on 22nd March:

[1] *Sic*: presumably *a* Canon of Hereford.

Dear Dr Pfatteicher,

The enclosed cable has just come from London, carrying word of Lord Salisbury's speech in the House of Lords and the latest advances in England and Denmark. These developments make necessary my presence on the other side, and I am planning to sail from New York on the *Aquitania* on Friday night.

I hope to see you before leaving. William Gilliland has been ill, and I want to drop in on him at State College on the way north. But we might be able to arrange a meeting late Wednesday, or Thursday or Friday. Will you wire me to the Highland Inn, Southern Pines, NC, saying what time would be most convenient.

With every good wish, believe me,

Sincerely,

Frank N. D. Buchman

On 27th March, after a brief meeting with Pfatteicher in Philadelphia, he was back in New York:

Dear Dr Pfatteicher,

Many thanks for yesterday. I want to send you a copy of the book *Group Movements*. I have also been reading a splendid chapter in Beverley Nichols' newest book on the place of the Oxford Group in his own personal life as well as the part it is playing in promoting vital Christianity in this day and age. A cable has just come urging me to proceed to Denmark direct. Forty members of Parliament were at a meeting yesterday: there are three houseparties this weekend at which five thousand people have registered. . . . On the fourth of April there will be a national houseparty at Ollerup which is to have its climaxed [*sic*] in a great Easter service.

I was interested in all you had to say and I am giving you my cable address—Buchman, Brownotel, London—and if you will feel guided to cable for me to return this year and it is within the realm of physical possibility, I shall naturally feel that I will obey your guidance. But if you will feel that in view of the work that is going on in these countries, it is of such value that I can be spared and that in a very sense[1] I am in the active work of the pastorate as an evangelist in this field to which established Lutheran clergymen acknowledge a debt that their own spiritual lives are being renewed and that there is an evident advance for the Kingdom of God in their parishes, then I might, in very truth, have a just right to take my part with those who are so splendidly serving in the active work in Pennsylvania.

I saw no-one else in Philadelphia save an old Lutheran of eighty-four years who is at Byberry and who looks forward to this visit whenever I can come. . . .

Faithfully yours,
Frank N. D. Buchman

PS Since we talked about Firestone yesterday, I thought you would like to know that one of the Firestone executives is sailing with me tonight for training.

This letter is characteristic at a number of points. Again the name of a prominent new supporter—Mr Beverley Nichols[2]—is dropped. There is the usual rather naïve reverence for numbers and size: forty Danish MPs, five thousand house-party-goers, a 'national' house-party 'climaxed' in an Easter service which must, of course, be boosted in advance as 'great'. By now, too, a London telegraphic address has been acquired, at one of the most distinguished Mayfair hotels. Since the 'old Lutheran of eighty-four years' was not a VIP, it is not clear why he is mentioned: possibly to explain why Buchman had no time to see other people in Philadelphia (including, it may be, ministers belonging to his faction rather than to that of Pfatteicher, who would accordingly find this paragraph reassuring), or possibly to emphasise his continuing care for the

[1] *Sic*: presumably 'in a very real sense'. There are other indications of haste in the typing of this letter, which Buchman cannot have read through before signing it.

[2] For Mr Nichols' own account of his relations with Buchman and the Group, see pp. 269-74.

pastoral needs of individuals. Certainly the letter's second paragraph is not without guile: the crusty Pfatteicher must have fumed, and Buchman must have known—and chuckled to know—that he would fume, at the suggestion that he should seek guidance on Buchman's movements and at the conditional promise attached to the suggestion.

The postscript, too, is interesting. Two years earlier, in January, 1934, one of the rich young converts displayed at an evening-dress rally of Buchmanites at the Plaza Hotel, New York, was Mr Russell Firestone, of the tyre-manufacturing family—who testified that, through Buchman's four Absolutes, executives and workers in his factory were learning to live 'non-skid lives'. (This is an early instance of the application of Buchmanite principles to industrial relations, later a major MRA activity; it may be assumed, too, that Mr Firestone was one of the industrialists who provided Buchman with generous financial assistance.)

But the most striking thing about these letters is the contrast that they present to the Keswick notes of twenty-eight years before. Those were uncouth scribbles, dashed off in anguish of spirit, the signature rambling uncertainly backward: these are skilfully composed and (in the main) well-typed, and the forward-sloping signature is mature and confident. And they bear, of course, the elegant letter-heads of such hotels as the Miami Battle-Creek and Brown's.

The dim boy from the small-town liquor-store, the young minister whose first experiment in group-evangelism had ended in disaster, was well on his way to the top of the world.

3

THE 'OXFORD' GROUP

Buchman in World War I—Who's Who: *a misleading entry exposed by A. P. Herbert—Mrs Dodge's thought for the day—A world tour that went wrong—Barred from the campus at Princeton—Dangers of 'enthusiasm'*

SOME TWO dozen major tours and campaigns, in America and elsewhere, are listed in Frank Buchman's last *Who's Who* entry, and no doubt there were many more: as his letters to Dr Pfatteicher suggest, he rarely seemed to be in one place for more than a few days at a time.

As we have seen, his longest stay was at Pennsylvania State College ('Penn State'), where from 1909 to 1915 he was, as he later put it, 'in charge of Christian work'. This was the job that he undertook after the visit to the Near East and to England (including Keswick) that followed the hospice *débâcle*. His next post gave full scope to his taste for roving. The Revd G. F. Allen[1] explains what it was in his contribution to *Oxford and the Groups*:[2]

> From 1916, Frank Buchman held the position of an extension lecturer at Hartford Theological Seminary. The post left him half the year free for travel, and the travel was used for missions of evangelism throughout the world from east to west. . . . From 1923, he resigned the Hartford chair . . .

[1] *Cf* p. 195. [2] Ed R. H. S. Crossman(Blackwell, 1934).

Professor Bengt Sundkler, of Uppsala University, Sweden, a historian of some early stages of what is now called the ecumenical movement, records[1] that Buchman was in South India in 1915, co-operating in an evangelistic programme 'planned on the characteristically American revival patterns, devised in the days of Moody'. Buchman 'stressed the need for direct "personal work" ', and Professor Sundkler quotes the testimony of another missionary, H. A. Popley: 'He has been able to put this vital subject before us in a way that has never been done before.'

These were the early years of the First World War (in which the United States was not involved until 1917). In some editions of *Who's Who* Buchman's record for this period reads: 'made a tour of India, Korea, and Japan, 1915-16; toured in the Far East, 1917-19'. This (by contrast with much else that was thought worth including in *Who's Who*) is almost too brief a summary; it is strange that the Hartford lectureship is not mentioned. No doubt over-condensation accounts for what might seem, at first sight, to be a slight discrepancy in the record. For in the editions of *Who's Who* for other years—e.g., 1938—the entry reads: 'served European War with a flying squadron, looking after war prisoners'.

This is an intriguing statement. What exactly, one would like to know, is a 'flying squadron', and what was Buchman's status in (or rather, to use his more indefinite word, 'with') it? Who were the prisoners whom he was 'looking after'? Presumably Germans, if he was on the Allied side. Or, as an American citizen with strong German antecedents and links, was he able, at least until 1917, to visit Allied prisoners in German camps—though hardly by 'flying squadron'? How, above all, was he able to fit in service in the '*European* War' with those extensive Far-Eastern tours—one of them, apparently, lasting for two years—and with the Hartford post, which cannot have been entirely a sinecure? *Who's Who* gives no clue; and the war prisoners vanish from later editions.

[1] *Church of South India: the Movement towards Union 1900-1947* (Lutterworth Press, 1954).

Unfortunately, the evidence about Buchman's life contained in *Who's Who* cannot be regarded as entirely reliable. Some years ago, Sir Alan Herbert pointed out that these biographical entries—for the wording of which, as is customary, their subject was responsible—fell short, in more than one respect, of the standards that might have been expected of a professor of Absolute Honesty.

Under '*Educ*', Buchman's entry reads: 'Muhlenberg College, AB, AM, DD, LLD (Oglethorpe); studied Cambridge University, 1921-22.' Since he took the trouble to mention that one of his doctorates was not conferred by his own old college, it is surprising that the second half of this entry should be not merely vague but so inaccurate as to be misleading. For, in fact, Buchman never studied at Cambridge University at all. He spent six months at Westminster College, a Presbyterian theological institution which is, geographically, in Cambridge, but is not a part of the University and is not to be found in the University Calendar. Even so, the entry might have been justifiable if Buchman had attended University lectures, as outside students sometimes do: Herbert ascertained from the University authorities that Buchman had never asked permission to do so.

Herbert's analysis of another item in Buchman's *Who's Who* entry was more complex, but no less devastating. This was an important item, for it purported to record the start of the movement that was to grow into Moral Re-Armament. One would suppose that special care would have been taken to ensure its precise accuracy. The reverse was the case: in successive editions of *Who's Who* the facts were more and more blurred—and, if one hesitates to say that they were blurred deliberately, it is only because, despite the mounting evidence of dishonesty, it is not easy to believe that a religious leader who could attract the whole-hearted allegiance of some fine-spirited and even of some intelligent men and women, would resort to such shabby trickery. Nor is it clear why a man of considerable astuteness, as Buchman often showed himself to be, should 'stick his neck out', quite unnecessarily, by printing statements about himself which could readily be checked and, if untrue, used to his discredit. Nor can it be said that the data were simply supplied to *Who's Who* by some secretary, without Buchman's knowledge: he would have had to be consulted about the personal details of his early life at least (including his education); and Herbert's exposures were so widely and repeatedly publicised that Buchman must certainly have been aware of them. It is strange, too, that so many of his followers should have remained faithful to him after these exposures; but the history of credulity among religious devotees would need an encyclopaedia to itself.

The basic facts about the start of Buchman's movement seem to be that it was built up gradually and informally from 1918 (when he held his first organised 'house-party' in China) until the formation of the First Century Christian Fellowship in 1921. The name 'Oxford Group' was first used in 1929 in South Africa: its innocent originator is said to have been a railway porter who scribbled the phrase on labels stuck on the windows of the reserved compartments in which a team of Buchmanites—mostly, as it happened, from Oxford, some being Rhodes Scholars—were travelling. The South African press picked up the tag, and the Buchmanites (as one of their supporters was to put it, much later) 'submitted to the appellation'.

In the light of these facts, the manipulation of the *Who's Who* entry is curious. When Buchman first appears in *Who's Who*, in 1928, we read that he '. . . became the centre of a new religious movement known as A First Century Christian Fellowship, 1921'. The name of Oxford does not appear until 1931, when the entry has been changed to read: '. . . originator of the Oxford Groups . . . became the centre of a new religious movement known as the Oxford Group Movement (A First Century Christian Fellowship), 1921.' Looking at the 1934 entry, one may find some significance in the fact that 1933 was observed as the centenary of the Oxford Movement proper—the Tractarian or Catholic revival in the Church of England. There was much publicity for this centenary, and it is not surprising that the Oxford Group Movement, as it had begun to call itself, should have enjoyed, by accident or design, some of the overflow of this *réclame*. At any rate, in this edition we find that, after thirteen years, the First Century Christian Fellowship has been dropped altogether—so that the Buchman entry now records that he '. . . became the centre of a new religious movement known as the Oxford Group Movement, 1921'.

In 1939 (as Herbert puts it), 'the year in which, by a happy chance, the Board of Trade is to be asked for official recognition, the epic swells . . ., and quite a new note is heard: ". . . visited Oxford in 1921, where in Christ Church the Oxford Group was founded." '

Herbert comments that the redraft of the entry must have been 'intended to suggest that in 1921 a new movement was deliberately "founded" with the name of "Oxford Group" '. He emphasises his point with a simple analogy: 'It would be one thing to say "After thirteen years I have decided to change my name from Buchman to Benson". It would be quite another to adjust the records so as to suggest that the name was Benson from the beginning.' He adds: ' "Small things", you may say. But if "absolute honesty" is so frail in small things, can it be trusted in the great?'

In the interests of Absolute Honesty, however, it must be recorded that this misleading entry was changed in later editions of *Who's Who*. Here Buchman's entry reads: '. . . visited Oxford in 1921 where in following years the Oxford leadership grew; travelled 1929, with a group of Oxford men in South Africa, where they were given the name Oxford Group by the press, their work since spreading to more than sixty countries.' No doubt the greater accuracy of this entry is the excuse for its discursiveness; but, by the end of his life, Buchman was occupying, in the British *Who's Who*, considerably more space than could be spared for Americans whom many Britons would consider more deserving of it—80 lines compared with 55 and 33 lines for Presidents Eisenhower and Truman, respectively, 38 for Professor Reinhold Niebuhr, 24 for Greta Garbo, and 23 for Robert Frost.

It must be supposed that this last entry was changed in order to dispel the misleading impression drawn attention to by Herbert. But the fact that it was changed makes it even more surprising that Buchman did not have the false entry about Cambridge University changed, too, though Herbert repeatedly drew attention to it (and in *Who's Who in America* he was said to have studied at 'Westminster College, Cambridge University'—still inaccurate but slightly less misleading). Possibly he was Guided not to do so because such a change would have marked a victory for a vigorous critic of the Group, as distinct from what could have been said of the other change, that it was merely a 'clarification' or 'amplification' of something which had been misinterpreted. If this is the case, this was surely a decision which disproves the Group slogan, 'Frank's guidance is always right': it would have been easy, and to his credit, to say that, since misunderstanding had been caused by the loose wording, the entry would be corrected in the next edition of *Who's Who.*

It may even be that, when he first went to Cambridge, Buchman—who knew, in 1921, little about the structure of English universities—genuinely thought that Westminster College was part of the University. It would have done him no harm to admit his error when it was pointed out. As the jaunty MRA jingle has it: 'Sorry is a magic little word.' But there was a streak of obstinacy in Buchman: perhaps it was partly this that made him so successful in detecting and overcoming obstinacy in others. There was trouble with the publishers of *Who's Who*, who resented aspersions on the accuracy of their highly reputed reference-book. But the Cambridge entry was not changed—and Herbert was able to observe, with some justification if unkindly, that Buchman had 'no more right to have claimed to have studied at Cambridge University than a man who reads a book in a Cambridge bun-shop'.

Throughout his middle years the progress of Buchman and his movement, though considerable, was by no means steady. There were spectacular ups and downs: fate seemed to deal favours and unpleasantnesses with capricious impartiality. Sometimes the same incident is interpreted, by supporters and by antagonists, in diametrically opposite ways. In one year he might be the host or guest of millionaires and royal personages, and able to use their names or their money to advance his cause—and then, in the same year, might come a sharp setback or humiliating snub, such as that delivered in July, 1937, at a Foyle literary luncheon in London, by Miss Margaret Rawlings, the actress. She had been invited as the 'guest of honour' without realising that the luncheon was in honour, too, of Buchman; and, despite intense advance counter-pressure and the numbing impact of a floodlit para-military parade of young Groupers, carrying banners, singing choruses and shouting slogans, she had the courage to say, in front of 2,000 other guests—many of them Buchmanites—that, to her, 'this public exposure of the soul, this psychic exhibitionism, with its natural accompaniment of sensual satisfaction', was 'as shocking, indecent and indelicate as it would be if a man took all his clothes off in Piccadilly Circus'.

For a time, when in New York, he lived in considerable comfort in a house in West 53rd Street belonging to John D. Rockefeller, jnr (but leased to a Changed lady). Here, in 1926, he entertained Queen Marie of Rumania to tea; he invited two hundred other guests, including eleven prominent citizens of Allentown, to meet her. Though this function secured gratifying publicity, it does not seem to have been an unqualified success: the Queen had a cold and did not stay long, and when (presumably not within earshot of the two hundred other guests) she asked Buchman to read her sins in her face, he promptly replied 'Pride and self-satisfaction'. (This dashing remark offsets, rather endearingly, some of the perennial accusations of snobbery; or perhaps Buchman had ascertained, before tea, that his guest was not really a top queen.)

The lists of those attending Group functions in this period read like a digest of the Social Register, Debrett, and the *Almanach de Gotha.* Some of the richest American families were usually represented; from the House of Lords would come Lord Addington, Lord Noel-Buxton, or Lord Rochester; from Holland, Count John Bentinck; from all over Northern Europe, an assortment of baronesses, including such splendidly Firbankian figures as the Baroness de Watteville Berckheim, who was thought to be of Latvian origin; from Austria, Baron Franckenstein; from Germany, Frau Katherine von Hanfstaengl, mother of Hitler's favourite, 'Putzi' Hanfstaengl.

It cannot be assumed that all of these were Changed and dedicated Groupers, but at least they had been induced to attend a Buchmanite house-party or assembly or *soirée*; and theirs is the kind of name that predominates in the Buchmanite guest-lists of the inter-war years, no doubt because a base had to be secured before the major attempts to infiltrate the Labour Movement in the West, and the ideological offensives in Asia and Africa (if these were fully foreseen in those years, which seems doubtful).

The Group had, indeed, made several tentative forays outside the Protestant and Anglo-Saxon countries which were most congenial to it, but its main excursions in Africa, for instance, were to the least African of African countries—the Union of South Africa. Here it was warmly welcomed, and the Deputy Prime Minister, Mr J. H. Hofmeyr, in a valedictory tribute, praised it in words that make sad reading now[1]—sad, and as empty as many of the other rhetorical endorsements of MRA extracted from politicians and potentates down the years.

But it was still, on the whole, domestic America at its most gilded that provided the cosiest pulpit for Buchman. At one time he was befriended by Mrs Thomas A. Edison, widow of the inventor: his home-town newspaper published a picture of him, sprucely dinner-jacketed, at a dinner-party for 150 that she gave in his honour. She compared his teaching to her husband's incandescent lamp. In September, 1936, a typical headline on the society page of the *New York Times* read:

[1] See p. 174

NEWPORT PARTIES
FOR OXFORD GROUP
Mrs Beverley Bogert Holds
Reception—Mrs Cornelius
Vanderbilt Entertains
WILLING SPENCERS HOSTS

A few months before these social diversions, an important Group assembly had been held at Stockbridge, Massachusetts. In the course of it one guest had the privilege of lunching privately with Dr Buchman: she was Mrs Henry Ford, wife of the head of the great automobile dynasty; both she and her husband were consistent supporters of Buchman's work. Buchman himself often preferred to watch from the background at Group gatherings, but at this assembly he spoke. It is on record (*New York Times*, 3rd June, 1936) that he said, possibly in reply to a question about the nature and purpose of his movement:

> You may say spiritual revolution if you want to, or you can say Christian revolution, or you can put in any qualifications or terms you like. Our aim is the remaking of the world. We remake people: nations are remade.
>
> Write this down: the problems of the world reflect the people who live in it. With that as our basis I am going to ask Mrs Cleveland E. Dodge to deliver a message which she has condensed into a few words.

Mrs Cleveland E. Dodge's message was as follows:

> If war were declared today the even course of our lives would be turned topsy-turvy. We would mobilise for action under the Red Cross. Why not mobilise today for action in a revolutionary army under the Cross of Jesus?

Mrs Dodge's thought for the day may have been more remarkable before it was condensed (at whose behest?); but, within its frame of reference, it is less totally null than Buchman's own pronouncement. 'Write this down: *the problems of the world reflect the people who live in it.'* Platitudes abound in religious discourses of all kinds, but has any other religious leader in history dared to say 'Write this down' before emitting a dozen words so confused in syntax, so almost entirely without useful meaning, so shatteringly flat as these? To a Christian, the claim that such phrases were uttered under divine Guidance must surely seem blasphemous—an insult to the intelligence of God. Yet the report does not indicate even a squeak of protest, from Mrs Cleveland E. Dodge or from anybody else: so easily, in the atmosphere of a Group assembly, were people soothed by mellow-sounding, vapid verbiage.

There were several contributions of more solid interest than this. A Dutch Socialist parliamentarian, Mr J. E. W. Duys, testified that Changing, according to the Buchmanite prescription, 'had improved both his personal behaviour and his law practice'.[1] Mr Robert W. Hudgens, regional director of the Resettlement Administration for the south-eastern States of the USA, explained that it was his duty to keep his Federal agency 'out of politics', but that, soon after he had started work in New Orleans, Senator Huey Long had sent a representative to see him, 'to discuss organisation and patronage'. This must have been a ticklish moment: in the vocabulary of that most corrupt and dictatorial of politicians, 'organisation and patronage' could mean only one thing—the carving-up of whatever spoils were going.

Mr Hudgens dealt with the menace in what one must concede was an inspired way. He invited Huey Long's representative to pray with him, and suggested that they should then act under joint Guidance. One would like to have seen the fixer's face at this moment. He seems, however, to have reported back satisfactorily, for Mr Hudgens was able to tell the assembly: 'The next day Huey Long sent word that if I got into any trouble by being honest I should let him know'—a

[1] Duys is remembered, as 'a tragic case', by present leaders of the Dutch Socialist Party. They say that he wanted, but failed, to become party leader, and that in the war he 'went wrong', collaborated with the Nazis, and fell out with the party. He died soon after the war.

memorable and, from that quarter, surprisingly fragrant assurance. 'God', added Mr Hudgens, 'is the wisest political boss.'

The assembly, which lasted for some days, was held in a camp. The camp cook, Francis Flanagan, confirmed to reporters that the menu was planned daily by God, during the morning Quiet Time which, like all good Buchmanites, the cook observed. Unfortunately, no details of this menu—its adequacy, its nutritional balance, its gastronomic ingenuity—survive.

Another moving testimony to the value of Guidance was given by a vacuum-cleaner salesman named Henry Sutton. 'I was proud of being an Englishman', he said, 'but I was guided by God to hoist the Stars and Stripes daily at the camp as a gesture of complete surrender of national pride.'

Soon after this assembly, Buchman was away on his travels again. This journey was one that he was not to be allowed to forget: his destination was Nazi Germany.

But there were also darker and more dubious episodes during this period, to balance the successful assemblies and rallies and the holy jollity of the grand hostesses' hospitality. Two incidents may be cited—each quite different in kind from the other but both, one must suppose, extremely embarrassing at the time.

The incident that I find the more puzzling occurred in the early 1920s—probably, according to my information, in 1921 or 1922, years during part of which, as we have seen, Buchman was in England. He undertook to escort on a world tour a young American, the son of wealthy parents, who had got into trouble through excessive drinking. Apparently the young man had shown himself responsive to Buchman's influence, and it was thought that Buchman—who still, evidently, had plenty of spare time—would be an ideal chaperon, tutor, and guardian. On the face of it, a happy arrangement—and this is a well-known Buchmanite anecdote: the tour has often been mentioned in print, always, of course, greatly to Buchman's credit. It may be that there was more than one such tour; but the only one of which I have been able to check some of the essential facts ended in a disastrous, and mysterious, anticlimax.

The young man in question was nineteen years old. His parents paid Buchman in advance a sum sufficient to cover the cost of the trip for the two of them; even in those days, this must have been substantial. The end of the expedition remains inexplicable. When the two travellers reached Paris, the younger of them fell in with some boys he knew of his own age, and left Buchman; and Buchman, instead of communicating with the young man's family, simply left him in Paris and proceeded on his travels alone. Nor did he ever repay any of the money that had been advanced to him. The young man died some years later, in his thirties.

When I first heard this story, I found it incredible. Buchman had indeed once before—in his dispute with the hospice trustees—behaved in a violently impulsive, almost hysterical, way and had sought to solve a problem by running away from it. But years of fruitful experience lay between that personal crisis and this: he was now not only an ordained Lutheran minister, but the life-changer whose own life had, he claimed, been changed by the transforming vision at Keswick. He was also a well-brought-up, reasonably well-educated, American citizen. It seemed impossible that he could have been guilty of conduct so flatly contrary to common decency, common honesty, and Christian charity.

But this information came to me direct from an unimpeachable source—from the young man's own brother and sister, who are well-known and highly respected residents of Philadelphia and persons of unquestionable integrity. I discussed the matter at length with his sister, and we considered every explanation that might have exculpated Buchman. Perhaps her brother had positively insisted on breaking with him and staying in Paris? But he was responsible to the parents: he should have cabled and written to them, asking to be relieved of his charge—and he should have done this even if the young man had asked him not to. Even suppose a bargain struck between them, Buchman agreeing not to get in touch with the parents in return for some promise of good conduct: Buchman should surely, then or on his return to Philadelphia, have contacted them and at least offered to refund some of the money; or, if he had left the balance of it with their son in Paris, he should have told them so. Or suppose that a letter from him went astray: again, it is inconceivable that he would not have gone to see them on his return, to discuss their son's case with them; and, if he had enclosed a cheque with the letter, he would have discovered sooner or later that it had not been paid into their account.

Whatever general view one takes of Buchman and his movement, it must be admitted that such conduct as this seems quite out of character. The story is, on the face of it, a highly improbable one. Yet those who are best qualified to know the facts insist, with complete certainty, that it is true. I feel obliged to accept what they tell me, and to agree with them that there is no reputable explanation of Buchman's behaviour.

Another incident from this period that seems worth mentioning is more often referred to by critics than by supporters of MRA, for its flavour is certainly disagreeable. It was in the spring of 1924 that Dr John G. Hibben, President of Princeton University, barred Buchman from the university campus. His edict was stern. He said: 'As long as I am President of the University (and I think I speak for the whole administration) there is no place for "Buchmanism" in Princeton.' Buchman, accordingly, was refused permission ever to hold a meeting there.

The situation that made this ban necessary will be familiar to anyone who has encountered young Buchmanites in action, especially in a university: it is compounded of zeal amounting to fanaticism, persistent crude invasions of physical and spiritual privacy, high-pressure attempts at 'life-changing', an obsessive and often impertinent harping on sin, especially sexual sin, and experiments in Guidance which have sometimes led students to neglect work and cut exams.

There may have been, in some individual cases, some good

consequences of all this feverish revivalism; but at Princeton, as elsewhere, the less good results were twofold: quite serious academic and emotional disturbance, leading in a number of cases to actual nervous and mental breakdowns; and secondly —a result troublesome to authority but not unhealthy in itself —reprisals by students who resented the Buchmanite solicitations. At Princeton these reprisals took the usual turbulent forms but were concentrated against what must have been a particularly fatuous work of art: this was a bronze statue entitled 'The Christian Student' which portrayed a sweater-clad youth, with a Bible in one hand and a football in the other, gazing at the stars. Night after night empty gin-bottles were stacked round the Christian Student's legs; sometimes he was painted red, sometimes decked with brassières and other unsuitable objects. Some years later, in 1930, the statue was taken down officially and stowed in a garage.

Despite the ban on Buchman personally, his student followers continued their activities—so much so that, at one time, their opponents mockingly formed a Society for the Propagation of Moral Turpitude. More than two years after the ban, in October, 1926, the Philadelphia Society of Princeton was charged, at a students' open forum, with Buchmanite tendencies. A questionnaire was circulated and resulted in overwhelming anti-Buchmanite votes—in one case, 253 to 85. Controversy was so acute, and resentment at the Buchmanites' conversion techniques so widespread, that President Hibben appointed a nine-man enquiry, on which were represented the trustees of the University, the faculty, and the undergraduates, to investigate the whole matter.

Since the Princeton ban on Buchman has been quoted against him so often, two facts must in fairness be stated. The report of Hibben's enquiry cleared the Philadelphia Society of aggressive or undesirable methods of personal evangelism. This does not mean that such methods were never used at any time by Buchmanite students, possibly not members of this Society; but it was a substantial acquittal. Secondly, in 1930, Buchman paid his first visit to Princeton since the ban—to officiate jointly, with President Hibben himself, at the wedding of Sam Shoemaker, jnr, the Episcopalian clergyman in whose parish he had established his national headquarters. Hibben, asked by the press if this implied a lifting of the ban, said that it did not; but he would hardly have agreed to take part in this ceremony with Buchman if he had felt serious doubts about his personal integrity.

Several more or less obvious observations on this incident may be made. One is that 'enthusiastic' religion can be dangerous to impressionable adolescents, especially those also undergoing the strains of intensive bookwork and unfolding sexual awareness. Another is that those who stimulate such enthusiasm, though not directly to blame for manifestations that even they may find excessive, have some responsibility for guarding in advance against emotional explosions. A third is that—as I know from the subsequent testimony of men who were at Princeton at the time—the greatest damage in such a case is done to Christianity itself, since it is inevitably identified to some extent with the warped version of it preached by the Buchmanites and personified in the ridiculous bronze statue. It is, moreover, identified specially with that aspect of their propaganda which will most surely catch the attention of the sex-conscious youth or girl—a narrow, repressive puritanism utterly remote from the spirit of the Gospel.

4

'THANK HEAVEN FOR HITLER!'

Buchman at the Hotel Adlon—His relations with Nazi leaders—An interview in New York—Hitler as the 'front-line' defender of Christianity—'A Karl Marx in every Jew'?—An elusive Nazi document, and an SS analysis

THE YEARS immediately before the Second World War were years of exultant advance for the Buchman Group; but they were also years in which some of its associations and attitudes earned it deep and lasting mistrust—culminating as they did in the American newspaper interview in which Buchman himself thanked heaven for Adolf Hitler.

He was one of many thousands of people from all over the world who visited Berlin, where the Olympic Games were being held, in the summer of 1936. Unlike most of the tourists, Buchman was privileged to meet and fraternise with some of the leading Nazis. Whether this was at his request or by their invitation, the contact was no doubt thought mutually advantageous.

One of the British visitors to Berlin was Mr Kenneth Lindsay, MP for Kilmarnock Burghs and, as Civil Lord of the Admiralty, a member of the British Government. He had seen something of the Oxford Groupers in their early days, and in the Hotel Adlon Buchman recognised him and greeted him cordially—asking if there were anyone he wanted to meet: did he know all the people there he ought to know? Lindsay said he thought so.

Buchman persisted. 'D'you know Heinrich Himmler?', he said. 'No? Say, you ought to know Heinrich. He's a great lad.'

Lindsay was aware, as Buchman also must have been, that Himmler was head of the Gestapo—a secret police force already notorious for exceptional brutality. He asked to be excused from meeting this 'great lad'.

Buchman added that Hitler himself was being most helpful to the Group: 'He lets us have house-parties whenever we like.' He did not seem to think much of England or of Canada: England was in a terrible state—'seething with Communism'; and so was Canada. Lindsay disagreed: he thought that such an assessment showed that Buchman really knew very little about England or Canada.

This account of Buchman's conversation with Lindsay was given me by Lindsay himself, and I published it in the *Daily Express*. It cannot have escaped the notice of Buchman or the MRA agents in London, but the factual statements in it have never been controverted. It is, indeed, not possible to deny them: Lindsay was a reputable and credible witness. On 15th May, 1941, however, an interview with Buchman appeared in the Allentown *Morning Call*. He was questioned about his association with Himmler. He denied that he knew him. The interviewer referred him to 'published reports of Himmler's reputed adoption of the Oxford Group principles'.[1] Buchman replied: 'Half the lies they tell about the Irish aren't true.'

Only three explanations of this belated denial of Kenneth Lindsay's testimony seem possible. Either Buchman was bluffing when he boasted to Lindsay of his friendship with Himmler (for, unless he had met him or wanted Lindsay to think he had met him, he would hardly have called him a 'great lad'); or, when he was interviewed by the *Call*, his memory was surprisingly defective; or he was lying.

Perhaps the best evidence is that of a leading member of

[1] In fact, it was more often said that Himmler's wife, rather than Himmler himself, was well-disposed towards the Group.

MRA's 'inner ring'—Mr Peter Howard. In *The World Rebuilt*[1] Howard writes (p. 127):

> The fact is that Buchman never met Hitler, and Hitler was too cautious to get into Buchman's orbit. Nor was Buchman an intimate of Himmler or of any other member of the Nazi hierarchy.

There is a distinction here, clearly intentional, between meeting and intimacy. By denying that Buchman was 'an intimate of Himmler', Howard implies that he did know him, if less than intimately—and thus shows that Buchman's denial, published ten years earlier, was false. Nor is there even the thin excuse for Buchman that Himmler was a leader of a country with which America was at war; for the denial dates from seven months before Pearl Harbor.

A fresh problem is raised, however, by Howard's blunt statement that 'Buchman never met Hitler' and his further statement that 'Hitler was too cautious to get into Buchman's orbit'. For in the archives of the Franklin D. Roosevelt Library at Hyde Park, New York, there is a letter to President Roosevelt from Mr Harry W. Blair, then Assistant Attorney General, telling him of Buchman's forthcoming visit to Germany and asking him to see Buchman before his departure—with the following remarkable explanation:

> Herr Hitler has requested a meeting with Dr Buchman. It is a matter of embarrassment to Dr Buchman when speaking to the leaders in these foreign countries not to have been received by his own President.

This suggests a somewhat onerous extension of protocol. If the leader of every British religious or philanthropic organisation—the President of the Baptist Union, say, or the Chief Scout—is going to claim that, before he goes on a tour in the course of which he may meet a foreign head of state, he ought first to have audience of the Queen, because it would be 'a

[1] Blandford Press, 1951.

matter of embarrassment' to him not to have been so received, the Court Circular will be even longer than it is.

But the preceding sentence is even more interesting: 'Herr Hitler has requested a meeting with Dr Buchman.' Mr Blair had got to know Buchman when staying in Florida with his wife, who had been ill: the rest of his letter shows that he was thoroughly 'sold' on the Group, and in touch with Buchman. ('He can be reached directly at the Battle Creek Sanitorium, Miami Springs, Florida, or a message sent to me here[1] would reach him.') It is inconceivable that he would have made this statement about Hitler except on Buchman's authority; and it is unlikely that a lawyer sufficiently eminent to be Assistant Attorney General of the United States, trained in the weighing of evidence, would have reversed, and translated into a form so positive, a mere expression of hope for such a meeting on Buchman's part. Yet Peter Howard says that Hitler was 'too cautious' to meet Buchman. Is Howard mis-informed, or was Buchman, through his notable new ally, trying to put one across Roosevelt?

Whether Buchman did or did not meet Hitler, it was Roosevelt, not Hitler, who may have been, at this time, 'too cautious to get into Buchman's orbit'. A memorandum, signed 'K.', attached to Mr Blair's letter in the Hyde Park files, records that he was told by telephone that 'the President would like tremendously to see Dr Buckman [*sic*]' but that this was 'physically impossible' at that time.

Buchman arrived back in America, after his German trip, on 25th August, 1936. Next day the *New York World-Telegram* published its celebrated interview with him. The staff reporter who wrote it was William A. H. Birnie (now a senior editor of *Reader's Digest*). Since this interview was the start of the major public controversy of Buchman's life, and since his supporters have continued to complain that unfair use has been made of it by his critics, it seems desirable to quote it in full:

[1] The Assistant Attorney General's office in Washington.

HITLER OR ANY FASCIST LEADER CONTROLLED BY GOD COULD CURE ALL ILLS OF WORLD, BUCHMAN BELIEVES

By William A. H. Birnie,
World-Telegram Staff Writer

To Dr Frank Nathan Daniel Buchman, vigorous, outspoken, 58-year-old leader of the revivalist Oxford Group, the Fascist dictatorships of Europe suggest infinite possibilities for remaking the world and putting it under 'God control'.

'I thank heaven for a man like Adolf Hitler, who built a front line of defence against the anti-Christ of Communism,' he said today in his book-lined office in the annex to Calvary Church, Fourth Ave and 21st St.

'My barber in London told me Hitler saved all Europe from Communism. That's how he felt. Of course, I don't condone everything the Nazis do. Anti-Semitism? Bad, naturally. I suppose Hitler sees a Karl Marx in every Jew.

'But think what it would mean to the world if Hitler surrendered to the control of God. Or Mussolini. Or any dictator. Through such a man God could control a nation overnight and solve every last, bewildering problem.'

Dr Buchman, who is directing an Oxford house-party tonight at the Lenox, Mass. estate of Mrs Harriet Pullman Schermerhorn, returned from Europe aboard the *Queen Mary*, after attending Oxford meetings in England and the Olympic Games in Berlin.

A small, portly man, who doesn't smoke or drink and listens quietly to 'God's plans' for a half hour or so every day, usually before breakfast, Dr Buchman talked easily about world affairs while eight or nine Oxfordites—good-looking young fellows in tweeds—sat on the floor and listened.

'The world needs the dictatorship of the living spirit of God,' he said and smiled, adjusting his rimless glasses and smoothing the graying hair on the back of his head. 'I like to put it this way. God is a perpetual broadcasting station and all you need to do is tune in. What we need is a supernational network of live wires across the world to every last man, in every last place, in every last situation.

'The world won't listen to God but God has a plan for every person, for every nation. Human ingenuity is not enough. That is why the isms are pitted against each other and blood falls.

'Spain has taught us what godless Communism will bring. Who would have dreamed that nuns would be running naked in the streets? Human problems aren't economic. They're moral, and they can't be solved by immoral measures. They could be solved within a God-controlled democracy, or perhaps I should say a theocracy, and they could be solved through a God-controlled Fascist dictatorship.'

He looked around the room at the eight or nine young men drinking in his words, and straightened the crimson rose in his button hole.

'Suppose we here were all God-controlled and we became the Cabinet,' he said. 'You'—pointing at the reporter, who seldom ventures off the pavements of Manhattan—'You would take over agriculture. You'—a Princeton graduate beamed—'would be Mr Hull. Eric here, who has been playing around with a prominent Canadian who's Cabinet is material,[1] would be something else, and this young lawyer would run the Post Office.

'Then in a God-controlled nation, capital and labour would discuss their problems peacefully and reach God-controlled solutions. Yes, business would be owned by individuals, not by the State, but the owners would be God-controlled.'

The Oxford Group has no official membership lists, no centralised organisation, but Dr Buchman estimated that

[1] *Sic.* There may be an error in transcription, or a misprint, here. Elsewhere in the interview a few obvious misprints have been corrected.

'literally millions' listened in to his recent world broadcast from the meeting in England attended by 15,000 persons. Finances?

'God runs them,' he smiled. 'Don't you say every day, Give us this day our daily bread? And don't you receive?'

The group is built on the simple thesis that there is a divine plan for the world and that human beings, with faith and devotion, can receive God-given guidance in a 'quiet time' of communion. Most Oxfordites write down their guidance and then check it against the 'four absolutes' —absolute honesty, absolute purity, absolute unselfishness, absolute love.

'Those are Christ's standards,' Dr Buchman explained. 'We believe that human nature itself can be changed by them. We believe in answering revolution by more revolution—but revolution within the individual, and through the individual, revolution in the nation, and, through the nation, revolution in the world. It's as simple as that—Christian simplicity. And it's fun, too. We call each other by our first names and our meetings are always informal.

'I held meetings at the Republican and Democratic conventions. What Washington needs is God-control. Landon talks about divine guidance. Why doesn't he apply it? And the finest thing Roosevelt ever said was this—"I doubt if there exists any problem, political or economic, which would not melt before the fire of spiritual awakening".

'Oxford is not a one-way ticket to heaven, although that's a splendid thing and lots of people need it. It's a national ticket, too. That's the ticket we should vote in this coming election—God's ticket.'

Dr Buchman is unmarried, a graduate of Muhlenberg College, which awarded him a doctorate of divinity in 1926. He said he was 'changed'—Oxfordites use the word to mean the complete surrender to God control—by a gradual process.

'I was in England and I began to realise I was a sinner and there was an abyss between Christ and me,' he said. 'I was resenting my lost power and I was confessing others' sins when the real problem was mine. Then I went to church.

'A vision of the Cross. Of Christ on the Cross. An actual vision. I was changed then, but I've been changing ever since. A little even today, I suppose.'

'And when was the vision, Dr Buchman?'

'Let's see,' he said, and rustled some pamphlets in his hand. 'Let's see—what year was the vision?'

He looked around at the faces turned toward him. 'What year was the vision?' he repeated. One of the young men spoke up. '1908, wasn't it, Dr Buchman?'

Dr Buchman smiled at him.

'Of course,' he said. 'That was it. 1908.'

The interview began on the front page and was continued on page six of the newspaper. The continuation was headed: 'FASCIST WORLD RULED BY GOD, BUCHMAN IDEA/ Oxford Leader Declares That Would Solve "Every Last Bewildering Problem"/IS GRATEFUL FOR HITLER/ Asserts Spain Has Taught what Godless Communism Will Bring.'

This part of the interview was accompanied by a photograph of Buchman looking quizzically down at a young supporter on whose shoulder his hand rested. This photograph had a headline, 'THANK HEAVEN FOR A MAN LIKE HITLER' and a caption 'Dr Frank Buchman, who believes Hitler is Christianity's defender against Communism, with one of his young Oxford Group disciples, C. S. Wishard.'

Not unnaturally, this interview caused a furore both among the Oxford Group's friends and among its critics. Hitler had been in power for three years: much was already known in the West about the evils of the Nazi tyranny; the most active of its opponents—Trade Union organisers, Social Democrats,

Communists, religious leaders—were in concentration camps, others were leaving Germany as refugees; and—as Buchman himself in this interview showed that he knew—the persecution of the Jews had begun. Many Groupers must have been distressed by their leader's tribute to the Nazi dictator, and some, no doubt, left the movement in disgust. Conversely, the critics felt that what they had said about the Group—in particular, that its ethos was essentially totalitarian, tending to a kind of spiritual Fascism—was now justified.

MRA spokesmen, if tackled even today about this interview, never, so far as I know, repudiate what Buchman said and do not usually pretend that he was not accurately reported. They rely mainly on one or more of four lines of argument:

(1) *The 'thank heaven for Hitler' remark is 'quoted out of context'.* Certainly: it often is. But how could acres of context alter the plain meaning of the words? Buchman, having just visited Germany and being, no doubt, bemused by Nazi propaganda and the splendour of the Olympic Games, was honestly grateful for the rise of Hitler and honestly believed that he had 'built a front-line of defence' against Communism, which—again honestly—he equated with 'anti-Christ'.

In any case, if the context is examined thoroughly, it hardly exonerates Buchman. There is the one perfunctory phrase dissociating him from the Nazis' anti-Semitism: 'Bad, naturally.' But then, at once, he finds a slick excuse even for this: 'I suppose Hitler sees a Karl Marx in every Jew.' If these words mean anything, they must mean that Buchman thought it rather less objectionable to persecute Jews if they were also Marxists; for if he were merely stating this objectively, as the motive for Hitler's anti-Semitism, he would surely have added some further words of dissociation; he must have known, too, about the Nazis' theories of 'racial purity' and the Nordic *Herrenvolk*; and he must have known that Hitler did *not* see a Marxist in every Jew, since he had been busy confiscating the property of rich Jewish capitalists.

(2) *The interview, as published, was a 'garbled' version of remarks made by Buchman 'off the cuff'.* So far as I know, only one Buch-

manite has resorted to the slightly unworthy device (used by politicians who want to dodge the consequences of an indiscreet remark) of 'blaming the reporter'. Newspapers do sometimes publish reports which—usually through condensation and omission—distort what has been said in interviews; but this one ran to considerable length, and (except for the one line already referred to[1]) it reads like a straightforward, largely verbatim, account of what Buchman actually said. The words attributed to him as direct quotes are very much in his style of speaking. Much of the thought, too, is characteristic. In any case, I find no evidence, in the files of the *New York World-Telegram* or elsewhere, that Buchman at the time issued any denial or correction, or ventured to suggest that the reporter had misrepresented him. He would surely have done so if the interview had not fairly conveyed the substance of what he had said.

As for the 'off the cuff' excuse, that is even feebler. This was not one of those hasty interviews given as a ship docks and the reporters swarm on board. It took place, probably by appointment, in Buchman's 'book-lined office'. He evidently talked with the reporter for some time. He was surrounded by 'young men drinking in his words', and must have considered in advance what he was going to say to them (and to the press) about his German visit—and not merely considered but obtained what he believed to be 'accurate, adequate' Guidance from God about what to tell them. On his own showing, no man ever spoke less 'off the cuff'.

(3) *Buchman only fraternised with the Nazi leaders in order to 'change' them.* Mr Peter Howard has plugged this line consistently since his first Buchmanite apologia, *Innocent Men* (1941), in which he wrote (p. 83): 'I should think far less of Buchman if he went into Germany and only tried to find perfect Christians to consort with.' He went on to compare Buchman with Christ, who was 'always being reproved by the Pharisees for mixing with sinners'.

This seems to me a disingenuous argument. When Christ

[1] p. 69, *fn.*

told the woman taken in adultery that her sins were forgiven, he did not express warm public approval of her sins. He said: 'Go, and sin no more.' He forgave another sinner 'because she loved much'. Buchman in his interview, and in what we know of his conversations in Germany, did not follow the formula of hating the sin and loving the sinner; he loved the sin, too—or seemed to. His passing word of disapproval of one aspect of the Nazi régime was mild in comparison with his gratitude ('I thank heaven . . .') for what seemed to him Hitler's main achievement; though even he can hardly have mistaken the hate-filled paranoid dictator for one who 'loved much'.

Mr Howard went on to make a curious point—arguing that it was right that Buchman should have made these friendly contacts with Nazis because, in 1936, the Prime Minister had defended as 'highly beneficial' a meeting between a senior officer of the Royal Air Force and the Nazi Ribbentrop. To argue this in 1941 was both inept and cool; for by now Winston Churchill was Prime Minister—but the one whom Mr Howard was calling in aid was Churchill's old antagonist (and a former victim of Mr Howard's pen), Stanley Baldwin.

One may also observe that, in contrast with the sensational and painless conversions of other world statesmen claimed by MRA, Buchman seems to have made no impact whatever on the Nazi leaders. Perhaps he did not try very hard: after all, they were, in his opinion, defending Christianity. The headquarters of anti-Christ were further East. Come to think of it, it is puzzling that Buchman, feeling as he did about Communism, never went to Moscow to try to Change Stalin—or, later, Khrushchov. Presumably he was never Guided to do so: could this mean that his Guide did not agree with his identification of anti-Christ? Whatever the reason, it seems a pity that he never faced this supreme challenge: it would have been a fascinating encounter.

(4) *Many other prominent people, in Britain, Europe, and America, were wrong about Hitler.* Yes, indeed: Buchman is not alone in being condemned by the judgement of history; with him stand not only the open pro-Nazis, of whom there were in Britain

and America a few before the war, as now, but also the apostles of 'appeasement'. There, most notably, are Neville Chamberlain and his colleagues in the British Government, with such disastrous advisers as Sir Horace Wilson and Geoffrey Dawson (then Editor of *The Times*). There are the French politicians and industrialists with whom they conspired to betray Czechoslovakia. Some of these men were wicked, some merely foolish: their main folly was that, like Buchman, they feared Nazism less, and thought it less of a menace, than Communism.

But there is one big difference between these men and Buchman. Whether they were by profession religious men or not, they did not claim to be divinely guided in all that they said and did. They were ordinary fallible human beings, and some of them have since admitted, in their memoirs, that they were wrong. It would be a laudable demonstration of Absolute Honesty if Buchman and his supporters had done the same. They have never been able to do so—for if they did once make such an admission, on an issue of this importance, their fundamental theory of Guidance, in its special Buchmanite form, would be exploded. So this defence is as invalid, and for the same reason, as the 'off the cuff' excuse: 'Frank's Guidance is always right.' Hence all the wrigglings and evasions about the Hitler interview. Hence, too, the irritation with critics who are 'always raking it up', and the attempt to brush it off as 'old stuff', of no relevance today.[1]

It was still considered relevant, six and a half years after its publication, by the United States officials who had to consider a plea that some full-time MRA workers should be excused military service. (They were 'fighting a losing battle against induction in the Army', said Colonel Arthur V. McDermott, New York City draft director—adding that, in one case at least, 'the fraud and deceit' were 'palpable' and that in this case the record was 'reeking with hypocrisy and bad faith'.) Early in 1942, Draft Appeal Board 4, whose chairman, Mr Charles H. Tuttle, was a former United States Attorney, referred specifically to the *World-Telegram* interview and the

[1] *Cf* p. 280.

statements there attributed to Buchman, and delivered the following opinion:

> Careful research has established that the authenticity of these statements has never been repudiated nor their contents retracted by Dr Buchman.
>
> At the time when these statements were made, Hitler's whole philosophy of the divine right of might and of Germany and the Germans as the super-race, his program for the ruthless expansion of Germany by military conquest, his purpose to overthrow democracy in Germany and elsewhere, and his inhuman and unChristian call for persecution and destruction of the Jews, had been fully proclaimed to the world.

Mr Tuttle also observed that MRA was claiming an 'immunity not asked by or accorded to any other lay religious organisation', and spoke of its 'high-pressure methods to attain this special status'—methods which included the organising of telegrams and letters from 'holders of high public office'.

MRA propagandists point to the fact that thousands of Buchmanites served in the forces during the war as if this disposed of the matter and disproved the charges against Buchman. It does no such thing: it merely tends to show that these individual Buchmanites behaved decently, patriotically—and inconsistently. Their behaviour was inconsistent just because the Group could not, and did not, repudiate Buchman's endorsement of Hitler. Far from it: in 1941, on this very point, Mr Peter Howard wrote:[1]

> This fact is plain. The Oxford Group in Britain stands or falls with Frank Buchman. It is united to him by bonds of affection, interest, loyalty, and knowledge. The Group is the conception, life-work and inspiration of the man.

MRA is simply, as we have seen, the Oxford Group renamed and expanded. Some who do not know its earlier history may

[1] In *Innocent Men*, p. 94.

find its advertisements plausible; or they may be attracted by the enthusiasm of its advocates and the simplicity of its panacea for human ills. Before becoming involved in it, they ought to pause and consider the facts set out here—the basic fact being that this movement, claiming infallible Guidance, is the movement whose founder, without contradiction by his supporters, admired and praised the most abominable tyranny of modern times.

Here it seems right to refer to a document which was the theme of a letter in *The Times* of 29th December, 1945, signed by Lord Ammon and six other eminent persons.

They referred to 'a secret Gestapo report which has now been discovered'. They said that this report, prepared by the Reich Central Security Office, dealt with the aims and activities of Buchman and the Oxford Group; that it denounced them for 'uncompromisingly taking up a frontal position against National Socialism'; and that 'the secret police regarded the movement as "the pacemaker of Anglo-American diplomacy" '. They added this quotation from the report:

> The Group breathes the spirit of western democracy. It supplies the Christian garment for world democratic aims. The Group and the democracies supplement each other and render each other's work fruitful.

It may be remarked, in passing, that some theologians would not regard it as the business of Christianity to supply a 'garment' for any particular political system. Democracy, in its fullest expression, may be the system that approximates most nearly to a Christian philosophy of human equality and human rights—more so, indeed, than the theocracy hankered after by Buchmanites—but full democracy, economic, social, and political, does not yet exist anywhere in the world.

However, this enemy testimonial is clearly an impressive one, and it is natural that MRA spokesmen should often have used it when endeavouring to rebut the most embarrassing of the criticisms of their founder. Peter Howard, for instance, quotes the *Times* letter in full in *The World Rebuilt*, supplying also this information:

> The Gestapo report, *Die Oxfordgruppenbewegung*, was compiled in 1942 by the Head Office of the Reich Security Department. The discovery of this 126-page document during the German retreat from France was first disclosed in an Associated Press dispatch by the distinguished American columnist, DeWitt Mackenzie.

The letter in *The Times* suggested that a full translation of the document should be 'made available to the British public'. So far as I know, this has not been done. It is hard to imagine why, if a copy of it is or was in the possession of MRA and if the quotations in the *Times* letter indicate fairly the gist of it.

Unfortunately, the provenance and whereabouts of this document are one of the minor mysteries of the general mystery of MRA. *Time* magazine, with all its resources, was unable to locate it, and seems to have received vaguely evasive or negative answers when it tried to do so. I had the same experience, both in Washington and in Whitehall; and no trace of it could be found at the American-run Documents Centre in Berlin, which houses a considerable body of Nazi Party records.

This Centre does, however, have in its archives another Nazi document on the Oxford Group, produced by the SS Central Security Office in 1936—six years earlier than the one quoted in the *Times* letter. This was the year of Buchman's visit to Germany; the document is dated November, 1936, by which time he had been back in America for three months; yet, curiously, it makes no mention of his visit. Presumably its printing and distribution (restricted, for it is marked 'Secret') were delayed for some months after it had been compiled. Otherwise, the thorough and cautious Nazi bureaucrats responsible for drafting it (a task evidently carried out with care) could hardly have ignored Buchman's visit and have written, as they did, quoting an article in the *Nordschleswigsche Korrespondenz*:

Buchman is said to keep away from Germany for the time being, until the movement has taken root in Scandinavia. 'Everything Nordic, after all, is supposed to have a good name in Germany; if Oxford, therefore, were to be associated with tall blond Scandinavians of the same Lutheran upbringing, the movement would find easier the approach to their southern neighbours.'

None the less, the movement had already made some headway in Germany. Groups had been identified as functioning unobtrusively in Baden-Baden, Freiburg-B., Cologne, Stuttgart, Heidelberg, Darmstadt, Ludwigshafen, Offenbach, Bad Homburg, Butzbach, Hanau, Giessen, Marburg, Kassel, Essen, Hanover, Berlin, Leipzig, Munich, and Dresden.

This document is more balanced and objective in its assessment of Buchmanism than the later one seems to have been. On the one hand, it welcomes the movement as tending 'to make the Christian church less rigid': on the other hand, it sees in it 'a new and dangerous opponent for National Socialism', on the grounds that 'the Oxford Movement will bring a strengthening of the eastern Christian spirit'. This phrase, at first sight obscure, does not refer to the Orthodox East. It is an echo of the essential conflict between Christianity, cradled in an oriental religion—specifically, the Jewish religion—and the 'Aryan' racial myth: to the doctrinaire Nazi, Christianity was tainted with Judaism and with (to quote another phrase from the same passage) 'the oriental sense of guilt and atonement.'

On the whole, the conclusions reached in this document are unfavourable to the Buchmanites (for one reason, because 'their methods of suggestion make such an impact on members, particularly women, that they will be unlikely to co-operate with National Socialist organisations'). No absolutist régime can tolerate any potential domestic rival. But the document is not an incitement to active persecution: its object is to inform and to warn, and it concludes with strict instructions to police, mayors, and other functionaries that the Group is to be watched and reported on.

The document also includes evidence showing the Group in a light much more acceptable to the Nazis. This anecdote is quoted from the *Schleswig-Holsteinischen Landeszeitung*:

> A Swedish woman saw fit, after the National Socialist triumph, to use her considerable influence in her country to spread horror stories about the new Germany. Moreover she took part in public denunciations of the person of our Führer, Adolf Hitler. A short while ago she attended one of the larger Oxford meetings. There her conscience was sharply roused, and as a consequence she decided to write a letter of apology to Germany's Leader and to see to it that her change of mind became known in her own country.

If they know of its existence, it is not surprising that the MRA propagandists have made less use of this document than of the later one: they would have had to use it rather selectively. It is, none the less, clear that, though Hitler may have 're-quested a meeting with Dr Buchman', Buchman was by no means *persona grata*, at some time in 1936, with Himmler—'*Der Reichsführer SS*', whose ominous title appears on the front of this document. These two facts are, historically, not irreconcilable. Hitler himself may have had his own advance copy of the report and, piqued by its ambivalence, may have decided to see Buchman and weigh him up for himself; to see, perhaps, if he could use him. Alternatively, in police states as in democracies, security and intelligence organisations sometimes do their secret work in ways not known or approved of by the political leaders: in the United States the Central Intelligence Agency has occasionally deviated from State Department policy. It is even possible that those who drafted the report deliberately included material both for and against the Group in order to play safe on a matter on which there was no definite directive from a level higher than theirs.

Neither of these documents—the one, available, mixed in its judgement, the other, unavailable, alleged to be wholly hostile to the Group—seems to add anything useful to our knowledge of Buchman's attitude to Nazism in the 1930s. Straining tolerance to the limit, we may surmise that, in 1936, Buchman sensed some suspicion of himself among those whom he met in Germany, and feared that the work of his movement might be hindered. This could be one explanation of his over-effusive tribute to Himmler and of the ecstatic tone of the *World-Telegram* interview; he may have tried to curry favour with the Nazi bosses for the impeccable purpose of safeguarding his German followers. We may also surmise—since we cannot read it—that the missing 1942 document was, as MRA claims, wholly hostile to the Group. If this is so, it is not to be wondered at: by 1942 America was in the war, Buchman was siding unreservedly with the western allies, MRA was staging a 'patriotic revue', *You Can Defend America*, and rear-admirals and senators were more or less eagerly signing the familiar endorsements.

But these, as I say, are surmises. The testimony of Kenneth Lindsay and the *World-Telegram* interview are solidly factual evidence which has never been successfully contested.

5

GUIDANCE, NOT GUNS

Appeasement and Moral Re-Armament—The Munich crisis: 'France set a new fashion'—Some advice to Denmark—Influential support in Washington—A personal message from Roosevelt; and how it was organised

THE MONTH of September, 1938—one year before the outbreak of the Second World War—was the most critical month in all the inter-war years. German official documents published since the war show that a leading article in *The Times* of 7th September, suggesting that Czechoslovakia should cede the Sudeten area to Germany, and Chamberlain's offer to fly to Germany, so far from helping to secure peace, merely stiffened Hitler's attitude. He announced that, when he and Chamberlain met, he would present the German demands 'with brutal frankness'. So he did; and at Munich, on 29th September, Chamberlain and the French Premier, Daladier, gave him what he wanted. This was the shameful collapse to which the policy of 'appeasement' had logically led.

Throughout this year Buchman was more active and vocal than ever. His rallies and assemblies often coincided with moments of international crisis; and, examined in retrospect, much of what he said seems to have harmonised ominously with Hitler's interests. The slogan of 'Moral Re-Armament' was launched in May at a meeting in the East Ham Town Hall. Early in September a 'World Assembly for Moral

Re-Armament' was held at Interlaken: at this Assembly—three weeks before Munich—Buchman coined another slogan, 'Guidance or Guns'. Now, whether he did or did not so intend, the suggestion in these catch-phrases seemed to be that if people relied on MRA, and on Guidance, there would be no need for material re-armament or for guns. But what Britain needed at that moment was, precisely, guns. Successive governments had neglected their elementary duty of providing adequate national defence. If these slogans had any effect at all—and they may have had, projected as they were, with the Nazi-type flamboyance of the MRA rallies, among nations desperately troubled by the threat of war—the effect can only have been to lull people into a feeling that physical unpreparedness for war didn't really matter. Later, when Britain was actually at war, the Buchmanites denied indignantly that this had been the intention of these slogans; but the timing of their introduction, coupled with Buchman's open admiration for Hitler only two years before (and there is no evidence that he had changed his mind about him by 1938), seems significant.

Buchman was in London in November, 1938, and was interviewed on Armistice Day:

> . . . Commenting on the recent war crisis in Europe, Dr Buchman continued: 'France began to show that in a crisis the natural thing and rational thing is to listen rather than talk. France listened. France as a nation which sets fashions set [a] new fashion during the crisis. . . . One man, convinced, set a nation listening. Conviction took him to a cabinet minister and a nation acted. . . .'

From this panegyric one might suppose that, of all the nations of Western Europe, France at this time had the highest morale and the least corrupt politicians. As 1940 was to show, this is almost exactly the reverse of the truth. Again, there is no evidence that Buchman ever withdrew or corrected this misjudgement.

By now, disillusionment with Munich was widespread; but Buchman still seemed to be fairly content:

> 'On the fateful Munich day men and women everywhere attempted to make contact with the all-wise powerful force that might and could direct the destiny of nations. It became front-page news. Picture papers . . . recorded pictures of nations listening attentively. Every man carried in himself the possibility of having a plan for permanent peace and avoiding ugly catastrophe which no-one really wanted. . . .'

Woolly as these observations are, they appear to indicate that, in Buchman's view, the Munich pact—which satisfied most of Hitler's ambitions and made the Second World War almost inevitable—was a result of divine intervention; and that this intervention had been brought about, through a kind of automatic magic, by 'nations listening attentively'. It is an interesting sequence of processes.

Speaking particularly to his own country, America, Dr Buchman said: 'Shall we at last, as a nation, during our silence make a high resolve that we shall discover at all costs that silence is the answer to enduring peace? . . . For guidance comes in silence. Guidance outmodes guns. Guidance is better than guns.'

Earlier in this interview Buchman, explaining what happened during his own Quiet Times, said: 'I find that God's thoughts become my thoughts.' The quality of thought disclosed in the rest of the interview is such that theists must hope that Buchman's confidence on this point was as mistaken as his judgement of contemporary political affairs. It is hard to make any sense at all of such a phrase as 'silence is the answer to enduring peace'; but the mood is clearly one of passive acceptance, and the general trend seems to be towards a kind of ultra-Gandhism—non-violent *non*-resistance—which would have been singularly futile in western countries faced with the raging aggressions of Hitler. In the 1960s MRA offers to equip nations which did resist Hitler, and defeated him, with 'an ideology for democracy'. There is a certain effrontery in the offer, when one considers that in the 1930s MRA's founder was providing an ideology for appeasement.

Wherever he went, the treatment was the same. Some time earlier, speaking in Denmark, he had said: 'I challenge Denmark to be a miracle among nations, her national policy dictated by God, her national defence the respect and gratitude of her neighbours, her national armament an army of life-changers.' Guidance, again, not guns . . . but 'the respect and gratitude of her neighbours', especially her big neighbour to the south, didn't prove much of a 'national defence' to Denmark when Hitler chose to march in. No doubt Hitler could have crushed Denmark quickly in any case; but some small countries have managed to hold out against aggression by big powers for a considerable time—if their will to resist is strong. Hundreds of thousands, perhaps millions, of people in the Scandinavian and Low countries heard Buchman speak in those pre-war years. If his influence was as great as his devotees claimed that it was, he must have contributed substantially to the weakening of their will to resist. It may be only a coincidence—the matter is not provable one way or the other—but these same countries were the very ones that the Nazis overran most easily; while countries untouched by Buchmanism—small countries, too, not strong in armaments, countries like Yugoslavia, Poland, and Greece—put up the fiercest struggle against invasion. If Hitler was as helpful to Buchman in 1936 as Buchman's conversation with Kenneth Lindsay suggests that he was, he must have thought, in 1940, that he had made an excellent investment.

During and since the war, MRA propaganda has claimed that Buchman's influence in the Nazi-occupied democracies had results quite different from those suggested here: according to this version, dedicated Buchmanites led and inspired the Resistance in such countries as Norway and Holland, and witnesses have indeed been found to testify that this was so. Again, this cannot be absolutely proved or disproved, but the post-war MRA claim seems contrary to the logic of the pre-war Buchmanite position; and, without questioning the good faith of the MRA witnesses, I can only say that I have met a good many people, mainly Social Democrats, who were indubitably active in the Resistance in these countries and that, without exception, they have been astonished to learn of the MRA claim and have vigorously denied it. No doubt, like so much else in MRA propaganda, it is, without being totally untrue, greatly exaggerated.

In March, 1939, Buchman went back to America, after an absence of more than two years, with a large party of followers, including Bill Rowell, 'leader of 420,000 unemployed in London's East End', the Hon Miles Phillimore, 'who has been living and working with Rowell', Bishop Logan H. Roots, Frau (now called Madame) Hanfstaengl, John Vickers, son of the General Manager of Vickers Oils Ltd, Leeds, and several Oxford graduates. Interviewers found him as ebullient as ever and full of bombastic verbiage: 'The MRA slogan has caught on like wildfire in these troublesome days in England. . . . We are the repair crew for a disabled world. . . . Mankind will survive because mankind will respond to MRA'. In May he stated that he believed the European situation to be 'much better': an Allentown *Chronicle* reporter, quoting him on God's (i.e., Buchman's) 'Plan' for the world, wrote: 'He speaks of The Plan's followers in terms of "millions" and leaves you under the impression that The Plan is partially responsible for the improvement of the European outlook.'

This was two months after Hitler, breaking his own Munich pledges, had occupied the whole of Czechoslovakia. Everyone in the European democracies, including Neville Chamberlain, Daladier, and the other appeasers, now knew that Munich had been a disastrous failure and that war could hardly be averted. To say at this moment, as Buchman did, that things in Europe were 'much better' showed either a sinister and unconcealed devotion to the cause of Nazism or (more probably) crass ignorance, an infinite capacity for self-deception, and incorrigible frivolity.

Several months later, when in California for an MRA Assembly, he was involved in an escapade which even he may have found slightly too farcical—a visit to Mae West in Hollywood. According to the *New York Herald Tribune* of 19th August, 1939, Buchman instructed Miss West for thirty minutes in the principles of MRA. 'Miss West said she had become a firm believer in the doctrine'—adding 'I owe all my success to the kind of thinking MRA is.' She was also reported to have said to Buchman: 'Have you met W. C. Fields yet? You should. Moral Re-Armament is just the thing he needs. Give it to him in a bottle and he'll go for it.' It was put about subsequently that this meeting had been a stupid publicity stunt, and that Buchman was 'nonplussed' by it. He was not too nonplussed, however, to pose with Mae West for a photograph which has probably been published more often than any other ever taken of him.

On 27th August—just a week before the outbreak of war in Europe—he felt Guided to say, in a broadcast from San Francisco, that 'every nation and every individual' was 'responsible' for the international crisis: the Nazi war criminals might have quoted this exculpation at Nuremberg.

At the end of the year he was at Allentown for an 'old home Christmas visit', with—unusually for him—only one companion, Richard Van Dyke of New York City. The representative of the *Morning Call* caught him during dinner at an hotel, 'enjoying a cut of shoofly cake'. Though Britain, France and Germany had now been at war for nearly four months, and Poland as well as Czechoslovakia had been enslaved, Buchman's euphoria was undimmed. He reiterated the usual MRA clichés. He let fall a few important names, including Baldwin's. He reported 'a widespread response throughout Great Britain' to his lead. Queen Wilhelmina 'had already proclaimed MRA as a national policy'; King Leopold was following her example. (Both of them, in a few months' time, were to be victims of Nazism—the Queen as an exile, the King as a prisoner: the new 'national policy' would perhaps look a bit shop-soiled by then.)

There had been rallies, of course, during 1939, and a ten-day house-party to look after; and on Buchman's birthday—4th June—a 'National Meeting' in Washington.

Buchman's birthday was always kept by MRA as a great event, either because his admirers shared the instinct which causes other religious bodies to celebrate the nativities of saints, or because these observances gratified a certain infantile vanity in Buchman. This trait was shown also in his love of orders and decorations and the care with which all those that he received—from Greece, Western Germany, Formosa, and other friendly powers—were recorded in *Who's Who*: they made up about 11% of his entry. It must have been a keen disappointment to him that, though he was twice (in 1951 and 1952) recommended for a Nobel Prize, he never got one; possibly his supporters in Scandinavia were less influential than he fancied them to be.

But they were certainly influential in Washington. Any American of that time, looking at the finely printed invitation to this birthday meeting on 4th June, 1939, would have been impressed by the names listed on it. The eighty-five sponsors were almost all Senators or Congressmen and their wives; they included the Speaker of the House of Representatives, the Majority Leader of the Senate, Mr Harold L. Ickes, Mr Sam Rayburn, and Mr Harry S. Truman. In addition, ten messages were printed on the invitation—from Mr Cordell Hull (Secretary of State), ex-President Herbert Hoover, Dr Alexis Carrel, and others: several of these did not mention Moral Re-Armament as such, but confined themselves to such gnomic reflections as 'Civilisation today stands at the crossroads . . .' and demanded 'a re-awakening to those ancient truths on which the strength of democracy is based'. The biggest scoop was reserved for release at the actual meeting: President Roosevelt himself had been induced to send a personal message.

If it were possible to analyse this operation in all its phases, to trace the ramifications of the process which made possible the use of all these distinguished names, and the sending to this meeting of the President's message, we would have a classic case-history of the arts of political and personal pressure, wire-pulling, and lobbying. Some of those who allowed their names to be used were certainly not Buchmanites in the full sense of the word: one, for instance, Miss Frances Perkins (United States Secretary of Labour from 1933 to 1945), used to complain in desperation to her friends about the importunities of the Buchmanites: 'They *plague* me all the time!' (Being herself a devout Episcopalian, she was able to some extent to keep them at bay by telling them that when she had a load of sin to get rid of, she preferred 'the vacuum-cleaner of the confessional to the feather-duster of Sharing'.) At some point in such a process, the potential signatory who has been marked down as a key-man will, unless he has exceptional stamina, shrug his shoulders and say to his secretary, 'I *can't* waste any more time on these pests . . . But I don't really see how I can refuse to sign'—for the person deputed to get his signature will be someone to whom he owes (or from whom he expects) some kind of favour. The actual message that he signs can be as vague and harmless as he likes (which, again, makes it more difficult for him to refuse). His name is what counts—and as soon as this has been secured, it will be that much easier for the lobbyists to get the signatures of others who regard him with respect.

Roosevelt himself, politically astute though he was, seems to have been 'hooked' in just this kind of way; and it took quite a lot of evasive and protective staff-work to get him off the hook again after he had given this one message in 1939. Back in 1936, a week or two before the letter from the Assistant Attorney General already quoted,[1] Roosevelt had expressed an interest in the Oxford Group (and some criticism of it) in a private letter to an old friend, Mr Francis Call Woodman, a member of the Harvard Club of Boston, whom he had met by chance at a club dinner. Their exchanges, and Mr Blair's approach on Buchman's behalf, were quickly followed up by another friend, Mr Russell E. Sard, who wrote and asked Roosevelt, shortly before Buchman's visit to Germany, to see Buchman and have 'an unhurried talk' with him before he left—adding, with unconscious irony: 'It would be a relief, I am sure, to talk to someone who has something to *give* and not to *get*!' The reply to this, if any, and the sequel are not recorded;

[1] See p. 66.

but by 1939 the pressure was being intensified. Much of it, as in 1936, was applied through what in England would be called the old-boy network. On 15th February, 1939, for instance, Mr Hugh D. Scott wrote to remind Roosevelt that he had already telegraphed pressing the claims of Moral Re-Armament on him. 'I did this', he wrote, 'on the basis of our both being graduates of Groton and because I knew you as one who is profoundly interested in International Peace. . . . I was up at Groton not long ago with the Harry Rawles and had a wonderful time with the Rector and Mrs Peabody. Mrs Scott and I both send our best regards to Mrs Roosevelt.'

Whether these cosy intimacies worked or whether some of the distinguished sponsors of the meeting supplemented them with personal approaches, Roosevelt did agree to send the message, and it was in hand more than a week before the meeting. Such a message can never be of startling originality, but a good deal of care was taken over the text of this one (possibly because the President wanted to limit his commitment). At least three drafts were typed. The first draft read:

> Now, as in pioneer days, the underlying strength of America must consist in the moral fiber of her citizens. A program of Moral Re-Armament for the nation cannot fail, therefore, to heighten the effectiveness both of our nation's defense and of the will to peace of our people.

The final draft read:

> The underlying strength of the world must consist in the moral fiber of her citizens. A program of moral re-armament for the world cannot fail, therefore, to lessen the dangers of armed conflict. Such moral re-armament, to be most highly effective, must receive support on a world-wide basis.

The changes were made by Roosevelt himself (in his own hand, in the first draft): the most significant of them are, perhaps, the widening of the 'target' of the message, so that it is no longer America alone but the whole world that is to respond to it, and the deliberate substitution of lower-case for capital initial letters in the words 'moral re-armament'—the object of this change being, perhaps, not to identify the message too precisely with a particular organisation.

On 26th May one of Buchman's leading lieutenants, the expatriate British ex-tennis-champion H. W. ('Bunny') Austin, was received by Roosevelt at the White House and the message was handed to him. On the day after the meeting Mr Austin wrote a letter of thanks to Roosevelt. In it he took care to restore the initial capitals: 'Your vision of Moral Re-Armament as a world force is fast becoming a reality.' He also praised the message in terms that, naturally enough, erred on the side of fulsomeness. Carefully though he had supervised the drafting, Roosevelt can hardly have thought his own platitudes particularly epoch-making—but Austin wrote:

> . . . Coinciding so closely with the visit of Their Majesties to Washington, your message may have incalculable results. . . . The authority of your voice may well change the whole history of mankind. . . .

This was putting it a bit high. But Austin was addicted to such grandiose fatuities. A few weeks earlier, at a National Press Club luncheon in Washington, he had observed: 'Sportsmen morally rearmed can unite the world. . . . Sport and sportsmen must become the warp and wool [*sic*[1]] of a newly woven world.' (Nor does he seem to have learned, with the passing years, to avoid such absurdities. In 1963 he told viewers of British television what happened to his tennis when he met Buchman: 'I won the next two tournaments against all the best players in Europe . . . I thought—if Moral Re-Armament can do this for my tennis, what can't it do for the world!' Some viewers may have wondered what would have happened if his opponents, too, had been Changed.)

In any case, the Buchmanites were cockahoop at their successful invasion of the highest level in Washington political society—and, as so often happens, they could not let well alone.

[1] Or possibly a misprint in the newspaper report.

Only a month later Roosevelt was being pressed to send another message, this time to an MRA Assembly in Hollywood. On this occasion, again, a social contact was used for the approach. The request came in a letter, signed Helen Sargent Hitchcock (Mrs Ripley Hitchcock), which began:

> My dear Mr President,
>
> I shall always be grateful to Mrs James Roosevelt for giving me the rare privilege of having that talk at luncheon. It was good of you to promise to send a further message to the World Assembly at the Hollywood Bowl on July 19th at 8 o'clock in the evening. . . .

However firm the luncheon-table promise had seemed to Mrs Ripley Hitchcock, Roosevelt merely dictated a four-line note to his secretary, Stephen Early, telling him to send the same message as before (and ignoring the request, also contained in Mrs Ripley Hitchcock's letter, that he should read the message personally by telephone to the Assembly). All too soon Mrs Ripley Hitchcock was writing again, conveying Buchman's 'personal appreciation for the support which you have given this far-flung movement' and informing the President (perhaps in the hope of stirring him to further efforts of composition) that the message was being read on three separate occasions.

So it went on. In August a Florida editor asked for a message from Roosevelt for a gathering of Buchmanites from five southern states. (He got the same old message.) In November came a letter from no less a figure than Senator Harry S. Truman—and this was rather more troublesome, for Truman (who had just been on an 'inspection tour of the national defenses') enclosed a letter from Buchman the main purpose of which was to persuade Roosevelt to take part in an MRA 'world broadcast' in December. Truman wrote:

> . . . I sincerely hope that it will be possible for you to take part in this broadcast. I believe it would be advantageous if you could talk to Dr Buchman on the subject. I

> think he has some information that will be most interesting to you. He can come any time at your convenience. . . .

This could not be dealt with by a repetition of the familiar message. Europe was now at war; Truman, though not yet thought of as a future President, was a person of consequence in the Democratic Party. Roosevelt sent him a letter, marked 'PERSONAL', which read, in part:

> . . . I had previously received this invitation and have given it careful thought. I regret that I cannot accept.
>
> I note in the letter from Dr Buchman which you enclose that he feels now is the time to focus a message through which a philosophy of world peace and concord will emerge. . . .
>
> Timing is of the very essence of any action I should take in behalf of world peace, regardless of the vehicle to be selected through which to make an appeal. All things considered, I do not believe that this is the most favourable time for action on my part. . . .

Here Roosevelt's judgement was surely sounder than that of Buchman and the worthy, but still innocent, Senator who was Buchman's mouthpiece. This must have been among the highest stakes that Buchman ever played for—to try to induce the President of the United States to intervene in time of war between the warring nations, and to use as his 'vehicle' in doing so a broadcast sponsored by MRA. It is, of course, wildly improbable that such an intervention would have been successful; this may have been one of Roosevelt's reasons for rejecting Buchman's overture. But suppose that, by some remote chance or miracle, it had succeeded: suppose that this unorthodox *démarche* by Roosevelt had brought about an immediate armistice? Despite the suffering that the war was yet to cause, it may still be thought fortunate for the world that Buchman failed—for it must be assumed that, had he succeeded, Hitler (who would certainly not have accepted, in the winter of 1939, humiliating armistice terms) would have been left as overlord of most of central Europe, including Austria, Czechoslovakia, and half of Poland.

Roosevelt may well have seen this. Did Buchman see it?

No doubt Mr Peter Howard, who had not been Changed in 1939, did not know of this episode when, in 1941, he denied that Buchmanites were ever likely to back 'some mysterious peace move'.

No rebuff deterred Buchman for long. In June, 1940—his birthday, again—an 'MRA Week for National Unity' was to be held in San Francisco. Again came the demand for a presidential message; again the influential petitioner was referred to the year-old message—but this time with an intimation from the hard-tried Steve Early that 'just now, because of the unusual pressure of his official duties, the President has been obliged greatly to limit the sending of messages'.

One more item—an exchange of telegrams—is worth disinterring from the Buchman file in the Roosevelt archives. On 14th October, 1941, Mr Fred D. Jordan, of the *Bangor News*, Bangor, Maine, wired to Early at the White House:

> STATED HERE THE PRESIDENT HAS SPECIFICALLY ENDORSED BUCHMANISM OXFORD GROUPS MORAL RE-ARMAMENT MOVEMENT. WILL YOU KINDLY WIRE ME COLLECT VIA WESTERN UNION WHETHER THIS IS CORRECT.

Early wired back:

> THIS IS TO ADVISE YOU IN RESPONSE TO YOUR TELEGRAM OF OCTOBER FOURTEENTH THAT THE PRESIDENT HAS NOT GIVEN THE SPECIFIC ENDORSEMENT ABOUT WHICH YOU INQUIRE.
>
> STEPHEN EARLY
>
> Secretary to the President.

6

THE NEED FOR RECOGNITION

Missing a legacy—The 'Oxford Group' and the Member for Oxford University—The Buchmanites and military service—'We, the people of Britain . . .'—Mr Peter Howard leaves the Express*—A syllogism examined*

IN A letter to Pfatteicher dated 5th March, 1936, Buchman complained of his use of the word 'Buchmanism'. He wrote:

> We never even countenance the word, much less use it. It is a part of the sensational technique of the modern newspaper, and people have often been misled by it. . . . The term is used mainly by those who wish to escape the challenge that Christ is the power of God unto salvation to those who believe. The work of the Oxford Group is personal evangelism—none other than Acts 2: 47. Our thought was never to have any name, for our only organisation is the Church of Jesus Christ.

It is not clear just when 'our thought was never to have any name'; for in fact, as we have seen, the movement has had three names. But there was from the first a conscious effort to avoid formal organisation. 'A First Century Christian Fellowship' implied no denominational separation; the word 'Group' was fairly vague; 'Moral Re-Armament' still sounds more like a slogan than the name of a movement. 'You can't join', enquirers were told. 'There are no members—it's simply a higher quality of living.' Similarly, there was and is no regular subscription: the Changed give whatever they are Guided to give.

Then, in 1939, something awkward happened. A Dr Margaret Thackrah, who had died in 1937, left £500 in her will (plus 'certain residuary income', the value of her residuary estate being £11,183) to the Oxford Group. The relevant clause in her will must have seemed to her clear enough. It read:

> I give and bequeath five hundred pounds free of duty to the secretary or other proper officer (whose receipt shall be full and sufficient discharge) of the Oxford Group, whose offices are at present situated at Brown's Hotel, Dover Street, in the City of Westminster.

But of course, if you insist that you are not an organisation, that you have no church, no constitution or rules, no membership 'or definite location' (which is just what was insisted), you can hardly complain if a court of law takes you at your word and decides that you are altogether too nebulous to receive legacies that would-be benefactors have expressly willed to an organisation. That is, in fact, what Mr Justice Bennett, in the High Court of Justice (Chancery Division), did decide, on 9th March, 1939. In the words of the *Times* Law Report, 'the gifts failed as being void for uncertainty'. It was, said the Judge, 'a pure question of fact. Was there, or had there ever been, a body or society called the Oxford Group of which either Mr Wilson (who had said that he 'acted as treasurer') or Dr Buchman was the proper officer or secretary? The evidence failed to establish the existence of any such body.'

In view of all the publicity that the Group had already had, this may sound, to the non-legal layman, fantastic. But anybody who has had experience of the running of informal groups by high-minded amateurs, and the way in which money given to such people often seems simply to melt away (without the slightest suspicion of dishonesty), will agree that the Judge's main point was sound: if there was no real organisation, there was no one to whom a treasurer was responsible, and no one with any control over him.

Some information on the Group's finances came out in court. There had been banking accounts and offices since 1931. Full-time workers had their living expenses paid; and counsel explained that one item in the main account, 'recuperation and medical expenses in Germany' referred to 'payments to sanatoria for people who had been working for the Group and had broken down'. In eighteen months £7,872 12*s* 6*d* had been paid out through this account. The Judge pointed out that, of this sum, the auditor had seen receipts for only £2,576. Counsel explained that receipts were given for 'certain commercial transactions', but not otherwise. Mr Justice Bennett: 'There is a sum of £5,000 odd for which no receipts were produced.' He was also interested in an item in the main account which read 'Coronation seats, ball, boxes and tickets, etc—£409 1*s*.' It was explained that this referred to the entertainment of Group workers from overseas, and that 'this particular expenditure was made out of gifts expressly made for that particular purpose'. Counsel representing infant next-of-kin interested in the testatrix's residuary estate observed that this was 'a laudable object, but far removed from the promotion of religion'.

The costs of this case (which was brought by the executor and trustee of the will) must have far exceeded the sum in dispute. (They were presumably thought justified because it was a test case of some importance.) The case lasted for three days in the High Court, and a galaxy of KCs and junior counsel appeared for the various parties interested.

We may surmise that, on the night of 9th March or early next morning, there was a fairly intensive and gruelling Guidance session at Brown's Hotel and a lengthy exchange of transatlantic cables (for Buchman, then newly returned to America, had not been Guided to delay his departure in order to be present in court). 'Frank's guidance is always right': could his original guidance, that the Group should be loose and informal, have been wrong? It is doubtful whether anyone in England, in 1939, knew much about the allegedly haphazard administration of that hospice in Philadelphia, more than twenty years earlier. Since then, Buchman had coined one of his favourite sayings: 'Where God guides, he provides.' Had God, or hadn't he, provided the £500 legacy—and if he had, why hadn't he Guided the Judge to let them have it? It was all very confusing—but the usual process of rationalisation took charge and revised Guidance came through: in order to prevent any further loss of this kind, an application was made to the Board of Trade for a licence for the incorporation of a company, not for profit, under the name of The Oxford Group.

The controversy provoked by this decision raged for several months. It centred on what may now seem to be a narrow point—was the Group entitled to use the name of Oxford? It had, of course, used the name unofficially for some years, and could not have been prevented from doing so; but if this licence were granted, official sanction would be given to a claim and an association that many people considered bogus.

In support of its application, the Group was able, as usual, to present a large number of testimonials and petitions from MPs, mayors, and other public persons; but this time it encountered formidable opposition—led with spirit, in and out of Parliament, by Mr (now Sir) Alan Herbert. Sir Alan ('A.P.H.') is famous as a playwright, as the barrister-author of *Misleading Cases*, and as a member of the staff of *Punch*. Some of those involved in the controversy preferred to think of him primarily as a humorous writer; but on this matter of the Buchman Group he was completely serious. He was entitled to be; for he was from 1939 to 1950 MP, or Senior Burgess, for Oxford University, and as such he was aware of the resentment felt by many Oxford men, of varying religious and political views, at the appropriation by the Buchmanites of the name of the University.

Herbert's case against the Group was set out in a letter, more than a column long, in *The Times* of 3rd June, 1939 (the eve of Buchman's birthday meeting in Washington). He dealt with the two main points made by the Group's advocates—that it was 'a religious or semi-religious body, against whose work . . . nothing should be done', and that 'if the Groups were compelled to call themselves by any other name that good work would be hampered'. On the first point he said:

> When this question first arose I had the same feeling as the colleagues I have mentioned, that is, that this was a religious body with which there could be no quarrel except about its name. Since then I have seen and heard so much of the methods of the Groups that I have begun to doubt. Their campaigning in this affair has been most tenacious and, I regret to say, in my opinion, not strikingly Christian. I have carefully refrained from soliciting the aid of anyone not an Oxford man. But the Groups have been pestering not merely at the House but in their own homes innumerable members who have no connexion whatever with Oxford, but were naturally and rightly inclined to favour an apparently religious plea. There has been considerable *suggestio falsi*: e.g., that the Groups' opponents desired to prevent incorporation under any name, and that without the word 'Oxford' they would be cut off from their legacies, &c. When I explained to one correspondent that this was not merely a personal skirmish of my own, but that the Hebdomadal Council, the governing body of the University, was against the application he answered, 'Why do you bother about a few dons?' I explained to a lobbyer from Glasgow at the House that there has been real and frequent confusion between the Oxford Group and the Oxford Society, a body of old students—and, by the way, an international body also—officially recognized by the University, and he replied, 'Oh, that tripe!' Indeed, from the small respect which many of the Groupers seem to hold for the University it is difficult to see why they desire to use its name.

He also referred briefly to Buchman's falsification of his *Who's Who* entry.[1] On the second point he wrote:

[1] *Cf* p. 51.

Presumably, if some new name were adopted and made public by the very efficient propaganda machinery of the Groups, the intelligent testators would in future word their legacies accordingly; and, if not, I am informed on high legal authority, the Movement would not in fact be legally deprived of legacies so long as it was properly incorporated and its finances were properly conducted. Apart from money considerations, the suggestion that the Continental work of this religious movement is going to collapse because it is prevented from using an English name to which it is not entitled seems to me to be flimsy. Further, it is irrelevant; for though the Movement were even more celebrated and successful in Scandinavia than it is, the University of Oxford would still, rightly or wrongly, object to the use of its name. Hence (1) the letter which the Hebdomadal Council has addressed to the Board of Trade, and (2) the unanimous resolution of the Oxford Union Society—from which it will be seen that for once the generations of present-day Oxford are united.

This double-barrelled attack provoked an immediate reply, even longer than Herbert's letter, from a Group supporter whose name may have been calculated to carry weight with readers of *The Times* (including the President of the Board of Trade)—Sir Lynden Macassey, KC, a man eminent not only in the law but in the public services and in business. Sir Lynden had evidently been briefed by some person or body with an efficient press-cuttings library, for he had dug up an article written in *Punch* eleven years earlier by 'A.P.H.', and used this article (apparently anti-Group, though he quoted from it only one word, 'mischief') to suggest that Herbert was not so impartial as in his letter he had professed to be. He outlined the history of the movement since 1921, emphasising the connection with Oxford, such as it was, and the South African origin of the name 'Oxford Group'. He commented:

In submitting to the appellation, how can it be said by anyone desirous of fairly describing the origin of the name that they were giving a false name and address with intention to deceive. The name quickly passed into currency, not merely in South Africa, but later in Holland, Canada, Norway, Denmark, Sweden, Switzerland, and now in all the countries in which the Movement is working, for the same reason, that the pioneer leaders who took the work to those countries were in large majority members of Oxford University. . . . The conclusive circumstance which makes the use of the name 'Oxford Group' imperative is that it is the only name by which the Movement is generally recognized and its work known in all the 63 countries in which it is working. Whether incorporation does or does not take place under that name in England, the Movement will continue to be known by that name generally throughout the world. . . . Mr Herbert says, 'Let the Movement be called the "International Group Movement" '. It is difficult to imagine that he is serious if he is. No name would be more objected to in many Continental countries. If there is any word which has worse associations or more undesirable implications than the word 'international', as applied to any movement, it would be difficult to find it. Such a name would kill the Movement.

Sir Lynden did, however, disclose one slight concession: the Group, he said, had 'offered to insert in the memorandum and articles of association . . . a specific paragraph that they claim no such association' (Herbert having alleged that they had pretended to have 'a particular association with the University of Oxford'). He concluded by insisting that 'incorporation under any other name than that of the Oxford Group would result . . . in world-wide chaos'.

Herbert returned to the matter next day. Of the concession mentioned by Macassey, he observed:

Certainly I am aware that the Groups have offered, if they are permitted to take the name of Oxford for ever, to insert a paragraph in the articles of association (which the public do not see) that they do not claim any official association with the University. Indeed that is the final absurdity, of which I am glad Sir Lynden has reminded me. To go back to my parallel, it is like saying: 'If I may put "The Carlton" on my visiting cards I will write you a private letter to say that I do not really belong there.'

What Herbert could not then have known (or his answer to Macassey might have been even more pungent) was that, from that time onward, the Group itself would be using the name of Oxford less and less: within a few years Moral Re-Armament, or MRA, was to be the name by which it would be generally known throughout the world. So much for Sir Lynden's prophecy—grotesquely inflated, in any case—of 'world-wide chaos' if the name were changed.

Herbert, having amiably defended both 'A.P.H.' and 'the Senior Burgess for Oxford University' against the charge of inconsistency, ended with a sprightly coda which the more earnest Groupers must have found peculiarly galling:

> I am sorry that Sir Lynden Macassey does not think that 'International' is a suitable name for a body whose work 'is known in 63 countries'. But why in the world do they not use the name of the founder? It is now clear that it is not the name of our absurd little University which has conquered Scandinavia and softened, I understand, the heart of Herr Himmler, but the personality and doctrines of Dr Frank Buchman, an American citizen. Is it fair to let his name sink by degrees into the mists of oblivion when there is an opportunity to make it immortal in the Register of Companies? Is not now the time to add 'the Buchmanites' to the proud list which includes the Wesleyans, the Lutherans, the Calvinists, and the Puseyites—and even that almost forgotten sect, the Christians?

Every MP is accustomed to postal pressure campaigns, but the volume of letters that Herbert received on this issue is truly remarkable—their most unusual feature being that the great majority of them were letters of support. There were the official communications—the protest by the Hebdomadal Council and the resolution passed by the Oxford Union: a copy of this was sent to Herbert by the President of the Union, Mr E. R. G. Heath—himself destined to preside also, many years later, at the Board of Trade. There was a round-robin signed by 226 Oxford men and women, including 16 heads of houses, 180 professors, fellows, and others resident in Oxford colleges, and 30 MPs. There were literally hundreds of individual letters from senior and junior members of the University, including such eminent men—to take a few at random—as the Vice-Chancellor himself, Sir Cyril Norwood, C. K. Allen of Rhodes House, Dr Nathaniel Micklem, Dr H. A. L. Fisher, Bishop Walter Carey, the poet Alfred Noyes, and the cricketer Sir Pelham Warner. The Secretary of the Oxford Society (the official association of past and present members of the University) described the confusion between his Society and the Groupers which he was constantly having to clear up, especially abroad. A senior priest of the Oxford Mission to Calcutta (usually called 'the Oxford Mission' for short) reported a similar embarrassment. Dean Inge, in one of his celebrated *Evening Standard* articles, backed Herbert, while not censuring the Group except for its propaganda methods:

> Nothing more alien to the spirit of Oxford can be imagined. . . . It is a religious movement, and therefore its methods ought to be above suspicion.

He condemned as 'disingenuous' one argument that supporters of the Group were using—that some excellent products which happened to be made there, such as marmalade and motor-cars, used 'Oxford' as a trade-name without being thought to claim any association with the University:

> 'Windsor Soap' is not meant to imply that the Royal Family 'use no other'. The 'Gladstone Bag' was not intended to deter good Conservatives from taking these suitcases for the week-end. . . . Oxford men do not wish their university to be associated with Dr Buchman's

movement because they know that in this case Oxford is not, and is not intended to be, merely a trade-name.

Mrs Angela Thirkell, the novelist, wrote:

> Not only do I feel very strongly about the use of the word Oxford, but I have seen so much at very close quarters of their appallingly unscrupulous methods that I can only say with Mr Toobad 'The devil is come among us having great wrath'—I hope the rest is also true.

A parson, himself a Cambridge man, whom the Buchmanites would have regarded as a great capture—the Revd Pat McCormick, Vicar of St Martin's-in-the-Fields—wrote in similar terms of the dubious honesty of the claim.

Despite this influential and varied support for the Herbert campaign, the decision of the President of the Board of Trade, Mr Oliver Stanley, was disappointing to Oxford. In the House of Commons on 8th June, 1939, in a written answer, he announced that he had 'decided to grant to the association a licence under Section 18 of the Companies Act, 1929, to be registered by the name "Oxford Group" '. A few days later, tackled orally, he refused to see a deputation of MPs seeking to persuade him to change his decision: his power in this respect, he explained, was 'of a quasi-judicial character', and he had given 'the fullest consideration to all these conflicting views'.

Herbert appealed to him as 'the guardian of commercial morality' and referred to Mr Justice Bennett's 'severe comments' on Buchman's financial methods and records. Mr Stanley replied: 'One of the consequences of being registered as a company will be that the accounts of the Group will have to be kept in a specified form.' Herbert pounced on the Group's disclaimer of any 'official connection' with Oxford University and asked if this were not 'a final exhibition of the entire dishonesty of these canting cheats', who were 'obtaining money under false pretences'—thus earning himself a rebuke from the Speaker, who said that such words were 'only likely to lead to trouble'.

From September, 1939, Britain was occupied with business more important than the activities of the Buchmanites. Their chief antagonist joined the Thames Emergency Service on the day war broke out, and in June, 1940, became Petty Officer Herbert of the Naval Auxiliary Patrol. The Group vanished from the news.

Only for a time, though. Within a few years, in Britain as well as America[1] the Group was involved in even more painful controversy because it was seeking exemption from military service for some of its key workers, now described as 'lay evangelists'.

Again A. P. Herbert felt obliged to mount a campaign. Again there came a torrent of letters—most of them supporting him, but some backing the Buchmanites. A good few of the latter came from servicemen. There is no doubt that many young men who had been influenced by the Group served gallantly in the armed forces: they would probably have done so anyway, but their letters show, rather touchingly, that they had found in the Group something of value which they had not found in more conventional religion. Nor were many, if any, of the Group's adherents pacifists or conscientious objectors; and, once the war had begun, any who had felt drawn to Nazism or Fascism soon received more reliable, and safer, Guidance.

In reply to a question in the Commons by Herbert, on 11th September, 1941, the Minister of Labour, Ernest Bevin, explained, in precise departmental language, the rules governing the exemption of ministers of religion and lay evangelists:

> The National Service Acts exempt men in holy orders and ministers of any religious denomination from liability to be called up for service. Lay evangelists who are outside the scope of this exemption, but who have been engaged whole-time since before September, 1939, by a recognised religious body, in religious work analogous to that of a regular minister of a religious denomination, are reserved

[1] *Cf* p. 75.

by the Schedule of Reserved Occupations and Protected Work; they number rather more than 400.

Herbert did not ask a supplementary question; but Sir Percy Hurd asked if the Oxford Group were 'in that category'. Bevin replied 'No, Sir.' Mr George Mathers,[1] one of the Group's champions in the Labour Party, asked why Bevin took this view, since Groupers had been 'endorsed' as lay evangelists by eminent church leaders. Bevin said:

> Within the meaning of the National Service Act and their liability to serve their country, I am not prepared to accept the Oxford Group as a religious organisation.

Mathers and a Tory MP, Sir William Allen (who spoke of 'persecution'), pressed Bevin further, but he was not to be drawn.

On 7th October Mathers returned to the attack. Opening a debate on the Adjournment, he quoted at length from messages and testimonials, of a kind now familiar, from distinguished Americans, and remarked that Dr Buchman was 'highly respected . . . in log cabin and in White House'. (He did not know, of course, exactly how the single cautious token of respect bestowed on Buchman by the White House had been organised.)

Mathers spoke with eloquent Scottish sincerity; but, if he still hoped to persuade Bevin to change his mind, his speech was marred by an error of tactics and etiquette. When a Cabinet minister receives a deputation of MPs, it is understood that, since it is better that there should be a free exchange of views, the actual content of the discussion is to be confidential (except for a summary statement agreed for publication). Mathers not only referred to the fact that Bevin had received such a deputation on 10th April; he also quoted remarks that he alleged Bevin had made on that occasion, and said that he had formed the impression that Bevin's 'judgement was clouded

[1] Later Lord Mathers.

by his indignation' (at the pressure to which he had been subjected).

In particular, he enraged Bevin—who was never as thick-skinned as old parliamentary hands have to try to learn to be—by quoting and taking seriously what Bevin, if he said it at all to the deputation, may have meant as a humorous remark: a claim by Bevin that he knew 'far more' about theology than the Archbishop of Canterbury. Bevin, heaving his great bulk up to the despatch-box, interrupted to deny that this was what he had said.

A Tory, Sir Robert Gower, then interrupted to say that it was 'absolutely true'; and Mathers stuck to his recollection. But his battle was lost: Bevin would almost certainly not have changed his mind, anyway, but this personal attack, with the breach of confidence that it involved, must have hardened his heart. It may also have lost Mathers the support of some of his Trade Union and Labour colleagues, who revered Bevin as, outstandingly, their man in the Churchill coalition government.

This was a pity from the Group's point of view and also, just possibly, in the light of that unattainable ideal, absolutely impartial justice. Mathers cited three individual cases of Buchmanite 'lay evangelists' whose exemption—on the assumption that the Group was a *bona-fide* religious body—might well have seemed legitimate. But, quite apart from Mathers' tactical ineptitude, it must also be realised that the mood of the times was strongly against him. This was more than a year after the fall of France, but before Pearl Harbor: except for the Soviet Union, ravaged by Hitler's armies, Britain still 'stood alone', and there was a certain natural impatience with any who were thought, however unfairly, to be 'dodging the column'.

Bevin replied to the debate broadly and forthrightly. It was, he said, 'not a question of religion at all'. He spoke of the 'terrible responsibility' of having to order the lives of seven million citizens of military age, in accordance with the National Service Act, and 'holding the scales justly between citizen and citizen'. His action could be challenged in the Courts, but his expert advisers and he were convinced that 'by no stretch of imagination' could 'these men be brought within the terms of the express exemptions under the Act'. His strongest point was, perhaps, that laymen working full-time for other bodies, clearly religious but not denominational, were not exempt: he cited Toc H and the YMCA (who 'were told that they did not come within this definition, and patriotically accepted the decision'). Only the Group had instigated this high-pressure campaign.

He gave examples of the methods used to intensify the pressure:

> Mention has been made of two lord mayors. I am not going to raise prejudice but I should advise this Group to be a little more careful. The Lord Mayor of Hull told me that at 8 o'clock in the morning two men arrived, planted a document before him, and called upon him to sign it and send it to Mr Bevin. The Lord Mayor of Leeds told me a similar story. I have here a letter from the Mayor of Nottingham, who indicates the same kind of policy. A Member of this House, who is prepared to support what I say, brought me a message from the Mayor of Blyth to tell me that they called upon him, told a story and ended by saying, 'With Mr Bevin it can be understood because he is an atheist.' That is going a little bit too far.

Bevin was also entitled to claim that he had taken 'a generous view'. He had, in fact, agreed to defer for six months the call-up of eleven out of the twenty-nine 'lay evangelists' in question—the eleven to be chosen by the Group and to be aged 30-37—'to give them a chance to get other people to continue their work during the war'.

After this, little more had to be said. Some Members shouted 'Divide!' at the appropriate time—the Speaker, unusually, having reminded them that they might do so—but there was no vote. (A division on a back-bencher's Adjournment debate is rare, especially when a wartime coalition government is in power.) But A. P. Herbert spoke,[1] recapitulating some of the

[1] *Cf* p. 98.

arguments that he had used in his earlier forays. Now, for a change, with so powerful an ally as Bevin, he was on the winning side—though, as he put it, he still knew what he was 'up against with this vast, wealthy, and ruthless organisation, able at this moment to flood the country with a four-page leaflet on expensive paper, with a printed covering letter—and, by the way, with no printer's name on it according to the law'.

This document had been widely circulated as part of the campaign against Bevin's decision on the eleven 'lay evangelists'. (Why, one wonders, were so many people Guided to spend so much time, energy, and money on a campaign that was not only unsuccessful but, on balance, probably damaging to what would now be called the 'image' of the Group?) The document was a 'Proclamation' addressed, somewhat pretentiously, 'TO THE PEOPLE OF BRITAIN'. It read:

> The handful of men leading nationally the work of Moral Re-Armament are now being placed in military service.
>
> The national import of this decision is the reason for this letter.
>
> We and you, the remakers of the world, humble, hopeful champions of the new blood-bought charter of the freedom that is to be, must now pledge ourselves with renewed devotion to the way of justice and an inspired national courage.
>
> We, the people of Britain, whose King is by the Grace of God the Defender of the Faith, will give support and following to those who can build out of the resources of the Kingdom of God among us the moral and spiritual re-armament of our country.
>
> Britain's millions will once more find their voice in this next stage of the historic march of her moral and spiritual leadership, which has demanded of all her people not selfishness but sacrifice; not materialism but morale.
>
> These men have been enlisted since the last war, have undergone the training and discipline to fit themselves for

> special service in just such an emergency as we are now facing, have dedicated themselves to moral and spiritual re-armament, and have from the beginning been taking their rightful salient in front-line activity, building the lasting confidence and united determination so necessary for our immediate strength and ultimate victory.
>
> We believe that a nation fighting for freedom must have these men free to continue their work with every assistance and support.

This lush rhetoric was evidently composed with care and skill; but one omission is at first sight puzzling. Such phrases as 'exempt from military service' and 'reserved occupation' were commonly current; they were used in the newspapers, in the Commons debate on the lay evangelists, and in everyday speech. Nor was there any disgrace in being 'reserved': at various times during the war the Government held back men of many trades and professions in work essential to the war effort. Yet such phrases had, apart from their bureaucratic ring, a faintly disagreeable overtone: among the majority not in reserved occupations there were bitter jokes and rumours (mostly, no doubt, baseless) about people with 'a pull' who had wangled themselves out of the call-up—City men, perhaps, who had hurriedly bought farms and thus secured exemption for themselves or their sons.

If it was desired by the Group that those who signed or read this Proclamation should understand fully what it was about, one might expect to find in it a forceful demand that Bevin's decision be reversed and the work of the Group's lay evangelists classified as a reserved occupation. This was, after all, the purpose of the exercise, and it would have been both absolutely clear and Absolutely Honest.

There is no such demand in the document. The familiar phrases do not appear at all. Indeed, so sonorous and uplifting is its language that it is possible to read the Proclamation hastily—as, no doubt, it was often read by busy people—without realising that it was any different from what one irreverent alderman called 'the usual guff', and thus without realising that it was, at a critical period in the war, a weapon in an anti-Government pressure campaign. For it starts by simply stating that the MRA lay evangelists 'are now being placed in military service' ('placed in' is a curiously colourless alternative to the obvious 'called up for'); and, instead of adding 'This must be stopped' or some such forthright words, it goes on at once to refer to 'the national import of this decision' (no hint, even here, that the decision is thought wrong); and then deviates and swells into a kind of dream-sequence—a dithyrambic fantasia on blood-bought charters and inspired national courage which might have been and probably was the peroration of innumerable Armistice Day sermons . . . and still nothing about exemption or reserved occupations.

Then comes the remarkable paragraph that starts (a bit confusingly, since the Proclamation is addressed *to* the people of Britain): 'We, the people of Britain,[1] whose King is by the Grace of God[2] the Defender of the Faith. . . .' Here we find 'moral and spiritual re-armament' (without initial capitals), but the confusion is aggravated by the ingenious use of military metaphor: the lay evangelists 'have been enlisted since the last war . . . and have from the beginning been taking their rightful salient in front-line activity . . .' 'Enlisted'? 'Salient'? 'Front-line'? A simple reader of this might have supposed that the Buchmanite evangelists already were in the Army, and that it was there that they were to be 'free to continue their work' (why not, indeed?); and such a reader, his reflexes stimulated by the invocation of God, King, 'sacrifice', 'morale', and other conditioning instruments, may well have thought that it would be downright unpatriotic not to sign or support the Proclamation.

It may also be noted that—so soon after the struggle to keep,

[1] This phrase must have been drafted by an American, or by someone strongly under American influence: to many Englishmen it would have recalled merely the petition of the tailors of Tooley Street.

[2] Yes, but more precisely by the grace of Pope Leo X, who conferred the title on King Henry VIII in 1521 for apologetics remote from Buchmanism.

and the action to register, the name 'Oxford'—there is no mention in the Proclamation, despite its solemn and formal character, of the Oxford Group. For one reason or another, the prestige of the name no longer seemed so compellingly attractive as it had in peacetime; and many who would have heard of the Oxford Group and might vaguely have recalled the pre-war controversies (and even, perhaps, Dr Buchman's thanks to heaven for Hitler) did not associate them with the still relatively new catchword of Moral Re-Armament.

It seems legitimate to conclude that those who framed this Proclamation did so with the deliberate intention of minimising awkward questions from those invited to sign it and—by the adroit use of such emotive words and phrases as those just quoted, and the omission of other words, phrases, and facts, relevant but less appealing—maximising support among the uncritical. In function as well as in tone, therefore, it may be likened to the hypnotic prose of an advertising agency copywriter—to a television commercial for soap, perhaps, or beer: it sells its product by the manipulation of its victims' predictable reactions, by the selection and suppression of facts, and by saying what is literally true but may be, by suggestion, misleading.[1]

The passage in Mr Peter Howard's booklet, *Fighters Ever* (November, 1941), in which he quoted the text of this Proclamation contains other statements which were also literally true. One was that the 'civic heads of over 250 cities and towns' had signed the Proclamation, 'together with hundreds of other

[1] Similarly grandiloquent prose, and similar methods of whipping up support, are still favoured by MRA. In 1963 there was in many places in Britain a house-to-house canvass by MRA agents collecting signatures to a 'People's Declaration' in favour of honesty, purity, etc. ('As subjects of Her Majesty the Queen, . . . we pledge ourselves and call on our Parliamentary representatives to pledge themselves likewise, humbly, hopefully, passionately, to build a Britain governed by men governed by God.') It was stated that when a million signatures had been collected the Declaration was to be 'sent to the Government'. The Declaration, printed in red and blue, bore no indication that it was an MRA product; in some cases at least, considerable persuasion had to be exercised before the canvassers would admit its true origin.

Aldermen and Councillors, elected representatives of more than 11,000,000 people in these islands . . .'. So they were; but did anybody, even Mr Howard, suppose that all 11 million people supported them in this action? Municipal representatives are elected for a variety of reasons, many of them local (and the polls are often low). On this matter—a matter of 'national import', and certainly a matter of national policy—Parliament was the representative body primarily concerned; and Parliament had agreed, without a division, to support Bevin. One might argue from this that the people of Britain as a whole—all 40-odd million of them—were in favour of Bevin's decision; but it would be misleading to do so. (For one thing, 174 MPs, whose constituents may or may not have agreed with them on this issue, had signed a motion against it.) Is it more honest—is it Absolutely Honest—to brandish the impressive figure of 11 million as if, in this context, it had any meaning at all?

Fighters Ever was largely concerned with the call-up controversy, but it consists also of general propaganda for MRA and is worth examination as a sample of the quality of that propaganda.

It was of special interest in Fleet Street, for it gave Mr Howard's own version of the events leading to his departure from the *Sunday Express*. He had the usual newspaper staff contract, forbidding employees to engage in outside work 'unless special permission has first been obtained'. He explains that, in his case as in others, this provision had been interpreted liberally: he had helped to write a book and a film script and he had broadcast, 'without the permission but with the knowledge of the management'. This is rather a fine distinction, since the management, knowing of an intention to broadcast and disapproving of it, could have prevented it. Now he felt moved to write a book about the Oxford Group, to be called *Innocent Men* (presumably a deliberate echo of the title of an earlier book which he had helped to write, the best-selling *Guilty Men*); and on this, he says, 'the thought came to me that I should seek formal permission before publication'.

He next tells how he approached his editor, who 'doubted whether I would be given permission to write a book on the Oxford Group', and how 'on application to the management' he was 'put off on various pretexts'.

But the Group was under public attack: 'I had to insist upon an answer.' He was told that he 'could not write a book on that particular subject and still remain on the staff of the paper'. His employers 'did not ask to see the script before they gave their decision . . .'

So he left—and it was within the recollection of the late Sir Leslie Plummer, MP, then Assistant General Manager of the *Express*, that *Innocent Men* came out with such remarkable speed that (especially in view of wartime delays) it was evident that it had been written and printed, its publication having been negotiated privately, while Mr Howard was still on the *Express* staff, still ostensibly awaiting permission to write it.[1]

No doubt some of the events of what must have been a distressing period in Mr Howard's career soon became telescoped in his memory. A clue may be found in his statement that 'the thought came to me that I should seek formal permission before publication'. If these words are here used to indicate Guidance, this was one occasion, at least, when Guidance was consistent with common sense and the honouring, however belatedly, of a contract; though Mr Howard's use of the words 'before publication', taken with the paragraphs that follow them, is perhaps another instance of MRA's habit of preferring literal truth to Absolute Honesty.

There is also the strange business of the secret letter. Writing to Bevin on 14th September, 1941, A. P. Herbert had mentioned a letter which he enclosed with his own. 'If we ever have a debate about these gentry', he wrote, 'I should like to use the letter, but as it is marked SECRET, I don't know what I

[1] I showed this passage to Sir Leslie a few months before his untimely death: he confirmed its accuracy, and referred me for a detailed account of the episode to a statement by him (describing the chest-thumping drama of his last interview with Mr Howard) printed on p. 19 of the Minutes of Evidence (34) taken before the Royal Commission on the Press, 1948.

can do.' (His own letter, but not of course this enclosure, he released to the press.)

The debate, as we have seen, did take place. The terms in which Herbert had referred to the letter showed that it must have been from someone in an official position: letters from private persons may be 'private' or 'personal' or 'confidential', but they are not 'secret'; that term is used when some question of security is involved. Yet Mr Howard seems to have thought that Herbert, when he spoke of a secret letter, was referring to letters about the Group from members of the public. Describing the debate—in that somewhat feverish style which makes the reading of his many contributions to the Buchmanite scriptures hard work for those who care for English prose—he declared:

> Did he read his secret letter? Yes, siree. He read three of them. . . .

He then quoted the three letters that Herbert had read out in his speech—one from an old clergyman, one from a Scottish minister, one from a guest-house owner. Each of these correspondents had written to Herbert spontaneously, describing personal encounters with Buchmanites and testifying to their strongly pro-Nazi attitude (in at least one case, admittedly, before the war). Mr Howard added:

> These are the secret letters. Each one is secret in that Mr Herbert did not disclose the name of its sender.

This is a flagrant misuse of words. It is common practice, in Commons speeches or newspaper articles, to quote from a letter without naming its writer (and a minister of religion or a guest-house owner might be embarrassed by this kind of publicity). There is no doubt of the authenticity of the letters: by courtesy of Sir Alan Herbert, I have read them. Also, though Mr Howard did not mention this fact, Herbert had checked the *bona fides* of one writer—the Scottish minister—with three well-known MPs who knew him personally. Even Mr Howard did not dare to suggest that the letters were faked—but he did say:

After years of rummaging in every garbage can, that was the best Mr Herbert could produce. Three secret letters—from a nation of 44 million people over whom the Group have no control at all, at all. Anyone in these islands can write a stupid letter . . . or claim to have met someone who said something about the Oxford Group.

The short answer to these comments is: (*a*) Herbert did no 'rummaging'—he received literally hundreds of unsolicited letters, mostly condemning the Group, from people in all walks of life; (*b*) as already indicated, these letters were not 'secret', in the usual or technical sense of the word; (*c*) the fact that they were anti-Group does not make them 'stupid'—they were plain recitals of personal experiences; and (*d*) they were not from people who had 'met someone who said something' but from eye-witnesses giving their own first-hand accounts. Such flimsy evasions as Mr Howard's must, surely, have been inspired by panic.

It may be felt that, after all this time, it is unnecessary to disentangle these trivial controversies so laboriously. On the contrary, it seems to me that, since MRA is making a renewed bid for public esteem, especially in countries in which the Oxford Group, if it was ever heard of, has long been forgotten, there is a distinct advantage in dissecting the things said on its behalf in its earlier years, before it had acquired its full modern protective gloss. Moreover, the Buchmanites claimed then, as they claim now, that all their important activities were conducted under Guidance: they were 'God-controlled' men. Mr Howard, then still a neophyte, would have been careful to be sure of his Guidance: it would have been 'checked' and 'cross-checked'. He was a trained and fluent professional writer. The shoddy arguments that such a man, in such circumstances, deploys—or rather, sends spinning in all directions at once, like the balls of an incompetent juggler—discredit the Guidance and expose the God-control as an illusion.

Another slovenly argument in *Fighters Ever* is an example of a logical error common not only in MRA but in many other emotional cults (such as some of those described by Monsignor Knox in *Enthusiasm*). The error can be illustrated by a simple analogy from literature: a young poet is ignored or slated by the critics; he remembers that great poets of the past have also been ignored or slated; he and his friends therefore assume, and proclaim with passion, that *because of this* he must be, as a poet, among the great ones. He may be; but it does not follow logically that he is, merely because he has shared with them the experience of being ignored or slated.

The falsity of this syllogism is obvious as soon as it is pointed out. Yet, century after century, religious reformers and revivalists of one kind or another, encountering obstacles and criticism, identify their critics with the Pharisees or tyrants or infidels who have oppressed Christians since the first century AD, and slide painlessly—indeed exultantly—into the assumption, which is wrong in ninety-nine cases out of a hundred, that their difficulties are in the authentic tradition of the saints and martyrs of the Church.

Thus, in *Fighters Ever*, Mr Howard writes that the attacks upon the Group 'are themselves strong evidence that the Group is precisely what it describes itself to be—namely, a vital Christian force'.

This is as if our young poet were to say: 'The bad reviews I've been getting are themselves strong evidence that I am a great poet.' In either case, the claim is manifest nonsense. However, Mr Howard goes on to explain:

> For why? Every Christian revival throughout history has been assailed by mankind. And in each case the charges made have been identical.

He then compares the 'persecution' of the Group with the sufferings of Christ himself, St Paul, Wesley, General Booth, and St Ignatius Loyola. Proportion, humour, taste, modesty: there is perhaps, in such a comparison, some shortage of these qualities; and there is a difference in degree between being the subject of a speech or article by A. P. Herbert, however sharp, and death by crucifixion.

But what of the 'identical' charges? Is there here some significant similarity which may serve to authenticate Buchmanism as 'a vital Christian force'? Mr Howard lists some main criticisms of the Buchmanites: they were said to be 'disloyal to the nation', they were 'making a good thing out of religion', their methods were sensational. 'All that has been said about Buchman, and more, was said about Wesley, Booth, and many others.'

No doubt; but this, in itself, proves nothing. The charges may be true in one case, untrue in another; or true or untrue in both. Especially in matters of religion, human beings are both conservative and lazy. Any movement for reform will excite antagonism—but this does not mean that *every* movement that excites antagonism is good. In the long history of Christianity many a grotesque heresy has flourished for a while and withered away. To revert once more to the analogy of the young poet: he is attacked because his verse is 'incomprehensible' and because he uses vulgarisms from everyday speech. Precisely the same things were said about Wordsworth and about T. S. Eliot; but that does not necessarily put him on a level with Wordsworth and Eliot. Mr Howard has (or had, in 1941) still to learn the elementary lesson that similar effects may have different causes.

He quotes Christ's condemnation of those whose forefathers killed the prophets. He does not reflect that many who were not authentic prophets must also have been among those killed.

7

MRA AND LABOUR

A new look for the old Group—'An ideology for democracy'—MRA hospitality—Tea with Mme Laure—Campaigns in coalfields and docks—Condemned by the ICFTU—A surprising testimonial from Dagenham

SINCE THE end of the Second World War, the areas of activity of MRA have been enlarged, and its strategy modified accordingly. Even those who do not agree with the movement's aims and methods will admit that there must have been, at some point, a thorough attempt at a realistic reappraisal of the way the world was going (or possibly a series of bright hunches, interpreted as Guidance). In Britain, for six post-war years, the Labour Party was in office: the Conservatives were to recapture power, but this was clearly a period of social and economic change. Even more momentous were the developments in Asia, Africa, and Latin America, where industrial, social, and political revolutions were all occurring at once. The old empires were dying—more or less painlessly, or in bloody agony. It was a new version of Hardy's 'time of the breaking of nations'; and some of the broken, and remade, nations did indeed desperately need guidance, of the most practical kind.

In such a world, and to its newly literate audiences, the old image of the Oxford Group—the evening-dress sessions in ritzy ballrooms, the clean-limbed Blues confessing adolescent peccadilloes, the Keswick revelation and the revivalist terminology in which the message had been wrapped—would seem hopelessly out-of-date and irrelevant. New targets had to be selected, a new 'package' devised. At the same time, it was important not to frighten off the wealthy and conservative supporters, especially in America, who had helped to finance the Group's enterprises and missionary journeys.

Perhaps a date as far back as the 29th May, 1938, may be taken as the start of this climacteric, for it was then that, speaking at East Ham Town Hall—a Labour stronghold in a working-class district of London—Buchman first publicly proclaimed the slogan of Moral Re-Armament. On that occasion he said: 'Forget all about Frank Buchman and that one day he had a quiet time and now you have a movement in fifty-two countries. Britain and the world must re-arm morally.' The injunction to 'forget' the founder and his conversion experience was not, perhaps, meant to be (and has not been) taken literally; but the words imply a new emphasis.

So MRA is no longer the simple revivalist movement—the experiment in individual Christian evangelism or, as someone called it, 'a Salvation Army for the middle classes'—that Dr Buchman was promoting in the 1920s. It is a high-powered ideological crusade, with apparently unlimited funds. It intervenes busily in actual political and industrial situations. In its propaganda the necessity of 'God-control' and 'life-changing' is still urged; but—though there have been, since Dr Buchman's death, some signs of internal policy differences—the main purpose is 'to equip democracy with an ideology adequate' for the struggle against Communism.

The MRA policy-makers were shrewd enough to see that, in this struggle, it was useless merely to ally themselves with their customary supporters on the political Right—with pillars of the British establishment or American industrial tycoons. The rise of democratic Socialism naturally attracted the attention of a movement whose tactic had always been to capture key men everywhere; so, particularly since the war, there has been a determined attempt by MRA to infiltrate into the Labour and Trade Union movements of the West.

This effort, on which enormous resources of money and energy have been spent, has met with limited success. In Britain and other countries some individual Labour men of what may be called, without offence, middling rather than outstanding ability and position—a regional organiser here, a member of a Trade Union executive there—have been Changed. With others of all political views, a number of rank-and-file Labour men and women have accepted the hospitality of Caux, with all expenses paid, or the more modest favour of a coach-trip to the Westminster Theatre, London. A few Labour MPs have stayed at MRA's 'VIP hostel' in Charles Street, Berkeley Square: one, Tom Oswald, a well-liked ex-miner and former secretary of the Scottish group in the Parliamentary Labour Party, gives this in *Who's Who* as his permanent London address (with the MRA telephone number). Christopher Mayhew, MP—Under-Secretary of State for Foreign Affairs, 1946-50—once spent a week at Caux: he tells me that five or six years ago it would have been fair to describe him as a 'fellow-traveller' with MRA, but that he 'always resisted' complete involvement and has 'cooled off' in recent years. One MP, John McGovern, threw in his lot wholly with MRA, and for some time before his retirement from Parliament in 1959 seemed to find Buchmanite world tours more worth-while than the drudgery of Westminster; or, as *MRA Information Service* put it (2nd July, 1960), 'has during the last five years travelled over 150,000 miles to proclaim an ideology which supersedes the class war'. This paper adds that McGovern 'celebrated his golden wedding . . . at a banquet given in his honour at Dr Buchman's home in Melbourne'. Some of his Scottish colleagues, reading MRA's personal publicity for him and seeing the colour photograph of him—dapper, sun-tanned, and radiant—on the cover of *MRA Pictorial* (New Year, 1960), must have felt with some chagrin that they had, inexplicably, underrated him.

Beneath his portrait was a familiar MRA text which

provided a theme for this *Pictorial*—'MEN MUST CHOOSE' (abbreviated from a saying of William Penn—'Men must choose to be governed by God or they condemn themselves to be ruled by tyrants'—which, to the indignation of some Quakers, is much used in MRA propaganda). 'Ye can tell John has chosen', said one of his old friends, ruefully—and he pointed to an article or statement by McGovern on an inside page. It was headed 'I STAND WITH ADENAUER'. More recently McGovern chose his side in domestic politics, too: an interview in the *Sunday Express* of 8th March, 1964, quoted him as saying that he intended to vote Conservative in the coming general election, and that he was 'wholeheartedly behind Sir Alec Douglas-Home'.

Opposite McGovern's article was one by Mme Irène Laure, a French Socialist of whom Dr Adenauer (according to *MRA Pictorial*) 'once said that she had done more than any other living individual to bring reconciliation between France and Germany'. This may have been Adenauer's opinion, or part of a message drafted for him by MRA; others might give some credit to Winston Churchill for having initiated the idea in a speech at Zurich University on 19th September, 1946—the year before Mme Laure's first visit to Caux.

Mme Laure's article begins:

> As a Socialist I believed passionately in the brotherhood of man. But as a Marxist I was fighting the class war against the employers and as a Frenchwoman I hated Germany. . . . At Caux, when I saw a German step on to the platform to speak, I at once left the hall. When I was introduced to Frank Buchman, he asked me just one question, 'What sort of unity do you want for Europe?'

This, apparently, did the trick. Despite her long years of Marxist conditioning, the magic of Buchman and of Caux taught Mme Laure that (the shatteringly obvious aphorism is hers) 'hate can never create unity'. The sequel? 'I apologised to the Germans for having willed the total destruction of their country.'

It may occur to some Socialists, reading this, that for all

MRA's build-up of Mme Laure (pre-Caux) as a 'convinced Marxist', her outlook seems to have been determined largely by emotional nationalism. Socialists do not generally will the 'total destruction' of any country or indulge in such gestures as walking out of a hall in which a German is to speak: in the Second World War, in Britain at any rate, almost the only opposition to indiscriminate or 'obliteration' bombing by the RAF, and to the policy of unconditional surrender, came from Socialists; and it was the Conservative Lord Vansittart, rather than any Socialist, who inveighed against Germans as Germans, not merely as Nazis. However, Mme Laure—a former Resistance fighter whose son was tortured by Germans—had an understandable excuse for her bitterness; and since she was clearly in many ways an admirable woman, I accepted with alacrity an invitation from Jennie Lee, MP, to meet her at tea on 31st July, 1963.

It was impossible not to like Mme Laure at sight. She is a tiny woman with a lively manner, full (one would judge) of human affection: her face is a pure oval, serene yet mobile, almost holy; her grey hair is drawn straight back.

Miss Lee, it should be explained, is no Buchmanite. On the contrary, she disapproves intensely of MRA—partly because of the extraordinary ineptness of some MRA agents' past approaches to her but, more profoundly, because she sees that, despite its talk of 'revolutionary change', MRA's philosophy is essentially conservative. Indeed, had she known when she first met her that Mme Laure was a Buchmanite (and was in London to attend an MRA Assembly), I doubt if she would have pursued the acquaintanceship.

After some general and friendly talk she said to Mme Laure, courteously but firmly: 'The abstract noun is often the enemy of concrete action. You see, I cannot forgive your movement for never denouncing those Tory gentlemen who sign motions supporting MRA—and then come into the House and vote against measures that will relieve human suffering. . . .' She was thinking, I knew, of Aneurin Bevan's great achievement, the National Health Service; and this was to the point, for

Mme Laure had been talking to us as a Socialist, describing the misery and hunger of millions of Asia, and asking, with a wealth of abstract nouns, what was to be done about it. She seemed to think the MRA formula, in all its vagueness, an adequate solution: we preferred 'concrete action'.

I thought of a characteristic rhetorical evasion by Dr Buchman (one still quoted with pride, and applied to various situations, by MRA). He was once asked to state in specific terms his 'programme' for India: his *programme*, not his hopes and aspirations, which no doubt most people would share. He replied: 'Empty hands will be filled with work, empty stomachs with food, and empty hearts with an idea that really satisfies. That is Moral Re-Armament for East and West.' It may be Moral Re-Armament for North and South, too, but it is not a programme: it is an incantation.

Aloud, reverting to the MPs who sign motions when pressed to do so by MRA lobbyists, I ventured to suggest that one of MRA's strategic errors, throughout its history, had been to rely too much on big names as such, on its long list of endorsements by the famous (about as convincing as endorsements of soap by Hollywood film-stars), on formal backing by functionaries, rather than (in its own terms) on truly Changed men. Mme Laure made no comment; her interpreter, an American woman, seemed slightly disconcerted.

At one stage in the conversation, Jennie Lee and I raised the well-known point that I have already dealt with in this book—Buchman's admiration for Hitler.

'That,' said Mme Laure, brushing the point aside, 'is mere propaganda.'

I cited the precise words and date of the *New York World-Telegram* interview. I fancied that a shade of disquiet passed over Mme Laure's face—but she insisted, her mouth set: 'To me, that is a lie.'

This seemed excessively subjective. I gave more of the circumstantial details. This time she said: 'Newspapers are not always accurate.' I said that I was fully aware of that, but that I did not believe that anyone could read this interview with care and not be convinced of its essential authenticity; and that, in any case, it had not been contradicted at the time.

It was no use. It dawned on me—as I might have realised from the confused thinking in her *Pictorial* article—that, besides being an extremely nice and good woman, Irène Laure was an extremely simple woman: simple not as a child or a great artist is simple, but simple with a kind of peasant obtuseness. To reason with her, even on the basis of Socialist axioms that we might have been expected to accept in common, was like trying to argue logically with a personally kindly aunt who belonged to some terrible, rigid, puritanical sect—the Exclusive Brethren, or something like that. When one range of subjects is approached, such a mind is closed. There was practically no communication between us.

MRA had at least succeeded in dividing one French Socialist from two British Socialists.

It is not, of course, only since 1945 that MRA has tried to influence the Labour and Trade Union movements of the West. As I have suggested, there has been, in accordance with the traditional MRA strategy of capturing 'key people', a more intensive concentration on this aim where Socialists have actually been in power (as, for instance, in Scandinavia); but ever since the earlier days of the Oxford Group, the prevention and cure of industrial discord was a professed object of Buchman and his disciples.

On 6th May, 1940, Buchman reported that in California MRA was 'striving to create' what he called 'a Maginot Line for industrial co-operation and national unity'—a metaphor that must have seemed singularly unfortunate a few weeks later, when the 'impregnable' £30-million Maginot Line was outflanked and broken by Hitler's army and became 'the tombstone of France'.

Equally unimpressive, in a different way, had been a luncheon in Buchman's honour at the National Trade Union Club, London, in November, 1938. This event was quoted in America as evidence of the Group's successful incursion into the British Trade Union movement: it was reported there to have been 'described as the largest and most representative in the club's history'. As those familiar with the British Trade Union movement of that time will be aware, this was not saying much: the club, now long defunct, had no long 'history'; its name was well-meaningly pretentious; its premises were small and drab.

The luncheon was held on the club's top floor. There had been some talk of holding it at a restaurant. 'I'm glad we've kept this *upper room*,' said Buchman.

He was in his most vapid and repetitive form. Tracing semicircles with his right hand, he said: 'Take British Labour. British Labour's cradle is a spiritual awakening. [*Slower*] British Labour's cradle is a spiritual awakening. Or let me put it this way: British Labour was cradled in a spiritual awakening.' His peroration contained such inspired phrases as '*By* Labour, *through* Labour, we may come to a better understanding *of* Labour'.

A veteran Trade Union leader, Ben Tillett, had been induced to move the vote of thanks to Buchman. He did so in a manner markedly less respectful than the Groupers present can have cared for. 'I've enjoyed your speech,' he said. 'I loved the Yankee-doodle of it.'

Many claims of MRA's success in solving industrial problems, usually by defeating Communist conspiracies, have been made: some may have some relation to the truth, some are almost certainly baseless; but, in the nature of the case, it is hard to get factual proof or disproof rather than expressions of opinion. Through my own political affiliations—through, for instance, the Socialist International—I have many contacts in countries in which MRA has operated. In almost every case, when I have enquired about MRA activities, I have been assured, by Social Democrats of unimpeachable integrity, that the claims are false or greatly exaggerated. One sceptical opinion was expressed in 1959 in the weekly review, *America*, by Fr Robert A. Graham, SJ, who wrote: 'MRA now claims to have had a major share in saving Western Europe from Communism. . . .

These claims are not taken seriously by those in a position to know the details of the developments in question.'

To some extent one can assess the plausibility of a claim when it is sufficiently specific; and some of the most specific of MRA's claims have concerned the British coal industry. On 16th January, 1952, for instance, press reports of an MRA 'Assembly of the Americas' at Miami, Florida, attributed to a British delegate, 'Bill Birmingham, Union Secretary of the Mosley Common Pit, Lancashire, second largest coal-mine in Britain', the claim that, as a result of MRA activity, 'production had increased from 11½ to 15 tons per man per shift', while, simultaneously, wages went up from 37*s* to 52*s* a day. The increases had occurred, he said, when the mine 'started operating on the basis of what is right rather than who is right'.

One must assume that Mr Birmingham was at one point misreported, or that the report was misprinted: 11½ tons is an impossibly high figure for output per man per shift (OMS). But he must have testified that there had been some improvement, or those organising the Assembly would not have thought it worth putting him up to speak. It is as well to check such claims from as authoritative a source as possible, and I therefore asked Lord Robens, Chairman of the National Coal Board, for his comments on Mr Birmingham's speech. Lord Robens replied:

> Mr Birmingham's claim about the beneficial effects of MRA on the pit's results in the early 1950s simply cannot be substantiated. OMS at the face fell markedly in the years following 1947 and at no time was a face OMS of 100 *cwts* ever achieved. Overall OMS was steadier, though here, too, there is no evidence of a sustained improvement. The figures, in *cwts* are as follows and should be compared with the figures of 11½ to 15 *tons* per man shift in Mr Birmingham's statement:

Year	*Face OMS*	*Overall OMS*
	cwt	*cwt*
1947	75·9	21·1
1948	72·6	20·8

Year	*Face OMS*	*Overall OMS*
	cwt	*cwt*
1949	72·7	20·8
1950	64·6	22·2
1951	66·9	23·9
1952	64·1	21·9

The figures of overall earnings per manshift in the same period went up from 27*s* 5*d* to 38*s* (as compared with the figures of 37*s* to 52*s* a day quoted by Mr Birmingham).

The MRA campaign in the coalfields was at its height in the earlier years of nationalisation. Its 'results'—so exuberantly boosted in MRA propaganda—were summed up, succinctly and coolly, in an official statement by the National Coal Board, issued in 1953 in response to an enquiry by the *Daily Telegraph*, which, like other newspapers, had been deluged with this propaganda. The statement was as follows:

> MRA has made some extravagant claims about productivity and labour relations in British pits. These were based mainly on a drive made by the movement shortly after nationalisation. Neither in the coalfields nor at headquarters is there any lasting or even temporary justification for such claims.

This campaign now seems to have been allowed to sink into oblivion. This is hardly surprising, if all its achievements are as hollow as that reported by Mr Birmingham at Miami—where, of course, there was no National Coal Board spokesman to correct him.

Possibly the main weight of the crusade is switched, as its pretensions are exploded in each, from one industry to another. The story of MRA and the docks was much the same as the story of MRA and the mines; and the pattern of the approach to key men among workers and management was, and is, fairly regular. Sometimes there is a substantial distribution of tickets for the local showing of an MRA film, or a trip to the Westminster. Then, MRA teams call for 'softening-up' chats at the homes of

Trade Union officials and shop stewards, especially those who are working at places where there have been many disputes and are known to be themselves militant. The wives of men active in the Trade Union movement are as accustomed as the wives of MPs or local councillors to evenings at home on their own, since their husbands may be out on Union or political business four or five evenings a week. So, whether the husbands are at home or not, the MRA reconnaissance teams—more personable and pleasant-spoken and, usually, more subtle in their methods than Jehovah's Witnesses—do not find it hard to get inside a typically hospitable working-class household. No actual Changing is attempted here; but, after some confidence has been established, at a psychologically suitable moment the invitation to Caux, for husband and wife together, is sprung.

The man may have his doubts. He knows that some of his best mates at work regard MRA with deep mistrust. But these young folk who have been calling on them seem all right . . . and what's wrong—as they point out—with going to see for yourself? No strings, no commitments: make up your own mind when you're there. And it certainly makes a nice change for the wife—a holiday at a Swiss mountain resort, all expenses paid. It is not to be wondered at that many accept and that, of these, quite a few succumb to the intense, hypnotic pressures of Caux. This must have been the technique used on many of the most active men in the docks—Jack Manning, for one, who had been associated with the Beaverbrae strike in 1949. He went to Caux, and he fell.

The National Coal Board's statement cutting MRA down to size on the coal-mines was published on 19th December, 1953, in an article by John Herbert in the *Daily Telegraph*. Mr Herbert was in pretty close touch with what was going on in the docks. He knew Jack Manning, and Manning invited him to an MRA meeting at Canning Town, at which 'not a dramatic opportunity was lost': there were personal conversion-stories, MRA songs in fervent chorus, Scandinavian girls in national costume. (Meetings staged like this may well appeal to many people, regardless of what they are in aid of, more than the average drab political party meeting.)

According to Mr Herbert,

> MRA claims a great response to its work among the 27,000 dockers of the Port of London. In the past three years I have not been able to find the names of more than six who admit to its principles. There are probably a few more, but these six men are the 'bridgehead'. . . . Pictures of such men as Mr Manning, one of the six, and their statements recur time and time again in MRA books and magazines. Derision is the normal response when MRA is mentioned among dockers.
>
> Within ten months of joining MRA Mr Manning boasted that since the Beaverbrae strike 'there has never been a dock strike in London, and Communists have had to shift their efforts to other docks'. The inference was that MRA was the cause of this change of spirit. In addition, he said that two dock disputes had been settled by application of its principles.

These achievements would have sounded impressive anywhere but in dockland (for instance, in the luxury of sun-drenched Miami). Unfortunately, the claim was untrue. Mr Herbert pointed out that there had been at least three major London dock strikes since the Beaverbrae strike. Arthur Deakin, who, as General Secretary of the Transport and General Workers' Union, was in a position to know the facts, described Mr Manning's boast as 'absolute nonsense'. Another MRA Changee, Alfred Bryan, an ex-Communist London Transport worker, repeated Manning's claim to Mr Herbert; the MRA official who introduced them did not correct the misstatement. Mr Herbert, tactlessly, reminded Mr Bryan of the strike in April, 1950, of 14,000 London dockers; of the tally-clerks' strike which paralysed the Port of London in 1951; and of the strike (also in 1951) which led to the trial and acquittal of seven dockers charged with conspiracy.

Predictably, this article provoked a considerable correspondence, starting with a letter signed by six Labour MPs 'vitally interested in Trade Union affairs'. This letter was a long one—ten inches long: it filled, by a coincidence, as much space as that part of Mr Herbert's article which had dealt with the MRA claims on the mines and the docks. It made no attempt to contradict factually his statement of the facts about strikes and productivity. It accused him of 'misstatements' but did not say what they were; it simply repeated the success-story of Caux ('since the war 68,000 persons from 118 countries . . .', including Dr Adenauer and M Schuman). Vague claims of 'solid results' in industry were based on the general statement that many Trade Unionists went back to Caux 'again and again', and constantly reported 'new progress in applying to their industries the basic principles of MRA'. Were these men to be 'discredited as unreliable witnesses by a stroke of Mr Herbert's facile pen'? Perhaps not; but they would have seemed more manifestly reliable if their six champions, or whoever drafted the letter for them to sign, had been able to quote one set of hard facts and figures that could be checked.

Major-General George Osborne de Renzy Channer, of Aston Bury, near Stevenage, also wrote attacking Mr Herbert—with the teasing question, 'How can he measure something moral and spiritual with a material yardstick?' This was a curious challenge. It might have been valid in any context but this—for it had escaped the Major-General that 'a material yardstick' (increased productivity in industry) was precisely what MRA was using to measure its claims.

But the best and most startling letter came from Philip Leon, of University College, Leicester, author of *The Philosophy of Courage*, a thoughtful apologia for the Oxford Group. It was startling because Mr Leon supported MRA, yet accepted some of Mr Herbert's criticisms of it:

> The weakest point in the movement is undoubtedly the habit . . . of constantly looking for and, often prematurely, advertising results.

> At best it is the prophet's hope ingenuously identifying the future with the present. . . . *At worst it is the propagandist's ingenious turning of a blind eye on inaccuracies he hopes will help the cause.*

The sentence here italicised is at once an admission and an accusation, of the utmost candour. What, if Mr Leon was right, becomes of Absolute Honesty?

I have chosen to recall this 11-year-old skirmish because it is a clear-cut example of a recurrent pattern of controversy about MRA—none of the aggrieved defenders of the movement refuting any of the critic's charges, one of them admitting and aggravating the main charge—and because, on the docks, Mr Herbert's information was specific and unanswerable. His article stands as a permanent condemnation of the basic claims and everyday operations of MRA: even if it had rectified its promotion methods, as advised by Mr Leon, the deliberate 'inaccuracies' would still be on record.

No such rectification has been undertaken. My own latest enquiries, among colleagues intimately acquainted with the docks and their problems, show that there has been no essential change in recent years, but, as in the coalfields, an apparent falling-off in MRA's activity and influence. One Labour MP writes to me: 'MRA has got nothing whatever to do with peace in the docks. . . . To the best of my knowledge, they have made no impact in Dockland, but are willing to tell "white lies" to justify their activities.' And Mr R. J. Mellish, MP for Bermondsey, who knows the problems of the docks as well as anybody, tells me: 'MRA claims about peace in Dockland are false'.

The formula 'what is right rather than who is right', used by Mr Birmingham at Miami, is a favourite MRA slogan in industrial disputes. It is an ingenious formula: it sounds 'fair enough'. Yet its very plausibility can subtly conceal a built-in bias. Disputes of any kind (personal, industrial, international) are settled, says MRA, when men Change and submit to

Guidance (to be checked, in case of doubt, with MRA headquarters). *In practice*, in an industrial dispute, this merely means that the workers modify what has seemed to them a just claim, while the employer, perhaps, treats them a little more benevolently—not a bad thing in itself—but remains still firmly in control of the business. There is no radical social critique here, no examination of the possibility that the whole structure of ownership and management in an industry may be unjust and inefficient and may need recasting—as, for instance, the coal industry in Britain was transferred from private to public ownership, a transfer now accepted by all British political parties, including the Conservative Party.

In the inter-war years of slump and mass-unemployment, coal was the most extreme example of what was wrong with British industry. I know of no evidence that MRA, then or since, has ever proposed a solution of an industrial problem that would involve taking an industry or a firm out of the hands of private owners, however inhumane, incompetent or irresponsible they may have been. For, clearly, the 'what-is-right-not-who-is-right' formula bars recrimination about such failings and therefore excludes the basic question of ownership: the entire agenda of MRA's round-table get-together of management and workers *must* be concerned only with making the existing set-up work more harmoniously, through the smoothing-out of personal dissensions and prejudices. Without even the contemplation of more radical reforms than this, how can MRA claim, as it does, to be 'an ideology of revolutionary change'? In this context, it is an ideology of *no* change—no fundamental change—a recipe for preserving the *status quo* essentially intact, with perhaps some slight amelioration of its harsher features.

If this analysis is correct, it is surprising that any Labour supporter should have fallen for MRA's pretensions; but it is much less surprising that it should make a powerful appeal to industrialists bothered by Union 'agitators' and anxious for peace (on, roughly, their own terms) in industry. It is natural that they should see in MRA an up-to-date version of the old pie-in-the-sky revivalism, and should, with conscious cynicism or quite sincerely, lend it their support.

A hymn by a Victorian bishop, intended to stimulate alms-giving, contained three lines that have been purged from the more refined modern hymnals:

Whatever, Lord, we lend to thee
Repaid a thousand-fold will be—
Then gladly will we give to thee . . .

Industrialists with a feeling for utilitarian piety do not often calculate its benefits in such crudely usurious terms as that; but industrialists are among the rich men who have been Guided, on innumerable occasions, to make handsome gifts to MRA, in cash and in kind; and it would be unrealistic to suppose that they have done so without the slightest *arrière-pensée*—without reflecting for a moment that such gifts could be an insurance against 'trouble-makers' and thus a lucrative investment.

There is nothing irreverent in the use of such language in this context. The very word 'investment' occurs in a long report on the world distribution of the pamphlet, *Ideology and Coexistence*,[1] read into the US *Congressional Record* on 31st March, 1960, by a pro-MRA Representative, Mr Wolf from Iowa: this effort was described as 'a priority investment for free men who . . . are determined to see freedom extended to the whole world'. (A rhetorical echo of Dulles' policy of 'liberation'?)

Evidence that this policy had previously paid off handsomely was contained in a report from Caux in June, 1949, by J. M. Roberts, jnr, Associated Press Foreign Affairs Analyst, who wrote: 'At breakfast a millionaire baker talked with great enthusiasm of his complete freedom from labour trouble since he adopted the principles of MRA.' There was another revealing note in the obituary tribute to Buchman in his own home-town newspaper, the Allentown *Morning Call* (an excellent and independent newspaper, but always carefully briefed by Buchman's closest associates):

[1] *Cf* p. 156.

> Dr Buchman's beliefs had appeal among some industrial workers . . . and probably helped blunt some of their enthusiasm for collective action against management.

Most remarkable of these indications of what MRA is really about when it tries to stop industrial unrest is a saying attributed to John Riffe, American steelworkers' leader and sometime Executive Vice-President of the CIO. According to Peter Howard's biography, *Frank Buchman's Secret*, Buchman once said: 'I am not going to lure you by hopes of material success.' Yet MRA constantly exploits the crude materialism of the words that Riffe is said to have uttered, 'to a Senator', when he was dying in 1958. *Ideology and Co-existence* quotes the message thus: 'Tell America that when Frank Buchman changed John Riffe he saved American industry 500 million dollars.' To industrialists who had already contributed to MRA funds, this was an assurance that their money had not been wasted: to those who had not yet contributed, it was a fairly broad hint to do so.

Riffe's death-bed testimony is a favourite MRA text. If (as is possible) it is genuine, the actual words must have been taken down at the time, and must be known. It is strange, therefore, that there should be a slight, but significant, change in these words as printed in the *MRA Pictorial* that appeared only a month or two before *Ideology and Co-existence*. Instead of 'he saved American industry . . .', we find in the *Pictorial* 'he saved *this country* 500 million dollars'. The other version seems calculated to appeal primarily to industrialists: this version has a wide appeal, more in keeping with the general tone and theme of this issue of the *Pictorial*, aimed specially as it is at Labour and Trade Union readers, whose interpretation of the other version of the Riffe text might well be the one that I have suggested. The difference can hardly be accidental: whether it is in accordance with Absolute Honesty to tamper with the wording of what is presented as an actual quotation is a matter for the consciences of the Buchmanite chiefs.

Serious Trade Union leaders in Britain and in Europe have

reacted sharply to what Arthur Deakin described as MRA's 'unwanted interference' in trade disputes. In July, 1953, the Executive Board of the International Confederation of Free Trade Unions, meeting at Stockholm, considered and amended a report on MRA which its General Secretary had been asked to prepare, and circulated it for the information of its members.

Members of the ICFTU Executive had been asked for their views on MRA as they had seen it at work in their own countries and organisations. In the report as circulated, the views of members from New Zealand, Canada, India, Denmark, Germany, the USA, France, Japan, Great Britain, and Italy were quoted. Of these, only the Japanese and Italian members had anything to say in favour of MRA (and that not without qualifications). The Japanese member, T. Nishimaki, expressed his 'personal opinion'—not, apparently, that of his organisation, the Joint Council of Japanese Trade Unions—that 'MRA could give considerable strength to the Japanese workers', but added that 'it might give rise to useless friction within the democratic trade union movement'. The Italian member, Giulio Pastore, stated that the Confederazione Italiana Sindacati Lavoratori 'was favourably disposed towards the social ideas of MRA'; but, though the workers responded in good faith to these ideas, 'unfortunately they have found that it is otherwise with the employers'. He said: 'Many employers have visited Caux and delivered fine speeches about social progress, but once they returned to Italy they forgot all about it, thus proving the truth of the Italian proverb, "The wolf can lose his hairs, but not his viciousness".'

All the other members whose views were reported were unanimous in their condemnation of MRA:

> The New Zealand Federation of Labour stresses the fact that they neither have nor desire to have any relations with MRA. Some officials of affiliated unions are reported to have paid visits to Caux, with their families. . . . Their travelling expenses were not paid by the trade unions, nor

did these people go as delegates of the New Zealand Federation of Labour.

Canadian workers regard MRA with suspicion, distrust, and even open hostility. Although MRA succeeded in gaining a few labour supporters in the 1940s, these people were very soon disillusioned and left the movement.

E. Jensen (De samvirkende Fagforbund i Danmark) wrote that DSF had nothing to do with MRA. They considered that Buchman's statement that MRA had created industrial peace in Denmark was 'immoral', since it in no way corresponded to the facts.

Similarly strong views were expressed by Walter Reuther, from the United States, on behalf of the Congress of Industrial Organisations, and Arthur Deakin, of the British Trade Union Congress. Reuther recalled that at the CIO Convention in 1951 a resolution had been drafted expressing opposition to MRA. No formal vote was taken on this resolution, since such a vote might have been misinterpreted as an anti-religious gesture; but 'no doubt was left about the feelings of the vast majority being in strong opposition to MRA'.

Deakin said that many British trade unionists had been invited to Caux, Florida and Washington:

> Once there, they were asked to give their views on various subjects. Their personal statements were then represented for propaganda purposes as being the views of whole groups of workers.

He also mentioned MRA's interference at a delicate moment during an unofficial dock strike, involving the ports of Bristol, Liverpool, Southampton and London. The strike-committee had called a week-end conference in London. 'MRA invited the strike leaders to a conference on the same day, and promised to pay all their expenses.'

The report's 'conclusions' emphasised MRA's lavish display of wealth, derived from unknown but dubious sources; mentioned cases—e.g., in Sweden—in which 'employers have exercised very strong pressure on their workers to get them to join MRA'; and commented on attempts by 'small groups' to operate MRA 'directives' in factories—directives which 'seldom correspond to the will of the majority'.

The final conclusion, and recommendation, consisted of a single short sentence: 'It is our view that MRA should be prevented from encroaching upon trade union preserves.'

Nor was this an isolated or snap decision by the ICFTU. There were further enquiries from affiliated bodies in various parts of the world. In response to these, the attitude adopted at Stockholm was reaffirmed. Three years later, in November, 1956, the Executive Board passed a resolution bluntly 'advising trade unionists, in view of the continued interference of MRA in industrial matters, to sever all connections with that movement'; and the warning was repeated in June, 1960, after the distribution of *Ideology and Co-existence.*

These sharp rebuffs by the ICFTU must be among the severest set-backs that MRA has received. In this case, obviously, MRA could not indulge in its usual McCarthyite smear and allege that anybody who criticised it was a Communist or 'Communist-inspired'. Against Deakin, staunchest of right-wing Labour leaders, and against ICFTU, whose separate existence arises from its refusal to co-operate with the Communist-led Unions in the World Federation of Trade Unions, such a charge would have been so absurd that even MRA could not have hoped to get away with it.

One more claim from the past reads curiously in the light of later history. The brochure of the Mackinac Assembly in 1952 contains this testimony from the Superintendent of the Assembly Building, Ford Motor Co, Dagenham, Essex: 'Not a single grievance has left the assembly floor since we started applying MRA. Production and efficiency rose to 100·4%, the highest since the war.'

Production and efficiency are still high at Ford's of Dagenham; but it would be a slight exaggeration to say that 'not a single grievance' had been heard of from there in recent years. Perhaps 'applying MRA' doesn't work for long?

8

WHERE THE MONEY COMES FROM

'Sacrificial giving'—Henry Ford's 'generous hospitality'—A donation from Miss Boot—'Maximum economy at minimum expense'—An embarrassing cut-price flight—A Department of Justice tribute—Official subsidies?

HAVING CONSIDERED the real (if sometimes unconscious) purpose of the Buchmanites' interventions in industry, we naturally turn to the question that is most often asked about MRA: 'Where does all the money come from?' It is a question that could be answered in comprehensive detail only by those—the MRA people themselves—who prefer to answer it in general terms. They always say that their lavish expenditure—on newspaper advertising, on the printing and distribution of such pamphlets as *Ideology and Co-existence*, on travel, on the maintenance of their properties—is paid for 'through the conviction and sacrificial giving of thousands of fellow-citizens'. They cite such homely instances as that of a girl who sold her piano and sent them £20.

There is no reason to think that this is untrue. Probably many small gifts helped to make up the £21,000 which Lady Dollan, wife of a former Lord Provost of Glasgow, handed over to Dr Buchman at Mackinac on his seventy-seventh birthday, 'on behalf of the housewives of Britain'. MRA has tens of thousands of active supporters, in Britain, the United States, and elsewhere. Many of them are of modest means: all, we can be sure, are Guided to give what they can to the cause (and, since they are also Guided not to drink or smoke or use cosmetics, they have the more to give). Even critics who may wish that the cause were a different one cannot cavil at that.

But giving by the rich can also be 'sacrificial' (some rich men find it acutely painful to part with their money); and it would take a good many second-hand pianos to raise the millions spent by MRA. Moreover, MRA is fortunate in that much of its real estate and other capital assets was acquired before the war: such assets will have appreciated enormously in market value.

In London, many of the full-time workers live at the houses, or hostels, in Charles Street, Berkeley Square. They are maintained by sympathisers who have covenanted to give nearly £32,000 a year—plus free vegetables from the country and twenty cars (some of these on loan). Since these full-time workers receive no salary, they presumably pay no income-tax —unless the vigilant officials of the Inland Revenue have ruled that their not inconsiderable income in kind must be taxable. In general, it may be said that these fortunate, but doubtless frugal, MRA workers live, as their founder did, on a kind of sanctified expense account.

The names of most of the benefactors and the size of their gifts are kept secret. According to the *New York Times* of 29th September, 1954, 'a small group of donors, including a group of wealthy elderly women, contributes fairly large sums annually'. Such details as have from time to time been disclosed, or leaked into the newspapers, are an indication of the stratospheric level of opulence of some of MRA's best friends. A representative of *Time* magazine, attending a Guidance session at Caux one Sunday, heard a spokesman announce that MRA was short of a million dollars for some specific account or object: an elderly American woman pledged $100,000 if four others would do the same; the half-million was reached in fifteen minutes; the deficit was covered the same day.

In January, 1950, it was announced that Mrs John Henry Hammond, senr, a member of the Vanderbilt and Sloane families (and mother-in-law of Benny Goodman, the famous jazz clarinetist), had given her estate at Dellwood, near Mount Kisco, Westchester, to MRA. The estate included a 'beautiful country home' in the Georgian style (in which Mrs Hammond was retaining one room for her own use), formal gardens and swimming-pool, cottages to accommodate fifty people, and a 277-acre farm. Its value at that time was assessed at $175,000. Similarly, a wealthy Englishwoman, Miss Irene Prestwich, made over to MRA her 40-room Cheshire house, Tirley Garth, and her capital. This has been for more than twenty years a major MRA indoctrination centre: during the war a fortnightly news-letter, printed in the house, was sent to 2,000 servicemen. In an interview published in the *Chester Chronicle* on 4th May, 1964—her eightieth birthday—it was stated that Miss Prestwich was 'in the unusual position of paying rent to live in her own home.'

One absentee from the list of Buchman's known benefactors was Henry Ford. His absence is puzzling, for he and Mrs Ford were close personal friends of Buchman and Ford went on record as saying: 'The objective of MRA is one in which I strongly believe.' If a man as rich as Ford believes 'strongly' in a cause, one would suppose that he would feel obliged by conscience to contribute handsomely to it. Buchman himself explained, not altogether convincingly: 'We had that kind of friendship where money was neither expected nor given.' Mr Howard, in *Frank Buchman's Secret*, says: 'Henry Ford never gave nor left Buchman a cent of money. But he offered generous hospitality to Buchman and his friends.'

It is impossible not to assume that if Buchman had needed money badly at any time, and had asked Ford for it, he would have got it. Probably the need never arose. Mr Howard names three American pioneering industrialists—Firestone, Edison, Ford—as friends of Buchman: 'all knew him well and all were deeply influenced by him'. Ford is the only one of the three whom he singles out as a non-donor. Presumably both the others helped: either of them, single-handed, could have financed MRA for a long time.

Pre-war Japanese supporters of MRA included Takasumi Mitsui, 'brother of the richest man in Japan', and Takashi Akiyama, a millionaire Tokyo industrialist and financier. Mitsui attended an MRA Assembly in California in 1939, where he spoke feelingly of 'partnership' in industry: his own workers were described by an American editor who interviewed him as 'practically slaves—earning a few cents a day'.

In 1960, gifts of money in the United States (in addition to gifts in kind and service) totalled $3 millions. The gifts in kind were pretty valuable, too. A house in Washington (MRA's 'embassy') was a gift from wealthy converts. The budget for an MRA play, *The Good Road*, was estimated in 1948 to be around $100,000 a week. Among those who contributed towards the cost of this production were Admiral Byrd and a member of the Firestone family of tyre-tycoons.[1] The programme of the play, when performed in America, included a note indicating that such contributions constituted 'legitimate deductions for income-tax purposes'.[2]

Another stroke of luck came MRA's way in the same year. According to the Camden (New Jersey) *Courier*, 'Jack Currie, who quit a $25,000-a-year job with a top cosmetics company to devote his full time to MRA, helps handle the finances of the group. He has given $20,000 to the cause recently.' Mr Currie was quoted as having said: 'Some big contributor always comes through in time.'

Other donations have included a large sum[3] from Miss Boot, whose fortune was derived from the highly reputed

[1] *Cf* p. 48.

[2] A short announcement in the Palm Springs *Desert Sun* on 11th March, 1959, stated that MRA's budget for 1959 was $14 millions. Contributions ('tax-deductible') could be sent to a local PO box-number.

[3] Said to have been £100,000—a figure which Miss Boot (now the Hon Mrs Holman) refuses to confirm or deny, describing an enquiry on the matter as 'an impertinence'. However, Mr Willoughby R. Norman, Chairman of Boots Pure Drug Co Ltd, courteously confirms that she 'has been a life-long supporter of the Movement and has contributed generously to it'.

chain of chemists' shops, and 100,000 of that useful currency, Swiss francs, taken to Mackinac in 1955 by Dr Oscar Leimgruber, Chancellor of the Swiss Confederation. The £132,000 needed to buy the Westminster Theatre, London, is said to have been contributed by more than a thousand people; but one of the most generous of them was almost certainly Mr R. Stuart Sanderson, a Galashiels woollen magnate, who was largely responsible for negotiating the deal.

These impressive figures do not mean that money is squandered with unnecessary extravagance. On the contrary, it has always been a boast that, as Peter Howard put it many years ago, MRA practises 'a maximum economy at the minimum expense'. Thus, when Mr Percy B. Ruhe, of Allentown, went to Caux, he met Mrs Erich Peyer, whom he described as 'one of a very small group of German and Dutch citizens who had pledged their personal fortunes in order to buy the entire property for MRA'. (Other accounts say that three Swiss supporters persuaded 120 wealthy Swiss to put up a million francs.) They had to find a big sum—£200,000 or so.[1] But that was considered a 'bargain price': the tourist trade had not yet recovered from the war, the hotels were shut or in difficulties, most of their 1,250 rooms empty. Over the years, the cost of the repairs and maintenance of this multiple property—some of it not taken over in very good condition—must have been heavy. Only gardeners and maintenance men are paid employees. There are about forty of these: their annual wages bill must amount to at least £20,000.

Nor is it always as expensive as it might seem for MRA teams to stay at good hotels when moving round the world. Again according to Mr Howard, 'the hotel-keeper sees the generous way so much help is given . . . and meets generosity with generosity'. I do not know whether this was true of Brown's Hotel, Buchman's London headquarters for so long, or of the Waldorf-Astoria in New York, where a team of a hundred

[1] Mr Geoffrey Williamson in his book, *Inside Buchmanism* (Watts, 1954), quotes a figure of £80,000; but this would appear to be for Mountain House only—one of three hotels that were acquired.

Buchmanites from Europe stayed in March, 1934.[1] (They included Mr Bernard Bourdillon, formerly Secretary of Chatham House, two Dutch baronesses, and Mr George Light, 'chairman of the Warwickshire Unemployed Association and known as a Labour agitator'[2]; and they brought with them news of a striking propaganda achievement—the printing of an Oxford Group slogan on four million British milk-bottle tops.)

The cost of producing the *Ideology and Co-existence* pamphlet, high as it was, might have been even higher—if it is true, as claimed by MRA, that '200 tons of paper were specially made for the British edition at a minimum profit by the British paper industry'.

Occasionally this practice of 'maximum economy' has led to embarrassment for those who have sought to help MRA in ways that ill-disposed persons could represent as improper. There was serious trouble in Washington in August, 1955, when it became known that Mr Harold E. Talbott, Secretary of the Air Force, had put three large military aircraft—C 119 Transports—at the disposal of 192 Buchmanites and that the United States Air Force had flown them, at cut rates and by a devious route, from Manila to Switzerland. The purpose of the tour was to present the MRA propaganda play, *The Vanishing Island*, to African and Asian audiences. Thanks to preliminary pressure on high government officials, the tourists were allowed to take the aircraft where they liked: their itinerary turned out to be flexible. In Iraq, where government hospitality had been laid on for a smaller party—60 MRA guests, not 192, had been expected—they decided to split into sections: some of them

[1] Inspiring an unknown poet to compose a limerick:

There was a young man of Peoria
Where sinning grew gorier and gorier:
By confession and prayer
And some savoir-faire
He now lives at the Waldorf-Astoria.

[2] Extensive enquiries within the Labour Movement have failed to establish that this is an accurate description of Mr Light, though many remember him as a well-liked Labour supporter and lecturer.

would visit Damascus, some Amman. According to the Washington columnist, Ruth Montgomery, 'It was then that the delegates first ran into trouble with the Air Force'. She added (New York *Daily News*, 20th August, 1955):

> Arriving in Egypt the other day, the group next demanded that one plane, due to rest there a few days, immediately refuel to carry a part of them on a 'special' trip to Nairobi.
>
> The 18-man crew, already in a near state of mutiny over its distasteful assignment, adamantly refused because the trip was not on the original 11,000-mile schedule. The delegates hastily notified their converts in high places to apply pressure to the Air Force, and when some of the officials protested that the play was receiving a great deal of unfavourable publicity, Buchman's No 2 leader, Ray Purdy, shrugged: 'Oh, that's all Communist-inspired.'

Communist-inspired or not, most of the criticism came from people not usually thought of, even by Mr Purdy, as Communists. Sherman Adams, Chief of Staff at the White House and Assistant to the President, took the view that the play might do serious damage to the cause of democracy in Asia. United States ambassadors cabled protests; and John Foster Dulles, Secretary of State, notified them, and envoys in countries still to be visited, that the MRA company had no official standing. Vice-President Nixon himself tried to get the tour stopped.

Yet, only a few months earlier, Dr Buchman, in the course of a sermon on what he called 'the Electronics of the Spirit', had said:

> Plays . . . can bring the electronic answer to millions. Twenty-seven casts are giving the Moral Re-Armament plays in eight languages on every continent. In Hollywood, leading directors . . . actors, technicians and designers have given of their genius to create a new musical, *The Vanishing Island*, which has a captivating answer that reaches the heart of every man.

Why did it not reach the hearts of Mr Adams, Mr Dulles, and Mr Nixon? Not, surely, because of its anti-Communist message. The trouble was that it also exposed 'decadence' in the West: some of its rather crude satire was directed at corrupt American politicians.

All this was highly embarrassing for one Senator in particular—Senator H. Alexander Smith; for he was the father-in-law of Mr Ken Twitchell, jnr, a member of a leading MRA family and one of those responsible for organising this outing; and Senator Smith's daughter, son-in-law, and grandchildren were all taking part in the tour and performing in the play. Senator Smith did his best. He begged the producers to cut a scene showing a 'typical' democratic election candidate 'stuffing a ballot-box'; but, as he had to explain to his incensed colleagues, 'They told me it was too late.'

Similarly, Secretary Talbott's original executive decision had to stand. Yet it is unlikely that the White House, the Secretary of State, and the Vice-President combined were less influential, at that moment in Washington, than the friends of MRA. The decision itself is a matter of record: why it was not cancelled is a matter of speculation.

According to the Associated Press, Mr Talbott had 'let the Group use the planes at half the rate required by regulations for private citizens'. This may have worked out at even less than half the total cost of the trip. Contemporary reports state that MRA paid $123,906—the amount that would have been charged to Congressmen or government officials; and that the difference—some $135,000—had been met at the public expense.

There was, however, one peculiarly unfortunate circumstance—certainly not foreseen by the Buchmanites, and as painful to them as to anybody—which may have made it politically inexpedient for even the highest authority to countermand Secretary Talbott's instruction. On 1st August, some time after he had authorised these special facilities for the MRA tour, Mr Talbott resigned—'following an enquiry into allegations that he had misused his office in order to obtain business for an industrial engineering firm of which he was a partner'.[1]

It may well be that Mr Talbott had signed the authorisation, to oblige some MRA-minded colleague, in a fit of absent-mindedness; for he must have been fully occupied for some time in preparing to face these other grave charges. Towards the end of July he appeared before the Senate Permanent Investigating Sub-committee: he 'admitted that he had tried to get new business for Mulligan and Co, but denied that he had acted with impropriety, broken the law, or used his official influence to further his business interests'. Despite these protestations, he resigned before the Sub-committee's findings were published. President Eisenhower paid tribute to his 'unexcelled diligence' and 'fine accomplishment', but accepted his resignation, saying that the decision was 'the right one in the circumstances'.

In comparison with this abrupt and regrettable end to a career of some distinction, the bother about the MRA trip was a minor nuisance. Had the President exercised his power, just after the resignation, to countermand Mr Talbott's order, he would have been magnifying minor nuisance into major scandal; and he would have been involving the Administration in a breach of faith with the Buchmanites, to whom, however unwisely or even improperly, a competent executive official had given a commitment. Moreover, by taking such action he might have seemed to be suggesting that there was some sort of parallel between this incident and the events leading to Mr Talbott's resignation; that in one or the other case, or in both, the Secretary of the Air Force had been guilty of something worse than indiscretion; and that his own tribute to his departed colleague had, accordingly, been insincere.

So Eisenhower, well-advised, did nothing, and the Buchmanites enjoyed their world tour (in part) at the taxpayers' expense. It would not have occurred to them, but it must have occurred to some ironists that the scenes in their play which had caused such offence had, after all, a piquant, if tragic, relevance.

[1] *Keesing's Contemporary Archives*, volume 10, page 14,375.

It may be that some wealthy benefactor, anxious to restore the tarnished image of MRA, later reimbursed the Air Force for the excess cost of the tour; but I have seen no evidence that this was done. Nor, if it was done, could one ever be sure whether it would have been done if the affair had not broken in the press.

A less substantial, but equally unfortunate, use of public funds for, supposedly, the benefit of MRA came to light in 1949, after five Congressmen had enjoyed an expense-free trip to Caux. A resolution authorising the appropriation of $5,000 for this purpose from the House contingent fund had gone through Congress 'on the nod' at a moment when few members were present. This excursion aroused unfavourable comment when it became known not only that the five pilgrims had been chosen at random—the invitations being touted round like raffle-tickets—but that, even on arrival at Caux, several of them had had not the vaguest idea why they were there or what their journey was supposed to be in aid of. In this case, clearly, MRA was less to blame than its indiscreet supporters in Congress.

It will be seen that the sources from which funds are derived and the techniques of 'maximum economy'—the 'sacrificial' offerings of rank-and-file believers, the benefactions of millionaires interested both in insuring against labour trouble and in legitimate tax-avoidance, the 'generosity' of hotel-keepers and the zeal (excessive when exposed) of influential friends who can wangle privileges at the public expense—should be adequate to cover the cost even of MRA's massive operations. There does not seem to be much point, therefore, in speculating on a suggestion that has sometimes been made—that, during the period of the Cold War, MRA's services to the anti-Communist cause have been recognised by subsidies from official, but secret, agencies in the United States or elsewhere. The possibility of such assistance has been hinted at twice in recent years in the Beaverbook press—Mr Bernard Harris suggesting in the *Sunday Express* that it might have come from the State

Department, and Mr Sam White reporting in the *Evening Standard* that MRA was well-established at an important official level in France and might have received financial help from the *Deuxième Bureau.*

Subsidies of this kind would not be inherently improbable, though the Central Intelligence Agency might be a likelier American patron than the State Department. It was neither CIA nor the State Department, however, but the Department of Justice which in 1949, for some reason—as a result, no doubt, of long-sustained pressure and intrigue—issued a memorandum praising MRA as 'a world force having as its principal objective adequate ideological preparedness of free nations for the ideological conflicts in which the world is now engaged', and adding that MRA's objectives were 'recognised by the Department as worthy and helpful in the strengthening of democratic forces throughout the world'. It is worth noting the definition, presumably acceptable to MRA, of MRA's *principal* objective: by 1949, this was no longer the promotion of the Christian religion—the basis on which, ten years earlier, the President of the Board of Trade had authorised the registration of the Oxford Group.

However, such subventions are secret, and, as I say, they would not seem indispensable to an organisation with so many affluent private backers as MRA. Mr Ivan Yates, in a well-informed series of articles in the *Observer* in March, 1961, quotes Mr Roger Hicks, of MRA's 'inner ring', as saying: 'Industry is coming to realise that unless it supports MRA, there will be nothing left for it to support.' Frank Buchman, when tackled on finance, used to ask, with airy amusement, 'Isn't God a millionaire?' According to the poet Cowper, 'God moves in a mysterious way / His wonders to perform.' It seems best to leave it at that.

9

A SOUND INVESTMENT

Ideology and Co-existence—*Communists and anti-Communists—Detroit Methodists under suspicion—World distribution of a booklet to 'roll back Communism'—The conspiracy complex—Sacrifice or self-preservation?*

We have already noted a fundamental change of emphasis in Buchmanism—a change that coincides roughly with the years in which the slogan of 'moral re-armament' has grown into the name of the movement. Whether it can or cannot still be classified as a Christian movement or sect, it is clear that MRA has become primarily a morale-building and propagandist instrument in the Cold War. There is, of course, no inconsistency between this development and Dr Buchman's praise of Hitler in 1936; but in recent years Communism has been far more obsessively omnipresent in the MRA scriptures than it was in the early days.

There is a constant harping on 'ideology'. The word occurs in MRA propaganda with wearisome frequency: MRA is equipped with 'the strategy, the unity, and the commitment of a superior ideology', and 'the Summit Strategy Conferences at Mackinac and Caux provide ideological training in Moral Re-Armament without which our deterrent material re-armament programme would be wasted'. The star displayed in an MRA brochure one Christmas was not identified as the star of Bethlehem but as 'the star of an ideology which illumines the road from heart to heart, class to class . . .'.

This tendency is illustrated most vividly in the publication to which reference has been made—*Ideology and Co-existence*. This narrow grey 32-page booklet was first published in September, 1959. On its first page a 'choice' is presented starkly: 'The choice for America is Moral Re-Armament or Communism.' (This aphorism has been recited dozens of times, with slight variations, by MRA supporters: here it is attributed to Admiral William H. Standley, a former United States Ambassador in Moscow.)

The text of the booklet opens with the words: 'We are at war. World War III has begun.' From then on, the general line is an anti-Communist line as naïve, as crude, and almost as extreme as anything perpetrated by the John Birch Society. Indeed, those familiar with extremist movements of the Right in America will recognise the shrill note of intolerance and fear which was once sounded at America First rallies and still inspires the occasional recrudescence of the Ku Klux Klan. I do not suggest that MRA shares the Klan's racialist prejudices: it is the *tone* of the booklet that unpleasantly recalls these phenomena.

Specifically, the booklet opposes East-West trade, recognition of the Peking Government, and nuclear disarmament; and its central theme is that 'peaceful co-existence' means death to the West. Since all the major political parties in Britain are in favour, at least in theory, of almost everything that this booklet opposes, it might have been better, tactically (though there are some minor differences between the American and British editions), to rewrite it more thoroughly for British publication. But both are spiced with quotations from Lenin whose value is, at best, doubtful.[1]

Sometimes it descends to mere silliness, as when it quotes this utterly meaningless statement by a Canadian ex-Communist MRA convert, Gerry McManus: 'In Canada and the United States the floodtide of Communism washes over the nation

[1] See p. 239.

every day.'[1] Equally incredible is the statement: 'A recent Finnish visitor to the Kremlin was told that the greatest obstacle to the advance of Communism was Moral Re-Armament.' Only the most gullible reader would fail to ask a few questions about this unidentified Finn and his obliging Kremlin contact.

Then there is the bitter experience of one Theodore Guething, 'a machine-tool manufacturing executive', who testified at Mackinac:

> We American businessmen don't like being fooled. As chairman of a committee I helped raise $140,000 for one of the largest Methodist churches in Michigan. Last week the Detroit Conference of the Methodist Church adopted a policy which couldn't have been written better by Mr Khrushchov himself.

This sinister policy included 'total world disarmament, admission of Red China to the United Nations, an end to selective service, curtailment of civil defence, and the establishment of Berlin as a free city under UN supervision'. All or most of these aims, again, have been advocated in respectable liberal quarters in the West. So it looks as if, like it or not, Mr G. were going to go on 'being fooled' . . . until he breaks with MRA and wakes up to some of the facts of political life.

Silliness degenerates at one point in the booklet into psychopathic fantasy. We are warned: 'Communists frequently do not show themselves as Communists. They find they can infiltrate more effectively, for instance, as anti-Communists.' Now, this may be literally true in some cases of actual espionage: it might be practicable and useful for a secret service to train a few agents to pose (for many years) as their own opposites, as is said to be the practice of the FBI in America. But, before printing this suggestion, MRA ought surely to have paused to consider its dangerous implications. Is *every*

[1] This curious belief is not held by MRA only on the other side of the Atlantic. Mr Peter Howard, 'sales of whose books have passed the 3,500,000 mark in many languages', said at Mackinac in 1959: 'Britain . . . is almost taken over by Communist thinking. We have been brainwashed.'

ardent and vocal anti-Communist to be suspected of being a Communist in disguise? If so, what about the most apparently dedicated anti-Communists of all—the Buchmanites themselves? And is the converse true? Are the toughest Communists really anti-Communists? How *do* you know where you are, or who is who? That way madness lies . . .

Yet this is not just a momentary slip on the part of the compilers of *Ideology and Co-existence*. In an excellent article on 'The Mind of MRA', in *The Spectator* of 8th December, 1961, Mr Bamber Gascoigne remarked:

> In any other context MRA workers would recognise much of their conversation as slanderous gossip. Communism and homosexuality are the two charges which tend to be levelled most sweepingly at a wide range of public figures. I was informed, for instance, that Walter Reuther is a Communist; and that this explains why he made such a violent attack on Khrushchov during the latter's visit to the States, because some time ago all the leading Communists were ordered to start behaving as vehement anti-Communists for security reasons. Kennedy's Secretary of Labour, Arthur J. Goldberg, is also supposedly a Communist; and in fact started the very steel strike which he is now given credit for having helped to stop. When I asked for proof of this I was told an elaborate detective-story about a girl who had worked in Goldberg's office in the '40s; she was at that time connected with Communism and has recently started working for Goldberg again.

Mr Gascoigne asked his informant 'why, if they had such clear proof, they didn't reveal it and have Goldberg discharged'. The MRA man said that it was 'not their job to take that sort of action, it was their job to change people'. This did not quite square with what he later told Mr Gascoigne:

> A friend of ours only a few months ago got 227 homos and Communists sacked from the State Department—and within a month they were all back in their jobs.[1]

[1] These gangs always seem to operate by the 200—or this piece of gossip

This is the kind of unverifiable story, dressed up with a plausibly precise figure, that the late Senator McCarthy first gained notoriety by airing. (He said: 'I have here in my hand a list of 205—a list of names that were made known to the Secretary of State as being members of the Communist Party and who are, nevertheless, still working and shaping policy in the State Department.' Despite frequent challenges, he was never able to establish a case against any of the 205: they were, of course, mythical.)

Even McCarthy at the height of his power (which was several years earlier than this) might have had some difficulty in getting exactly 227 officials sacked simultaneously. The original inventor of such a tale must be completely unscrupulous and cold-blooded: he lies not so much because he enjoys his own fantasy as because he calculates that the provision of such fantasies helps him to retain power over the feeble-minded fanatics who spread them. He is a Machiavelli rather than a Mitty. It is difficult to identify, lurking among MRA's figureheads, any of sufficient distinction or sophistication to fill the part of the Prince; but the kind of fable quoted by Mr Gascoigne—with examples of which MRA folklore is replete—is in the authentic tradition of religious and political persecution. Such lies have been used, thousands of times in human history, to excuse the suppression, torture, or massacre of minorities—of witches, of gipsies, of Catholics or Protestants, of Jews or Freemasons; and, now, of alleged Communists or homosexuals. The conspiracy complex is endemic at a fairly low level of human nature, and it is not the least of the charges against MRA that, by disseminating such malignant rubbish, it helps to feed it.

Even more sensational, in the same *genre*, is a didactic

may be, slightly garbled, the same story that Peter Howard tells in his latest book, *Britain and the Beast*: 'At one point, 264 homosexuals were reported to have been purged from the American State Department. Many of them moved from Washington to New York and took jobs in the United Nations, drifting back to Washington after a year or two.' How does Mr Howard, or Mr Gascoigne's informant, know? And does the UN employ at sight, without checking, anyone sacked by the State Department?

American novel which was published in England in 1959 by the Blandford Press. (It seems reasonable to regard this firm as MRA's 'front' publishers: they publish some books which sound innocent and useful and are not, so far as I know, 'ideological': books on gardening and bird-spotting, *Ponycraft*, *Pens and How to Use Them*, *Road to Philately*, *The Complete Toastmaster*, and *Have Fun With Your Son*. But they have also published most of the MRA propaganda books.) The novel in question is more purely comic than *Ideology and Co-existence*: it is recommended for reading aloud, late at night, in a cheerful circle of connoisseurs of this kind of *kitsch*. This is, in fact, what has happened to it on occasion, since some MRA workers have been so ill-Guided as to lend it to Cambridge undergraduates and others insufficiently simple to fall for its message. Indeed, I have myself wondered (taking the hint from *Ideology and Co-existence*) whether it was not written by a Communist *agent provocateur* seeking to make anti-Communism ridiculous.

The novel is entitled *The Pentagon Case*. Its author calls himself 'Colonel Victor J. Fox': his real name is Robert A. Winston, and he is a retired US air group commander who served, rather briefly, with the Central Intelligence Agency and was then 'appointed to a key post in the Pentagon'. His theme is a network of Communist agents operating in the Pentagon itself. Many factual details are thinly disguised as fiction—a reference, for instance, to 'the distinguished author of *Nagasaki* . . . published by a notoriously left-wing "humor" magazine[1] which devoted an entire issue to this single piece of anti-atomic propaganda which was straight down the Communist party line'.

I have read *The Pentagon Case* with care, and I find it hard to believe that a serious independent publisher would have accepted it without some special incentive to do so. (It was originally published in New York by Freedom Press Inc.) It is an extreme manifestation of the conspiracy complex: Soviet Communism is '*the*' enemy, and the impending Soviet attack is a case of 'when', not 'if'; ' "progressive" education is education

[1] This means the *New Yorker*!

for Socialism . . . and Socialism is only a euphemism for Communism'—the aim of 'progressive' education being deliberately to delay the literacy of potential American soldiers and technicians and to reduce their respect for authority; obscene books and pictures are a Red-directed 'anti-morale operation'; 'our greatest film comedian went over to the enemy years ago, while he was still in Hollywood'; and alert anti-Communists are kidnapped and turned into 'zombies' by pre-frontal leucotomy. Fortunately, the clean-limbed ex-Marine hero, Brett Cable (whose nostrils 'flare slightly' at moments of stress), comes through, with the help of a patriotic senatorial committee. No such load of comic nonsense has been foisted on the British public since the late Mrs Nesta Webster's *Secret Societies and Subversive Movements*.

It is worth paying special attention to *Ideology and Co-existence* because MRA itself obviously considered it of maximum importance. An altogether extraordinary effort was devoted to its distribution. It is doubtful whether any propaganda tract ever published has had so speedy and immense a circulation: MRA's boast is that this 'is believed to be the largest, simultaneous, global distribution of any single piece of literature in history'. But then, most organisations—political, religious, or philanthropic—have to consider costs. In Britain alone, the number of copies of *Ideology and Co-existence* distributed was more than 15 million. The 'outline of world distribution' printed in the US *Congressional Record* at the request of Mr Wolf,[1] shortly before the booklet was distributed in Britain, stated: 'A national distribution company employing 8,000 women, who will walk 350,000 miles in ten days, will cover 13,200,000 homes in the main urban areas.' (The figure was raised later.)

It may be thought strange that MRA, which can command such blind devotion from its adherents, should have added steeply to the cost of this exercise by employing commercial agencies instead of relying on voluntary help for distribution as well as for finance. Probably a task of this magnitude could

[1] *Cf* p. 134.

only be accomplished efficiently by professionals working on it full-time; and those who were making the distribution possible by their generous gifts could hardly be expected to go themselves from house to house, on foot or in their Cadillacs, and knock at doors or send their chauffeurs to do so, like political canvassers or washing-machine salesmen.

The printed 'outline' claimed a distribution of a million copies, in English or in Afrikaans, in South Africa; of 6,700,000 copies in Sweden, Norway and Denmark; and of 50 million in the USA. 'In the next few days 545,000 copies will go to every home in the Washington area.' MRA subsequently announced a total world-wide distribution of 75 million copies. (An earlier estimate was 86 million.)

This was indeed to 'saturate' the market—but how lasting were such effects as there may have been? Not everybody reads every circular dropped in at the door; but many people, one might suppose, would have at least a vague recollection of the delivery of so unusual and substantial a circular in their neighbourhood. Some three years after the British distribution of *Ideology and Co-existence*, the Granada television company was preparing a programme on MRA in its *World in Action* series. 132 people were asked if they had received the booklet. Only three said they had.

Such a massive approach, however, could hardly fail to excite some response. MRA, in a characteristically bombastic overstatement, said that the pamphlet had 'captured the attention of the world'. Whether '500 letters a week' in Sweden was an adequate response cannot be determined: we are not told how many weeks this went on for, how many of the letters were from Swedes already Changed, and how many more were Changed as a result of the correspondence. Without such additional data, one can only say that 500 does not seem to represent a very high percentage of Sweden's quota of booklets. However, a Swedish Post Office test showed that '72% of copies were actually read'.

In Norway, the 'outline' recorded, the General Secretary of the Communist Party 'turned up at the MRA office in Oslo and asked for literature. . . . He went away loaded' (with 'literature', one hopes). No sequel to this visit is mentioned; but MRA supporters in Oslo reported another incident which may be more significant:

> A well-known international figure was due to speak on Oslo Radio on nuclear disarmament and the banning of the bomb. Radio authorities said that since the distribution of the manifesto they could not afford to have him talk. People's eyes were opened. The talk was cancelled.

'Could not afford . . .'. This sounds as if they were afraid—of what sort of pressure? Does MRA equate open eyes with closed minds? Would it excommunicate a sincere nuclear disarmer?

From India came the assurance that 'there is no doubt that the handbook had a real influence in the defeat of the Communists in the recent Kerala elections'. This is part of a frequently repeated MRA claim: it is denied by some reliable authorities—by, for instance, Professor J. K. Galbraith, the economist whose book, *The Affluent Society*, gave the English language a new catch-phrase. I met Galbraith, then United States Ambassador in India, when he was on leave in Washington early in 1962. He was familiar with what had happened in the Kerala elections, without having been personally involved in them (as MRA had been). He did not believe that MRA had made any appreciable contribution to the defeat of the Communists. 'The causes of their defeat were entirely different', he said.

Again, this 'outline' included what seemed a noteworthy testimonial from a leading French democratic Socialist, M Guy Mollet. He was alleged to have 'invited' an MRA play to France 'to bring ideological clarity before Khrushchov's arrival in the Spring' (of 1956). In a recent letter to me, M Mollet states:

> . . . I would add that MRA refers to my name and my support quite improperly. And I authorize you, most willingly, . . . to make use of this denial.

However convincing the readers of the *Congressional Record* thought these claims, they must have been impressed by the sheer size of the operation; and some of them would have been moved by the need for funds to pay for it, also stressed:

> For the distribution to every home in America, $2,500,000 is needed. For the distribution to every home in Washington area, $35,000 is required.... Up to now, this operation in Europe and Asia is costing roughly $2,800,000....

One cannot estimate how much this exercise cost in Britain, An interim figure quoted for 'distribution' was $560,000—about £187,000. This may or may not include printing and other production costs. The total cost of production and distribution for Britain and Western Europe cannot have been much less than £1 million; for the world, between £2 and £3 millions.

No doubt as an extra guarantee of good faith and good value, the 'outline' quoted an ad-man's testimony:

> Don Belding, former chairman of Foote, Cone, and Belding, leading US advertising agency, and civilian aide to the Secretariat of the Army for Southern California, says, 'Moral Re-Armament is the strongest single force in the world today from the ideological standpoint in answering Communism. We must multiply it a hundred times to create a wave of ideological pressure that will roll back Communism. Major investment in this force is essential to maintain freedom.'

Some encouraging examples were given:

> Businessmen have raised capital assets and made them available. One man sold a block of apartments and gave $56,000. Many have sold life insurances, property, jewelry. A company lawyer who has already given all his capital pledged his life insurance. A married man who had just inherited $25,000 gave the entire amount....

And so on.... Admirable, it might be said: this is real dedication—'sacrificial' giving indeed. One might agree if, so far as could be judged, the motive of the givers were truly self-sacrificing and positive. In some cases it may have been: MRA—like other causes, good or bad—has always been able to inspire some genuinely unselfish devotion. But the whole tone of this document—inserted in the *Congressional Record*, where people of wealth and influence might be expected to see it—is that of a stockbroker advising a client on a sound investment or an insurance agent offering an exceptionally advantageous life policy. The appeal is, essentially, to fear and self-preservation; not to self-sacrifice. It closes with the punch-line:

> If this force does not win, people in the United States will not only not have their fortunes, they will not have their lives.

What man of substance, with a proper regard for his commitments, could fail to reach for his cheque-book?

10

AFRO-ASIAN EXPANSION

Seeking new allies—Christ and the oriental market—MRA as 'the ruling factor in Japan'; and a disappointment—A Buddhist at Mackinac—An African at Caux—Congolese brotherhood—'Racial unity' in South Africa

THE CRUCIAL switch from redemptive evangelical Christianity to anti-Communist ideology must have been welcome to some of MRA's influential American backers: it brought the movement into line with the foreign policy pursued in the post-war period by the State Department, and the language now used was more secular and less uncomfortable.

One reason for the switch (which MRA spokesmen would insist was one of emphasis only, not of basic belief) may have been that, in a world-wide ideological struggle, powerful allies were both necessary and, on certain conditions, available. Some of these allies would shun a proselytising movement recognisably Christian and Western. Despite the medical and educational work that many European missionaries had done, they were handicapped, in the epoch of the liquidation of empires, by their links with the old colonial powers. Too often the religion of the missions had not taken root and become an Asian or African expression of Christianity, absorbing what it could of the 'pagan' rites: it was an alien culture. In British colonial or ex-colonial territories, for instance, 'the English church'—trim, grey, Gothic, such as may be seen at Eastbourne or Camberley—was hung with frayed regimental colours and tended by district commissioners' or officers' ladies, who would polish the brass and 'do the flowers' just as 'at home'.

This picture would not be true, of course, of all the oversea dioceses of the Anglican Communion or of all European Protestant missions. It is true of some, it is a parody of others; it may not be typical. Particularly in some parts of Africa, churches which began as missions have become truly indigenous. But where there was this failure to communicate with the people of the country—where the clergy, perhaps through no fault of their own, were little more than chaplains to the white minority of settlers and soldiers—MRA, like the Pentecostal sects in some parts of the world, might have had a better chance of success than the conventional Christian missionaries, tied as they largely were to observances and vocabularies traditional in their own distant lands.

Even in some countries of Latin America, the influence of Roman Catholicism, once so triumphantly dominant, now seems much less secure—a thin ornamental icing on the rich dark cake of paganism. Visiting prelates from North America lament widespread and major lapses into aboriginal cults, an alarming growth of atheism, and a shortage of clergy so acute that a single priest—inevitably, to English imaginations, a Graham Greene character—may have to cover many hundreds of square miles and can provide each of his villages with a Mass only once every few months. No doubt this was why Cardinal Cushing, of Boston, 'befriended' (it is his word) an MRA team that he met in South America—probably in Brazil, where MRA has been active for some years, with the aid of local ex-Communists. He was to regret his friendliness. Too much was made of it in MRA propaganda, and he was even quoted as saying that he would welcome the setting-up of MRA centres in his own archdiocese. 'That's silly', he said, repudiating the report and reiterating the official Roman Catholic warning against MRA.[1]

Asia, and especially India, must have seemed to MRA and

[1] See p. 183.

its Washington advisers a key sector of the global struggle: MRA must, therefore, be so projected in India that it would not seem to the most devout Hindu or Moslem to be just another Christian mission. So we find that in MRA propaganda designed for the oriental market there is practically no mention of Christianity: Christ, if named at all, is sandwiched unobtrusively between Gautama the Buddha and Mahatma Gandhi; the suggestion is that, whatever your faith, you will be the better—a better Hindu or Buddhist or Moslem—for accepting MRA's rule of life; and this rule of life, so far as it is theistic at all, is consistent—despite the Ministerium of Pennsylvania—with a relatively undogmatic pantheism.

These tactics seem to have worked in Burma, Japan, and Thailand at least. The respected name of U Nu is quoted in MRA propaganda so often, and with so much circumstantial detail, that his can hardly be one of those endorsements which other eminent persons have been induced to give to MRA without fully realising what they were letting themselves in for.

Japan, too, has been responsive to MRA's blandishments (and is honoured as the nation in which MRA's ambitious centre for the whole of Asia has been established). During the 1958 'Summit' conference at Mackinac, an MRA public relations hand-out recorded the presence there of Masahide Shibusawa, 'great-grandson of the founder of modern industrial Japan'. Shibusawa seems to be almost fanatical in his devotion to MRA. In 1963 he was seen in Granada's *World in Action* programme, saying: '. . . the military forces in Japan are taking Moral Re-Armament as their compulsory training for their officers and men' —a statement which, it is to be hoped, is not literally, or 'absolutely', true, since such compulsion would surely be as indecent as the conduct of the legendary Chinese general, a convert to Christianity, who baptised his troops with a hose. It may also be felt that there is a certain incongruity between the rule of the Four Absolutes and effective training in the art of war: if there were ever another war in which Japan was involved, one might even hope that soldiers practising the Absolutes would be on the other side rather than among one's allies. ('Corporal

Shibusawa, I want you to take a party round that hill over there, to create a diversion and make the enemy think that we're going in from the flank.' 'Oh no, sir, sorry sir, that wouldn't be absolutely honest.')

At Mackinac in 1958 Mr Shibusawa read to the assembled faithful an article by Japanese Finance Minister Ichimada in *Mainichi*, a paper 'with a daily circulation of 3½m'. In the course of a glowing tribute to Dr Buchman, Ichimada wrote: 'MRA is now the ruling factor in Japan and has transformed the nation.'

Such sweepingly unqualified assertions are usually unsafe. The transformation, if it ever occurred, did not last: two years later, in June, 1960, an MRA full-page advertisement[1] quoted Prime Minister Kishi on MRA's 'massive impact' on Japan 'during the past six weeks'. This advertisement—which consists of the text of a statement by Dr Buchman himself 'on the occasion of his eighty-second birthday and the opening of the Moral Re-Armament world assemblies at Caux and Mackinac Island, June, 1960'—adds that 'a leader of the Japanese Socialist Party at a crisis point early this year played a key part in healing a fresh split in their ranks and prevented Communism from taking over'. It is hard to know what 'crisis point' is here referred to, and what split was healed, since the Japanese Socialists had, in fact, been divided organically since 1959: there were two separate Socialist Parties in Japan, both affiliated to the Socialist International.

Delegates from both these parties with whom I discussed the matter at the Amsterdam congress of the Socialist International in September, 1963, were also puzzled by this statement. One of them thought that it must have referred to the controversy about the proposed security treaty with the United States. Popular anxiety about this treaty was beginning to be mobilised at that time; but the dispute, far from being healed, was soon to erupt in serious violence. The 'leader of the Japanese Socialist Party', praised by Buchman for this imaginary or

[1] This was the advertisement, headed 'A Hurricane of Common Sense', which led to considerable controversy. See p. 237.

ineffective 'healing', was probably (these delegates said) Mrs Shizue Kato, a member of the upper house in the Japanese parliament and the wife of a middle-of-the-road Socialist veteran. She is known as a strong supporter of MRA. Delegates from both parties agreed that Buchman's statement was 'much exaggerated', and that MRA's influence in Japan is limited, as one of them put it, to 'a small circle in the upper crust'—by which, he explained, he meant 'financiers, some intellectuals, and a few students'.

Such crises and contradictions may be thought strange in a nation in which, two years earlier, MRA had been 'the ruling factor' . . . and June, 1960, was, as it turned out, an unfortunate moment for exploiting the name of Mr Kishi. Three months earlier, indeed, his position must have seemed secure. On 26th March there had been a momentous encounter of East and West: the West German Chancellor, Dr Adenauer, had visited Tokyo, and at his meeting with Mr Kishi, 'members of the 16-nation MRA force in Japan were on hand with the Cabinet and Diplomatic Corps to welcome the German Leader'.

MRA and Mr Kishi were by now heavily committed to each other. Their expressions of mutual esteem were soon to seem excessively flattering. MRA, said Mr Kishi, was 'giving a moral backbone to the whole world'; and 'Peter Howard conveyed to the Prime Minister Dr Frank Buchman's message: Japan and Germany can give ideological clarity to the world'. Students of modern history may find this an interesting choice of world-instructors.

Then Mr Howard addressed Mr Kishi in terms that would have brought a blush to the cheeks of most democratic politicians. Of Kishi's 'amazing visit to the countries of Asia with "the statesmanship of the humble heart" ', he said 'If leaders of nations like mine had learned that secret, the world today would be united'—a smart back-hander at Mr Macmillan, President Kennedy, and others, which it is to be hoped that they heard of and took to heart.

No doubt the tribute by Kishi used in MRA's June advertisement was written while this mood of complacent jubilation lasted. It must have been composed before 26th May, when 1½ million Japanese—150,000 of them in Tokyo—took part in mass-demonstrations against the signing of the treaty with the United States. From the point of view of the MRA propagandists, who presumably like their output to be at least plausible, there could hardly have been a more unfortunate coincidence. Not all the demonstrators can have been Communists or dupes of the Communists. Memories of Hiroshima—and, indeed, of painstaking post-war American attempts to coach Japan in the ways of peace—were still vivid: this treaty, with all its implications, re-opened many old wounds. For the demonstrations of 26th May were not an isolated phenomenon. On 4th June—Dr Buchman's birthday!—there was a railway stoppage. Protest strikes became riots; in the Japanese parliament, opposition members piled furniture against the Speaker's door to try to prevent him from putting the ratification of the treaty to the vote, and Mr Kishi himself was trapped in the building for twelve hours.

These disorders culminated in a profound humiliation, for Mr Kishi and for the United States Government: a goodwill visit to Japan by President Eisenhower, scheduled for 19th-22nd June, had to be cancelled. Washington was furious: Kishi and his colleagues had seriously misjudged Japanese public opinion and the probable reactions to the treaty. On 23rd June Kishi announced his resignation. Three weeks later he left office—not the only statesman to have been misled by those who persuaded him to believe, and to tell the world, that MRA had had a 'massive impact' on his nation.

To a leading Buchmanite like Garth Lean, this upheaval in a nation's life was 'a simple question of ideology beating no ideology'. In his pamphlet, *The Fight for a New World*,[1] he explains that Japan was 'being mastered by a great idea'—in this case, Communism—'that empowered a few Japanese students, in 1960, so to mobilise their fellows that an American President was stopped from visiting their country'. But was all

[1] 'Published May 1962 by the Oxford Group.'

the disorder and opposition that I have described only the work of a few Communist students? And, if so, what becomes of the Finance Minister's tribute of two years earlier? Had MRA, then, really been 'the ruling factor' in Japan? Was this claim, publicised by MRA, untrue or mistaken? Is MRA Guided so to publicise error? What, come to that, of another proud boast—that 'whenever MRA and Communism meet head-on, MRA wins'?

However, Thailand is probably a more dependable American satellite than Japan and, as such, peculiarly susceptible to the appeal of MRA. That 1958 Mackinac hand-out also reported an unwontedly flamboyant exercise in ritualism:

> The colorful assembly rose in standing ovation in the high-raftered hall as the Lord Abbot of Watmahadtat monastery, who is also Minister of the Interior for Ecclesiastical Affairs in Thailand, in his saffron robes presented a ceremonial gong to Dr Buchman. He struck the gong four times, saying that each powerfully ringing note symbolised one of the absolute standards of MRA. . . . It was the first time that such a high official of the Buddhist hierarchy has left Asia. He told Dr Buchman that Moral Re-Armament will be the 'beacon that will guide the destination [*sic*] of humanity'.
>
> As a token of the response of the Buddhist world to Buchman's leadership, the Lord Abbot presented him with a gold medal bearing the image of the Emerald Buddha.

Note the final sentence of this report. Whoever wrote it had a deft way with words: he knew how to get more than its full value from this gaudy little incident—how to use it both to suggest an intoxicating vision of MRA's ever-widening empire and to play on the vanity of the eighty-year-old founder. 'The response of the Buddhist world to Buchman's leadership' is most ingenious, for 'leadership' has two subtly differing shades of meaning, according to its context. One implies stature, the other office: in 'the nation responded to the war-time leadership of Winston Churchill', it is used in a broader, looser sense than in 'the Conservative Government under the leadership of Winston Churchill'. Here the two senses are made to overlap: only a slight rearrangement of words is needed, and Buchman is the accredited leader of the Buddhist world. A large number of devout Buddhists in Asia would have been astonished had they known what was being said in their name.

Nor were the Buddhists the only extraneous followers of the new Messiah. It must have seemed to the faithful at Mackinac that the millennium was at hand—for this hand-out was headed: 'World Statesmen Turn to Buchman for Answer'. A German Chancellor and a Japanese Finance Minister are, in a sense, 'world statesmen', but the term sounds more comprehensive than that—and was, perhaps, meant so to sound.

After visiting Caux in 1949 Miss Honor Tracy wrote, in an entertaining article in the *New Statesman:*

> Everything up here is a little larger than life. Smiles are wider and toothier and handshakes positively cripple. . . . The people attending the conference, too, are apt to be presented as rather more important than they are; from hearing the officials talk, you would suppose that this was the cream and flower of Europe.
>
> I drew the attention of the Press Officer to what looked like over-optimism in some of his hand-outs, and taxed him with having on one occasion told me a plain fib. He hung his head:
>
> 'I'm not Absolutely Honest yet,' he groaned. 'Sorry!'
>
> A remark of this kind immediately makes one a friend for life, but it would be helpful if MRA prefaced its publicity material with a note to say that as the editors are still in the process of Change, the contents should be taken with a grain of salt.

Four years after Miss Tracy had been there, another visitor described, in *Tribune,* his reactions to Caux. He was a young African named Abu Mayanja and he had been recommended to go to Caux by an Anglican cleric in Uganda.

His first impression was unfavourable: 'I was annoyed that

everybody went out of their way to treat me with special and condescending courtesy: that everybody, man *or* woman, held the door for me to pass through, as if I was an elderly lady. . . .' (This reaction may seem, to those with little experience of inter-racial tensions, irrational: condescension is infuriating, but 'condescending courtesy' is surely preferable to discrimination. On the other hand, condescension expressed in exaggeratedly polite gestures is itself a form of discrimination. White people should feel able to treat Africans as casually as they treat other white people: the fact that some of the more sensitive and liberal of them cannot do so is an awkward by-product of racialism. I am sorry for Mr Mayanja's over-courteous Buchmanites: they were trying hard. . . .)

His next impression was more favourable: 'I was always being introduced to European settlers from Kenya, South Africa and Central Africa. The reason . . . was openly declared to be to show me how Moral Re-Armament, through the application of the dictum that "change begins with me", was already changing the white oppressors of Africa, thereby solving the problem of race and colour tyranny. . . .' Again, it must be conceded that, so far as it went, MRA's object was good. Racial discrimination and prejudice are among the worst evils in the world, and anyone who is against them is on the side of humanity.

But it is no good being against them without adequate weapons—without a more profound diagnosis and a more lasting cure than MRA could provide. 'Diagnosis' and 'cure' are words that were often on Buchman's lips. His fundamental mistake was to suppose that social and economic evils could be diagnosed and cured in terms of individual human nature alone. So these journeys from Africa to Caux were wasted journeys: the settlers learned to treat with courtesy, and almost as equals, the individual Africans whom they met there; then they would return to Africa, well-meaningly enough, but with no mandate, no education, no Guidance for *collective* action to bring about radical change in property relations and in the whole social and economic set-up; and without these broader changes, improvements in personal behaviour—admirable in themselves—can have little impact on the major problems.

So strong are the pressures of economic interest and social custom (through which economic interest is expressed and safeguarded) that even the most striking personal improvement, however sincerely initiated, may not last long. One of the settlers whom Abu Mayanja had made friends with was painfully candid: he 'told me that Caux had changed him sufficiently to enable him to endure having lunch with me on the same table, but that he was afraid of going back to Kenya and doing the same thing there'. This example of Absolute Honesty can hardly have been to the taste of those in charge at Caux.

Mr Mayanja's account contains other details which show how intensive, yet how appallingly superficial—how frivolous, even—the Caux treatment was, and he is only one of many witnesses who have found the complete lack of privacy and solitude the most trying thing about the place:

> I found that I was always encircled. My solicitous friends could not bear to leave me alone. . . . For the two major meals . . . you were always 'fixed' on a table, with a number of people. At breakfast and tea, you would almost always be with . . . those people who had made it their special job to look after you. . . .
>
> The meals are *the* great times of MRA. They are the times when real, serious, individual conversion is put into motion. I wonder if you can imagine an ignorant, savage, non-Christian, young African being set on by four or five resolute men—all insisting that he had done something amiss, and that he needed change.

Mr Mayanja writes ironically, but it is clear from his account that, as one finds so often in studying this movement, the MRA people detailed to Change him were totally lacking in tact—and, one might add, in real courtesy. I cannot imagine any comparable assault on a human soul at an Anglican, a Methodist, or a Roman Catholic dinner-table, not because people of those allegiances do not hold their faith strongly but because they would regard such behaviour to a guest as intolerably bad manners: they would also know, incidentally, that nothing could be more likely to put off permanently anyone of even the slightest intelligence. If it were argued that visitors to Caux are there not just for fun and light social conversation, but as serious enquirers, and that a mealtime is as good a time as any other for providing information and administering persuasion, I would merely reply that there are ways and ways of doing things, and that the Caux way, as experienced by Abu Mayanja and others, is a singularly insensitive way.

Even more fatuous were the 'quiet times' that he was roped in for. After a few minutes with pencils and notebooks:

> . . . somebody would begin reading out to the company the divine message; he had been told . . . to exercise more discipline against the attraction of the female sex. He had also been told that Abu . . . was destined to be a great fighter for Moral Re-Armament.
>
> Then another and another—all saying, in various phrases, that God had told them that Abu was destined to bring peace, happiness, prosperity to Africa and to the world, through Moral Re-Armament. . . .

As more perceptive companions might have guessed, Abu was not the sort of man to fall for this heavily obvious flattery, even when it was supposed to come from so exalted a source. Not for the first or last time, Buchmanite Guidance was to be proved inaccurate; for Abu, when pressed to disclose *his* Guidance, would sometimes answer, 'quite truthfully', that he 'had been thinking about the girl who had served us at the meal-table'; then, realising that this was not quite what was wanted, would devise such pretentious MRA-type utterances as 'Africa will be the pivot on which world events will be balanced', or 'something equally silly'. Finally, feeling that he could not bear all this nonsense any longer, he said that he had been Guided to go back to London at once—Guidance which was diagnosed as having come not from God but from the Devil.

He left, all the same—to be met at Victoria Station by importunate Buchmanites, begging him to accept their hospitality in London; for, as others have discovered, often at the cost of great mental distress, it is only with extreme reluctance that MRA will release anyone who has looked like being a useful convert.

Abu Mayanja, stronger-minded than some, resisted these further solicitations and survived, to send Caux up sky-high in his *Tribune* article. Caux, it must be admitted, has survived, too . . . and it must also be admitted that the Buchmanites were right at least in their estimate of their young guest's potential usefulness: he has become prominent in the political life of his own land, being a member of the regional parliament of Buganda Kingdom and Minister of Education in the Kabaka's government.

Other Africans, not necessarily less strong-minded than Mayanja but possibly less sophisticated, have not been able to resist MRA's advances so coolly; and their initial response has provided material for some of MRA's claims. Except, possibly, for Algeria, the worst violence of recent years has been in the Congo. An MRA task-force went there six weeks before independence. Glowing tributes were obtained from leading Congolese politicians, many of whom were taken to Caux for training. Time on Leopoldville radio was made available to MRA every day. The MRA missionaries were particularly well-received in Katanga. President Tshombe said: 'We will all be brothers.' Events in the Congo since then have hardly confirmed this prophecy: inter-tribal enmity, aggravated by European financial interests, made Congolese brotherhood look more like that of Cain and Abel.

On MRA's particular claim to have reconciled two warring tribes, the Lulua and the Baluba, Mr Andrew Boyd of *The Economist*, an expert on African affairs, said in the *World in Action* television programme:

> It's quite true that these two tribes had been fighting and that their leaders were reconciled in August, 1961,

but that was only part of a much more general reconciliation, throughout the Congo, which had been achieved by months of patient diplomacy by United Nations officials—and the particular Lulua-Baluba reconciliation, *unlike the others*, fell apart very quickly. In fact, one of the two quarrelling leaders very soon found himself in gaol.

Such other practical good as has been done—with little publicity—has largely been done by the relief and welfare agencies of the United Nations, supplemented by the voluntary effort, in many lands, of such organisations as Oxfam, War on Want, and Freedom from Hunger. To those who have seen Congolese children dying from malnutrition and tropical diseases, it would seem that food, medical aid, and education, rather than propaganda about the Four Absolutes, would be the best weapons for the moral and physical rearmament of the Congo. Perhaps some of the MRA people on the spot did take part in this immense and urgent task of physical relief; they are not, I am sure, personally inhumane. I can only say that, among the hard-pressed UN and other relief workers whom I talked to when visiting the Congo, I met none who had anything to do with MRA. The only ones, indeed, identifiable as an organised body of professing Christians were some Belgian nuns who had courageously stayed on to nurse in their overcrowded hospital when the emergency had begun and doctors and other professional people had fled the country. Perhaps MRA was engaged in what would certainly have been the full-time task of Changing the directors and agents of the *Union Minière*.

The link between MRA and President Tshombe was still publicised for a time after it must have been clear that he was a somewhat off-beat convert, being notably truculent in his defence of the interests of the *Union Minière* and not conspicuously dedicated to Absolute Love and Absolute Unselfishness. At a time when it was convenient to him to leave the Congo, it was reported that he was going to attend an MRA gathering in Rio de Janeiro. This intention was frustrated by visa trouble: it had become known in Washington that Tshombe's private hope, in crossing the Atlantic, was not so much to assist the cause of MRA as to try to organise diplomatic recognition of his 'independent republic' by some of the more amenable Latin-American states.

But of all the African nations, the one in which humane and democratic and Christian values are violated most conspicuously is South Africa. Here, if there were any substance in the claims of MRA, and if these claims were to carry conviction in other African territories, Moral Re-Armament should surely stand up for human unity, human rights, and human dignity, and confront directly the monstrous crime of *apartheid*. Again, it may be that some individual Buchmanites have been among the heroes and martyrs of the South African resistance; but the main leadership of that resistance has come from the more conventional Christian denominations and from non-Christians—most notably, perhaps, from such Anglicans as Bishop Reeves, Trevor Huddleston (now Bishop of Masasi), Michael Scott, Archbishop de Blank, and Miss Hannah Stanton.

In fact, the record of MRA in South Africa, such as it is, consists largely of the usual outpouring of self-praise—of loudly proclaimed success which turns out to be, quite evidently, failure. Since 1929, when the Oxford Group acquired its name there, teams or task-forces of Buchmanites have visited South Africa on a number of occasions, and have had a warmly sympathetic welcome. Three of many illustrative quotations may suffice.

During that 1929 visit Buchman himself was with the team. One of the politicians whom he captivated was J. H. Hofmeyr, Deputy Prime Minister to Smuts. Hofmeyr, summing up the results of Buchman's visit, said that it had 'started a major and continuing influence for racial reconciliation throughout the whole country, white and black, Dutch and British'. The subsequent history of South Africa shows that this judgement—especially the words 'major and continuing'—was too sanguine; but, serious as South African racial division was even then, this was before it had been elevated to a philosophy of government under Malan, Strijdom and Verwoerd. In January, 1955, delegates from South Africa were present at an MRA World Assembly in Washington. Buchman's home-town newspaper, the Allentown *Morning Call*, summarised their contribution thus:

> Speakers from South Africa said MRA was replacing racial supremacy and bloody revolution in their nation with 'a new dimension of racial unity'.

Hofmeyr might have been excused for thinking, a generation ago, that things were going to get better in South Africa. The suggestion that they were already getting better in 1955—whatever 'a new dimension . . .' may mean—could have been made only by a fool or a knave.

In his birthday message ('A Hurricane of Common Sense'), as recently as 1960, Dr Buchman wrote, of the MRA film musical, *The Crowning Experience*:

> White and black leadership in South Africa want their Cabinet and the whole country to see this movie. They say it holds the secret that alone can cure the racial divisions that are tearing South Africa apart, dividing her from other countries, and undermining her economic life.

These words appeared just a year before South Africa left the Commonwealth. The most disgraceful tyranny since Hitler's—with which it has much in common—was already in power. We can be certain that the South African Government would not have allowed this film to be shown publicly if it had contained anything that seriously challenged the dogma of *apartheid*. Buchman referred to 'white and black leadership' as wanting it shown. Which white leaders precisely? And which black ones? At least Buchman could not pretend that all was well in South Africa; but he did not explain what had happened to the 'new dimension of racial unity' proclaimed, under his auspices, five years earlier. In fact, throughout the years in which his teams had been operating in South Africa and his propagandists had been churning out rapturous accounts of their unbroken series of successes, things had been getting steadily worse, racial passion and prejudice more violent, dictatorship more rigid and brutal.

We cannot blame MRA for the bloodshed, oppression, and fear that darken Africa. One cannot blame anyone or any movement for trying hard and failing. But it would be easier to feel sympathy with some of MRA's efforts if it did not pretend to have an infallible instant panacea; if only it would, just occasionally, admit to failure, forgo boasting, exaggeration and snobbish name-dropping, practise self-criticism, and cultivate the virtue of humility.

11

THE DOUBLE STANDARD

A tribute to Islam—'Top people' and The Crowning Experience*—Appeal to snobbery—Condemned by Rome—A fundamental change in strategy—A Christian assembly slandered: the slanderers rebuked but unrepentant*

However MRA may have developed in recent years, its original impetus was religious and Protestant. In the West, at least, its continuing appeal is largely to Christians—practising, nominal, and lapsed; and when its apologists have to answer awkward questions from known Christians (other than Roman Catholics) they rely heavily on language dear to the Evangelical, and assure these questioners that they are 'rooted in Christ'. Yet the ideology, as distinct from the religion, is commended to men of all religious faiths or none, and no attempt is made to convert, for instance, practising Jews or Buddhists to Christianity.

In the adoption of this double standard (as we may, without offence, call it) MRA is true to the example of Frank Buchman himself. He saw no inconsistency in saying that MRA had 'the answer . . . that unites the Moslem with all men who truly live their faith' and that the Moslem nations could be 'a girder of unity for the whole world', while he was at the same time assuring his less broad-minded brethren in the Ministerium of Pennsylvania that his teaching was based entirely on that of Luther. The religion of Islam, at its best, is one of the most elevated of the great world religions, but an orthodox Lutheran could hardly fail to recognise it, especially in Africa, as a potent and proselytising rival to Christianity.

It may be that Buchman's own attitude underwent some modification over the years, as he travelled the world and became friendly with potentates and holy men of various faiths. His tribute to Islam was uttered at the Mackinac 'summit strategy conference' in 1959, when the Shah had just made him a Commander of the Order of the Crown of Iran—an honour that clearly called for some reciprocal courtesy. His growing latitude in such matters is shown by the contrast between this statement and his answer to a question put to him many years earlier, in 1932, at a house-party at Briarcliff Manor, New York:

> The Trinity is certainly a part of the fellowship's tenets, and a Unitarian would cease to be a Unitarian if he became identified with the group.

This occasion must have been one of the last to be sponsored by the First Century Christian Fellowship under that name: for by now the Fellowship (though not yet removed from Buchman's entry in *Who's Who*) had been for some years changing into the Oxford Group. At any rate, it would be unthinkable now—or, probably, for the last twenty years of Buchman's life—that a Unitarian who stuck to his beliefs should be excluded from the fellowship of MRA.

In 1936 Buchman was still using the pious metaphors in which he had been reared. On 21st June of that year, he spoke of the 'atoning blood and work of Christ', and placed himself and his hearers at the 'foot of the Cross, where the blood of Christ will cleanse us from every sin'. It may be noted, however, that these words were spoken in Philadelphia—within earshot, so to speak, of the Ministerium's vigilantes. Similar expressions are still used by such Buchmanite clergymen as the Revd K. W. S. Jardine, a former Canon of Lahore, who testified as recently as 1960 that, after twenty years of missionary work in India, it was at Mackinac that 'the Cross of Christ became . . . a burning reality' to him. There may seem to be a certain incongruity between this devout language and, for instance, the telegram that Buchman once received from a number of distinguished Greeks (when the King of the Hellenes was conferring on him another of the orders and decorations that he so much enjoyed receiving); for this telegram assured him that 'the principles of Moral Re-Armament correspond fully to Hellenic civilisation, ancient and present. . . .' The gods of Olympus might have been taken slightly aback if required to practise Absolute Purity. But there is no need to assume any conscious hypocrisy in such apparent contradictions: no doubt Buchman was simply being, like the Apostle Paul, 'all things to all men'.

Since there is this persistent appeal to Christians, it is as well to examine the reactions to MRA of thoughtful Christians of varying allegiances. I have already mentioned one comment that is generally made: despite Peter Howard's tribute to Mr Kishi's 'statesmanship of the humble heart'[1], it has constantly been remarked by Christian critics of MRA that the Four Absolutes do not include the virtue of humility, and that MRA pronouncements are often tinged with a certain arrogance. This criticism is not really met by pointing to the generally admirable habit, recommended by MRA, of apologising to those whom one has wronged. For one thing, 'saying sorry' is not a monopoly of MRA—though in this as in other cases it might be supposed, from some MRA literature, that no one had ever practised any virtue, or done anything generous or unselfish, before Dr Buchman began his career as a 'soul-surgeon'. Again, there are situations and relationships in which what is called a 'grovelling' apology can be, whether the person making it realises this or not, an oblique manifestation of pride. It can even serve—as, no doubt through no intention of his, Dr Buchman's six letters from Keswick did—to put the other party in the wrong, and may thus be little more than a ploy in the social game that Mr Stephen Potter calls one-upmanship.

[1] See p. 165.

Humility has been described as the only specifically Christian virtue: its opposite is the sin of pride—the 'root sin', since it underlies so many of the others and can take so many forms. The more subtle forms of it can be, psychologically, the most serious; but one of the most obvious is snobbery. Dr Horton Davies, in the chapter on MRA in his *Christian Deviations* (SCM Press, 1954), says:

> The Oxford Group cannot be entirely freed from the charge of snobbery, social and spiritual. Their predilection for the company of the famous and the affluent . . . is well-known. Moreover, their attitude to the ordinary church-goer frequently savours of Pharisaism.

Several examples of this 'predilection' have been given already. Miss Honor Tracy's teasing rebuke,[1] on this very point, has clearly been ignored: one fairly recent example may be found in the film which Buchman was so proud of having sent to South Africa, *The Crowning Experience*—'Dr Buchman's soap opera', as Paul Dehn, the *Daily Herald* film-critic, called it. In his review of the film he deplored its 'sickening appeal to our sense of snobbery', citing this incident from it:

> A woman journalist . . . telephoning her news-editor in a state of euphoric radiance from the MRA conference at Lake Mackinac, says: 'This place is fantastic! There are top-level people here from all over the world!'

These amateur actors were indeed boosted as 'the most distinguished supporting cast ever to appear in an Academy Award qualifying picture'—a phrase that, perhaps, falls just short of Absolute Honesty, since the uninitiated might take it to mean that this picture had won an Academy Award, which it hadn't. Closer examination, however, shows that they were not, in fact, what a really discriminating snob would call 'top-level people'. They were the usual stage-army of converts who are trotted around to MRA rallies because their names sound impressive to the unsophisticated: 'Bunny' Austin (a tennis-champion of long, long ago), Gandhi's grandson (but nobody

[1] See p. 168.

who cuts much ice in India today), the 89-year-old Chief Walking Buffalo, a princess of 'one of the four kingdoms of Uganda', a Swedish MP, a vice-president of an American trade union. . . . Not performing in the film, but visible in it when the camera reverently explored a huge fresco showing Dr Buchman surrounded by his 'personal friends', were a few less doubtfully 'top-level people', all either dead or extremely old: Louisa Lady Antrim ('lady-in-waiting to three Queens of England'), Lord Athlone, General Pershing, Mr and Mrs Henry Ford, and Dr Adenauer. (It is never quite clear whether Buchman's 'personal friends' were among the Changed, or whether their VIP status earned them some sort of dispensation.)

Mr Dehn, after reflecting on this highly concentrated visual example of the Buchmanite trick of name-dropping, went on to say, much too optimistically, that people should be 'reasoned' into accepting MRA's anti-Communist ideology 'rather than be told, patronisingly, that they should turn Buchmanite because people more famous and/or aristocratic have previously been converted'.

This is not so unfair as it must have seemed to the Buchmanites. Who, seriously, would Change because an aged Red Indian chief and an ex-tennis-champion, as such, are paraded at a rally or in a film as Changed men? Who would be converted to a new quasi-religious ideology merely because it was commended by a former royal lady-in-waiting? Who, one might ask, but the most crawling snob?

In any case, even if the MRA strategy of Changing 'key' people first, in the hope that others will follow their example, were proved correct, 'top-level' people are not necessarily to be equated with 'key' people. 'Key' people (if the phrase means anything) are people with actual power or a wide range of influence—men like Hitler as Buchman saw him at the time of the *World-Telegram* interview. Of those just listed, only Adenauer could properly be so described.

Adenauer was one of the few major political leaders who seemed to take a genuine interest in MRA (as distinct from merely agreeing to sign messages in standard MRA jargon). Since he is a Roman Catholic, it was presumably MRA's anti-Communism rather than its religious aspect that attracted him; and his friendship with Dr Buchman seemed to grow steadily when Western Germany was consolidating its position as the late John Foster Dulles' favourite ally. Certainly, whether he dictated them all or not, no statesman has showered greetings and tributes on Buchman and MRA more profusely than Adenauer. In the course of one congratulatory message he remarked: 'A nation with an ideology is always on the offensive.' The thought might have been more happily expressed. Nor can the MRA leaders have felt that Adenauer was really one of them when, just before his retirement in October, 1963, he declared: 'There is only one foreign policy for a state—self-interest.'

In any case, knowing personally a good many West Germans, of varying ages, beliefs and economic backgrounds, I cannot think of any who are likely to be moved to undergo a conversion experience because their aged former Chancellor has endorsed MRA—and Germans are supposed to respond rather more readily to recommendations from above than the people of some other countries do.

On the whole, therefore, I regard MRA's 'key' people theory as largely mistaken, and I suspect that it represents a rationalisation of Buchman's own passion for mixing with 'celebrities'. He who in his youth had been so colourless and undistinguished, but had soon come to like 'hobnobbing with nabobs', seems never to have lost this appetite. To ordinary people, Christian or non-Christian, this was one of his—and is one of MRA's—most unattractive characteristics.

Other Christian reactions to MRA naturally vary according to denomination and individual temperament. I have suggested that a motive for MRA's major shift of strategy may have been its need, in a period of global expansion, of allies other than those who would be attracted by old-fashioned Protestant evangelism; and have cited the scrupulous credal neutrality of its appeal to the nations of Asia. But there was another international religious body, far older than MRA, whose support would be of value in many parts of the world, especially in the Latin South of Europe and America (where Buchmanism had made, on the whole, less impact than in the largely non-Catholic and Anglo-Saxon north): Buchman's eyes must have strayed admiringly and reflectively towards the Roman Catholic Church—not towards its theology but towards its world-wide organisation, spiritual power, and political influence. Here would be a formidable ally indeed.

But Roman Catholics are forbidden *communicatio in sacris*: despite the *détente* of the past year or two, they may not, as a general rule, take part in prayer or worship with Christians of other allegiances; and some of the Buchmanite practices were clearly, in their way, religious. It is not surprising, therefore, that MRA has been formally and explicitly condemned by Rome. This condemnation is contained in a ruling by the Holy Office, issued in 1935 and summarised thus in the (American) *National Catholic Almanac*:

> Priests may not take any part in MRA meetings and activities, and . . . lay persons may not accept responsible positions in the Movement. Participation in MRA involves dangers to the Faith, and has been forbidden by many Bishops.

It is true that this is not an absolute ban on lay participation, but faithful Roman Catholics must take seriously so grave a warning—a warning reiterated in December, 1957, by the *Osservatore Romano* (the official Vatican organ), which, while conceding the possibility, 'under certain conditions and within certain limits', of 'certain kinds of co-operation by Catholics', stressed the 'obvious and grave' dangers of 'indifferentism or religious syncretism'. It is confirmed at Archbishop's House, Westminster, that the ruling of the Holy Office still stands and represents the official attitude of the Roman Catholic Church.

In practice, the attitude to MRA of Roman Catholic prelates, priests, and laymen has varied—a phenomenon puzzling to those outside it who are apt, mistakenly, to think of the Roman Catholic Church as a monolithic and tightly disciplined body. MRA propaganda has recorded the approval of a South American cardinal, a Benedictine abbot, and some bishops, one of these being the bishop of the diocese in which Caux is situated. But, in an article in the June, 1956, issue of *Social Order* (St Louis 8, Missouri, USA), Fr Edward Duff, SJ, wrote: 'Since the bishop of Fribourg, Lausanne, and Geneva (a tri-city see) is commonly invoked as favouring MRA, it will be useful to set down the only statement Bishop François Charrière ever made on the subject (25th October, 1927)'—and quoted a long statement giving MRA a cautious and strictly conditional blessing, warning of 'a real danger', and saying that MRA 'of its very nature, however correct its solutions on secondary points may be, cannot represent in any adequate fashion the divine revelation which alone is capable of saving individuals and the world'. This was, of course, long before the condemnation by the Holy Office: I cannot trace any equally thorough statement by Mgr Charrière since Fr Duff quoted him in 1956; but his attitude to Caux in recent years is said to have been friendly.

In England the generally critical tone of comments and correspondence in the leading intellectual Roman Catholic review, *The Tablet*, has been qualified by praise for the movement from one eminent convert, Sir Arnold Lunn (who happens to have a special family attachment to Switzerland and has therefore seen something of the work at Caux). Sir Arnold has seen lapsed Roman Catholics return to the practice of their religion as a result of contact with MRA; and testimony such as this must be taken into account when the pros and cons of the movement are weighed.

On the other hand, Sir Arnold's belief that some improvement in MRA was attributable to the influence of Roman Catholics inside it was countered by another Roman Catholic convert—formerly a full-time MRA worker—Mr Edward Vogt, who explained that MRA only tolerated such influence to the extent to which it might serve to make the movement more attractive to Roman Catholics.

Apart from these local and individual deviations, the ban

would be regarded as binding by most Roman Catholics, and has been reinforced by the pronouncements of many prelates, including one so tolerant and ecumenically-minded as the late Cardinal Hinsley. This was a continuing handicap to closer relations between MRA and the Vatican. . . . But what if a movement such as this were not really a religion, in the strict sense of the word, at all? What if it explicitly disavowed any intention of being a kind of church, and was concerned almost entirely to promote a 'secular' ideology? That might make it easier for Roman Catholics to enter into full relations with it. This must have seemed to the MRA hierarchy, at some point a few years ago, to be the answer: the First Century Christian Fellowship was finally out; an Ideology for Democracy was in.

If these were the motives for the change of strategy, they are not necessarily discreditable to MRA; every organisation, every church or sect, has undergone comparable changes. They would be discreditable, I think, only if the strategy had been adopted because MRA's rich backers—particularly the American industrialists who have contributed so generously to its funds—had seen in it a convenient instrument for anti-Communist propaganda, or another 'voice of America' in the Cold War. That would indeed be to confuse means with ends, to *use* religion and God in a totally impermissible way, and to reduce what had begun, in intention, as a humane and 'life-changing' force to a mere quasi-spiritual McCarthyism.

One must assume that the MRA policy-makers, under the supreme and supposedly infallible leadership of Buchman, sincerely believed that they were Guided by God towards this change of strategy and emphasis. The change may well have helped to commend the movement in these wider areas, but may also, ironically, have had the effect of lessening its appeal to some of those who had at first encouraged it—for instance, to Anglicans and Protestants in Britain and elsewhere. Christians of these other denominations, too, have had cause to treat with reserve the approaches of MRA, for reasons which may be illustrated from an episode within my own experience.

An important Christian conference was held at Lausanne in

1960. It was called the Ecumenical Youth Assembly in Europe, and it was organised under the auspices of the Youth Department of the World Council of Churches. It was attended by some 1,800 delegates from many countries. Its president was Canon Edward Patey, of Coventry; I was one of three speakers invited to introduce the main themes for discussion.

For more than a year the secretary of this Assembly, Michel Wagner, a French Protestant pastor of experience and integrity, had been working full-time on the preliminary arrangements. Some time in advance, Pastor Wagner was visited by a team of MRA representatives from Caux. They said that they would like to send a substantial delegation to the Lausanne Assembly. Pastor Wagner, who had some knowledge of MRA and its methods, had no wish to see them 'capture', or seriously infiltrate, the Assembly; nor would it have been in accordance with his responsibility to the World Council of Churches to make such infiltration possible. Quite apart from his personal views, however, the constitution of the Assembly did not provide for the sending of delegates by churches or by any organisations: the delegates from each country were chosen by the Youth Department of the Council of Churches in that country (and did, in the event, include a few MRA supporters). Pastor Wagner explained this to the MRA representatives. They went back to Caux.

This Assembly at Lausanne happened to coincide, more or less, with the opening of the regular MRA Assembly at Caux. The press correspondents in Switzerland—Swiss, British, American, and others—went first to Caux for a press conference there, and then came on to cover the Lausanne Assembly. At Caux they were astonished to hear—and we were astonished when they reported it to us at Lausanne—a fierce onslaught on the Lausanne Assembly. MRA spokesmen told the press that our Assembly was 'Communist-inspired' or 'Communist-dominated', and that its president, Canon Patey, was a Communist. (He is not; but he explained that he had been to Moscow, at the invitation of church leaders, but had refused to go to Caux—which was enough, no doubt, for the loose talkers of Caux.) They went on to make slanderous personal attacks on others connected with the Assembly.

This conduct by the 'God-controlled' men of Caux shocked the officials of the World Council of Churches who were at Lausanne, and in particular the General Secretary, Dr Visser 't Hooft—a man held in honour throughout the world. So deeply did he feel the wickedness of this false witness by a neighbour that he issued to the press a solemn rebuke, protesting against the 'ridiculous and absolutely baseless rumours spread by members of this movement [MRA] against the Lausanne Assembly'.

The sequel was even more fantastic than the original attack. Presumably because Dr Visser 't Hooft was internationally famous—a 'key man' in the ecumenical movement—and perhaps because superior Guidance had reached Caux, the Buchmanites chose a curious and, in its way, daring method of extricating themselves from their false position. They did not apologise for what had been said. They simply denied, with every appearance of injured innocence, that the slanders complained of had ever been uttered at Caux! Now, there was no question that they had been uttered there, to pressmen, by a full-time MRA worker who frequently dealt with press enquiries. At least three experienced and reputable journalists had reported them to us; and the Geneva *Weekly Tribune* quoted M Paul Eberhart, the Lausanne Assembly's press officer, as saying that 'delegates and members of his staff had been approached by MRA people with the same allegations'.

A day or two later I happened to be in the office of one of these journalists when he was telephoning to Caux to try to find out more about this mysterious feint. The man whom he spoke to was in MRA's inner ring. I heard the journalist's end of the conversation, and he told me in detail, immediately afterwards, what the man at Caux had said; I still have the note of their exchanges that I made at the time. I will only say that the Caux end of it was a remarkable exercise in evasion—slightly uncertain and anxious at first, but gathering confidence as its own momentum carried it further and further away from Absolute Honesty.

12

ANGLICAN REACTIONS

A good address in Oxford—An Archbishop's endorsement—Dr Hensley Henson's Charge—'Frank's Guidance was always right'—Dangers and absurdities of Sharing —Free discussion with MRA found impossible

THE ENGLISH-SPEAKING countries, the world-wide Anglican Communion, and the Protestant churches—at their strongest in Northern Europe and North America—must from the first have offered a terrain for the securing of Buchmanite bases more encouraging than the Latin South or the non-Christian East. Moreover (to revert for a moment to the earliest days of his mission), England had been the land of Frank Buchman's own Change. It was, perhaps, natural that he should settle for a while in England when the time came to organise a coherent movement; and it was shrewd to take advantage of a private invitation to Oxford and make his first headquarters there.

As the movement developed, he formed useful friendships both in what is now called the Establishment and in the established Church of England, whose dignitaries he was thus able to approach from a good address and with impressive introductions—two essentials, in a society as class-conscious as England's, for those seeking to widen footholds into bridgeheads. Possibly England's unique interweaving of Church and State attracted him, too: key men here could be key men in both; bishops sat in the House of Lords, the Prime Minister chose the bishops. At any rate, Christ Church, Oxford, was an ideal letterhead.

His sojourn at Christ Church did not entirely escape adverse comment. Old inhabitants recall that, at the request of an ardent undergraduate disciple, Buchman was allowed to occupy rooms in college; and that, these rooms happening to remain, temporarily, vacant, he stayed on and on—not exactly, in so hospitable a House, overstaying his welcome, but staying rather longer than the college authorities had expected him to, or than they really liked strangers, even peripatetic evangelists, to stay. They also recall that the head of the college, Dean White, was reluctant to receive him; but that when Dean White died 13 years later, Buchman, forgivingly, attended his funeral (and someone who was missing no points made sure that *The Times* included his name in the list of those present).

The Chaplain of Worcester College, the Revd Dudley Narborough, was one of the Oxford dons who were disturbed by Buchman's activities. Many years later, in the Church Assembly debate on MRA on 15th February, 1955, Mr Narborough—by now Bishop of Colchester—recalled those early Oxford days. The *Report of Proceedings* (the Church Assembly's *Hansard* but, unlike Parliament's *Hansard*, in *oratio obliqua*) records thus what the Bishop said:

> . . . many years ago, when Dr Buchman first came to England, he [Mr Narborough] was a college chaplain in Oxford; Dr Buchman worked hard amongst the undergraduates at Oxford, and he got the most unfavourable impression of his handling of many of the undergraduates of his college. He went to him 'to have it out with him', and came away most dissatisfied with the outcome of the interview.

Since MRA has attempted to impugn the fairness of the Bishop's contribution to the study of MRA, it is worth noting that the *Report of Proceedings* also records that he added that 'he had the impression that since then the movement had improved immensely'.

Few such rebuffs came Buchman's way: in the inter-war years his influence on senior dignitaries of the Church of England, and among Anglicans everywhere, was considerable. They liked him and welcomed him quite unsuspectingly. It is strange to recall, nowadays—for such an event is unlikely to take place while Dr Ramsey is Archbishop of Canterbury—that Archbishop Lang 'commissioned' Dr Buchman and a hundred of his full-time workers, at Lambeth Palace, for evangelistic work in London. In 1933 the Bishop of London conducted a similar, but public, 'commissioning' service in St Paul's Cathedral. In July, 1934, Archbishop Lang, again, said: 'The Movement is most certainly doing what the Church of Christ exists everywhere to do. It is changing human lives. . . .' Nor was it only the lapsed Roman Catholics observed by Sir Arnold Lunn who returned to their churches after experience of MRA: among its full-time workers and supporters there have always been a number of practising Anglicans, Methodists, and other Christians.

This generous welcome, in the highest quarters of the Established Church, seems to dispose of the analogy sometimes drawn between more adverse Anglican reactions to the Oxford Group and MRA—most of them much later in date—and the cold stiffness of the Church in the eighteenth century which was a main cause of the Methodist schism.

If Archbishop Lang's handsome tribute was justified then—as some churchmen probably still think it was—what has gone wrong? Why, come to think of it, does MRA still have to go on quoting this old tribute (and other pre-war testimonials by the late Lords Salisbury and Athlone)? There have been three Archbishops of Canterbury since Lang—Temple, Fisher, and Ramsey. Presumably MRA would have welcomed, and may have solicited, testimonials from any or all of them.

Temple, according to his biographer, Dr F. A. Iremonger,[1] did feel able cautiously to commend the movement. His commendation is not quoted in MRA propaganda, possibly because it is qualified by a warning against 'dangers of a

[1] William Temple, *His Life and Letters*, Oxford, 1948, pp. 489-90.

serious kind' associated with the movement—for instance, 'the ignoring by members of the admitted limitations and consequent supposition that the Groups can be substituted for the Church'. Temple added that, during his mission to the University, he had found that 'the best folk in Oxford were those who had got into the Movement and had then got partially out again—not with any repudiation of it, but simply going on to a wider fellowship and outlook'. The leaders of a movement so total in its claims as MRA are unlikely to be satisfied with a tribute which says that 'the best folk' are those who have left them, even 'partially'.

When Lord Fisher of Lambeth was Archbishop of Canterbury, and earlier when he was Bishop of London, his relations with MRA were slight, and do not seem to have been happy. Some overtures by individual supporters of MRA did not lead to any public pronouncement by him. Lord Fisher is known for his forthright outspokenness on many topics: it may be surmised that he did not find the Buchmanites' methods of approaching him, and their professions of Absolute Honesty, convincing or attractive. Dr Ramsey, again, has made no public reference to the movement, as he surely would have if he had wished to assist its propaganda.

Why have these three Archbishops in turn chosen not to follow Dr Lang's example? Why, in respect of its religious pretensions, are most of the more prominent ecclesiastical supporters of MRA either those who were committed to it before the war (such as the Revd J. P. Thornton-Duesbery, Master of St Peter's College, Oxford, who is primarily a don rather than a cleric in the full stream of church life) or prelates in countries in which it has only fairly recently arrived, and in which there is a sharp and direct challenge to the Church from an anti-clerical, and usually Marxist, Left?

It seems to me that the answers to these questions, and the explanation of a perceptible 'cooling-off' by churchmen who, a generation ago, might have greeted the Buchman Group with tolerance or even with enthusiasm, are to be found, precisely, in the change of character and strategy that has been noted. 'Its Christian character', writes Lord Fisher,[1] 'has steadily been replaced by an almost exclusive concentration on fighting Communism as the first purpose of its waiting upon God'.

Even in Archbishop Lang's day, however, one English bishop, Dr Hensley Henson, of Durham, declared his emphatic disapproval of the Group in a diocesan charge[2] which remains a powerful indictment of Buchmanism from a religious and ecclesiastical point of view—its effectiveness being enhanced by a classical and trenchant prose style.

Dr Henson's comments echo, at one point, my own first reactions to the movement. He had read two books by prominent Groupers—one of them an American clergyman, the Revd Sam Shoemaker.[3] He remarks:

> The sincerity and enthusiasm of the writers are everywhere apparent, but so are their lop-sidedness, their perilous self-confidence, and their impatience of criticism, however reasonable and kindly. I read them both, as I read most of the Group's publications, not without sympathy, indeed, but with a melancholy wonder. I am attracted by the fervour; I am repelled by the assurance. Perhaps the repulsion prevails over the attraction. Such megalomaniacal self-confidence, such lack of proportion, such lack of charity, are without parallel in religious literature—except, of course, in the writings of the obscurer sectaries.

He is severe in his condemnation of the basic Group technique of Guidance. Originally, Guidance was secured in solitude, in the prescribed 'quiet time' each morning, when the Grouper would lie on his bed with pencil and paper, jotting down whatever thoughts—preferably 'luminous thoughts'—came to him, often about the trivial routine of daily life. It has

[1] In a private letter to the author.
[2] Published in book form as *The Group Movement* (Oxford, 1933).
[3] See p. 267.

always seemed to me extraordinarily presumptuous and indeed superstitious to be so certain that any stray thought, possibly prompted by any one of dozens of influences, from childhood memory, or something half-heard on the radio, to indigestion, is an infallible message direct from God. To many Christians such a procedure will also seem both frivolous and irreverent. As the Rt Revd M. J. Browne, Bishop of Galway, put it in his Catholic Truth Society pamphlet on the movement:

> Groupists actually speak of 'listening-in' to the Holy Ghost: whenever they run up against a difficulty they stop for guidance. Such an idea of God is crudely anthropomorphic, derogatory to God's honour, and contrary to natural morality. . . . Guidance as understood by the Groups encourages all kinds of illusions; it undermines the sense of personal moral responsibility, it leads to fanaticism.

These words will not seem too strong if some actual examples of Guidance are considered. We have noted the case of the camp cook whose menus were arranged under Guidance.[1] At Caux, not only meals but flower arrangements have been similarly planned. No doubt special care was taken in seeking Guidance for Dr Buchman's own dining-room, to which VIPs were invited. Miss Tracy[2] was lucky enough to 'work a shift with the angels in Frank's kitchen' on an occasion when private inspiration was supplementing Guidance deliciously:

> Girls, what you say we make a fig *soufflé* just for Frank's table? Pass me that tin, labelled For Frank Only. See that cherry jam? Made specially for Frank, by the King of Siam's mother. Hurry up with the fried chicken, Frank's Table has finished soup! More cream for Frank's Table! Butter for Frank's Table! Pudding for Frank's Table! This is none of Frank's doing: it's just how these devoted ladies show their gratitude for being allowed to work for him.

There may be a nostalgic echo of the gastronomic delights of Caux in a dithyrambic prose-poem on Buchman's excellences

[1] See p. 59. [2] *Op. cit.*

which formed part of a report from Mackinac in 1955, signed 'Yours in the fight,

Paul Campbell Doe and Peter Howard
John Wood Enid and Morris Martin':

> Our guidance on Frank's seventy-seventh birthday was that his greatest years are at hand . . .
>
> He lives a statesmanship—ambition-free—which will be normal for millions. It is astounding what he does by not doing it!
>
> He can . . . give the thinking for the next stage of history—yet he makes few speeches . . .
>
> He has never written a song, yet because of him a new music is being created . . .
>
> He has never cooked a meal, yet because of him there is a new perfection in the kitchen . . .

In this atmosphere of dedicated jollity, Guidance flows readily. One day a leading MRA woman noticed an unfamiliar and unpleasant smell—drains—and said so. Buchman overheard the remark, or it was reported to him. He reacted rather sharply: such a remark was too 'negative'. The woman at once sat down and sought Guidance. The Guidance came: Never make negative remarks. Presumably someone took positive action about the drains.

The climax of one of the most popular of the earlier Buchmanite scriptures, *For Sinners Only*, by A. J. Russell,[1] records a piece of Guidance of such shattering importance that the whole paragraph is printed in italics:

> *Then suddenly a flash came to show me that this book was to be written, followed by another giving me the title. I sat up startled! . . . 'That checks. It rings a bell', was the opinion expressed by Ray Purdy immediately I began to tell him what was in my mind. The urge had come not as a strong luminous thought or a soundless whisper in the atmosphere, but as sudden pressure on my brain.*

[1] Hodder and Stoughton, 1933.

Sometimes Guidance leads to uncivilised and inconsiderate behaviour. A pleasant little article in *The Times* of 14th September, 1962—the reminiscences of an obviously friendly and hospitable vicar's wife—recorded this incident:

> The greatest strain . . . occurred when members of the Oxford Group, as it was then called, descended on us, unexpectedly, but guided to our door in taxis, demanding beds. Frantic telephones to friends and sympathisers reduced the number in the end, but the shock was only equalled later by the arrival of two unbalanced women at midnight, who asserted that they had been sent by God to stay the night with us.

An even more surprising possible consequence of Guidance—surprising because here the Guided person was the Revd Geoffrey Allen,[1] Fellow and Chaplain of Lincoln College, Oxford—is mentioned in Dr Henson's book. Dr Allen had written:

> God is Lord of the whole of our time. If He wills that we should go to apparently fixed engagements, He will send us to them. If He wills that we should break free from them to be used for other work of His, He is able to guide us how without damage to others of his children we may be set free. We must . . . each new day allow God to redirect us. . . .

Dr Henson remarks, tartly:

> I have read this passage several times, and considered it carefully, but I have not been able to reconcile it either with piety or with good sense. It appears to be equally inconsistent with the character of God and the self-respect of man. If generally acted upon, it would make social life almost impossible. It suggests that the Almighty may first 'guide' His children to frame engagements, which, next, when they fall due, He may 'guide' them to break. Instead of directing his course by reason and conscience, illumined

[1] Now Bishop of Derby. See p. 202.

no doubt by the Spirit of God, but indestructibly free and responsible, the Christian is reduced to dependence on specific directions which he cannot foresee, may not understand or approve, and must not disobey.

This 'temper of mind', Dr Henson adds, 'is Pharisaic rather than Christian. It seeks the proof of Divine action in what is abnormal, amazing, even miraculous. Its view of inspiration is mechanical, and its treatment of Scripture literalist.'

Now it may be said that the examples of Guidance just given, deplorable or absurd as some of them are, are extreme examples dating from the exuberant youth of a movement which has now grown up. Certainly MRA looks more sophisticated, more 'glossy', more conscious of public relations, than the Oxford Group did. If there are any 'unbalanced women' in the movement—such as one may expect to find in any enthusiastic cult—they do not ring vicarage doorbells at midnight: they have rooms, efficiently booked in advance, at good hotels. MRA's clerical dons are as unlikely as any other educated adult to be suddenly Guided to chuck a dinner date.

But this mechanical theory of Guidance is as central to the belief and practice of Buchmanites now as it was to Frank Buchman when he first decided, at Penn State, to spend the hour from five to six o'clock every morning 'listening in to the orders of the day'. (As he put it, 'God just wakes me up, and I know that he wants to tell me something.') It could never be abandoned or seriously modified—though from fairly early days, possibly because there had been too many cases in which infallible messages contradicted each other, Guidance was increasingly sought collectively. The sillier 'luminous thoughts' may not often now come to light—and may, indeed, be suppressed, wisely if dictatorially, by the Guidance of MRA superiors—but the Buchmanites still seek Guidance with pencil and paper.

One of the most graphic descriptions of a collective 'quiet time'—an eye-witness account by a lapsed Grouper—is quoted by Dr Henson:

The team is sitting in a semi-circle around Sam. 'Well', Sam asks, 'what's the plan for to-night's meeting? Let's listen.' . . . 'Guidance-books' appear, pencils fly swiftly over blank sheets. Some peer glassily at the ceiling. Others close their eyes momentarily, and are invariably rewarded with two or three lines of guidance. 'Amen. What comes?', Sam asks, as the scrape of pencils and pens perceptibly diminishes in volume, thereby indicating to him that the details of God's plan had been fully communicated. Sharing begins. 'Any guidance about the motif?' 'It comes to me that J. ought to give a good wad on Sin. My guidance is that we shall get the pious crowd to-night', says B. 'That checks with my guidance', says another. 'Check', 'check', 'check', echoes from many of the team. 'That's it, Sin—that's what I got too. Sin is the drive for to-night.' (It should be noted that guidance is regarded as being practically infallible when a majority is in agreement.) The door opens. Frank walks in, and sits next to Sam. 'How far have you got with to-night's meeting?', he asks. 'It seems clear that sin is the motif to-night', Sam tells him. Frank interrupts quickly: 'Now wait a minute. I'm not so sure. I've got a feeling that it may be too early for sin. "Intrigue" is what came to me in my early quiet time. You've got to get hold of that important pagan bunch. Play with 'em—show 'em what they're missing. Give 'em the feeling that religion's more fun than cocktail parties. Suppose we have further Quiet, and check up on it.'

More Quiet. More writing. Frank was always a tonic. Every one writes more busily. Guidance comes more easily. The words 'intrigue' and 'hilarity' appear on many notebooks. 'Amen, what comes!', asks Frank. 'I got "intrigue" this time', says B. Sam seemed to have got different guidance too this time. (The phrases 'right guidance' and 'bad guidance' were in common use.) 'I check with you, Frank', he says. 'It came to me that I must be more flexible, and have no preconceptions.' 'Check', 'check', check', again echoes round the room. Frank resumes. 'Well now, I'll share my guidance—A battery of witness from young Oxford. They want to hear Oxford, so we'll let 'em. Crisp nuggets of witness. Intrigue the young pagan elements. Sweep 'em along. That's my guidance. Now I don't want to dictate. I may be wrong. I want you to check me.' But we knew better. Frank's guidance was always right.

Dr Henson comments on the 'blending of childishness, unconscious profanity, and astute management' exhibited in this scene; and adds:

> The history of Christianity contains so many paradoxes that hardly any extravagance is too gross to be credible. Yet the considering observer will reflect with amazement that the Groupists who figured in these grotesque proceedings were not illiterate fanatics driven crazy by persecution, but educated men and women who were not only tolerated but honoured by their contemporaries.

Almost incredible as the account of 'these grotesque proceedings' is—in particular, the fatuous sycophancy of 'Frank's guidance was always right'—it is confirmed in an interesting passage in the Church Assembly report already referred to,[1] which does not date from the youth of the movement, but only from 1955:

> We may also wonder whether . . . members of MRA have sufficient means for distinguishing between the genuine guidance of the Holy Spirit and the deliverances of their own sub-conscious minds masquerading as God's voice. MRA is not unaware of this difficulty and in practice individual guidance is not regarded as infallible. In the working vocabulary of the movement there are the phrases 'good guidance' and 'bad guidance'. Rules for distinguishing these have been drawn up by MRA writers, but, while satisfactory enough so far as they go, they are far too vague to be of any practical value. In practice the

[1] See p. 189.

criterion would seem to be that 'group guidance' has priority over individual guidance in cases of divergence, and 'the best guidance' would seem in fact always to be that of the inner permanent group and ultimately of Buchman himself. We may recall the statement commonly repeated in the movement: 'Frank's guidance is always right'; this is a statement believed to be proved by experience rather than an article of faith, but it is none the less potent for that. The essentially autocratic character of all this could easily lead to abuse, and in general MRA's teaching on guidance conduces to a dangerous depreciation of the place of common sense and the powers of the intellect in the religious life, and to a very questionable willingness to set aside agreements and engagements previously entered upon in deference to alleged direct revelation.

Although this sober report, in its anxiety to be fair to MRA, states that 'in practice individual guidance is not regarded as infallible', the concession is substantially qualified by what follows. Indeed, the report adds that the practice of Guidance may 'lead to a claim to virtual infallibility'. We have seen already that this claim, in turn, may lead to the most ruthless intolerance and to conduct falling far short of Absolute Honesty and Absolute Love.

Such can be some of the fruits of Guidance.

The other special religious technique practised in MRA is Sharing. A distinction may be drawn between Sharing 'as confession' (i.e., privately) and Sharing 'as witness' (i.e., semi-publicly, in Group session). Of Sharing as confession it can be said, in general, that it is in accord both with ancient Christian tradition and with modern psychological theory and psychiatric practice; and many Christians will agree with Dr Henson's expression of gratitude to the Buchmanites 'for the emphasis they place on a much neglected part of Christian ministry'. (It is not neglected by Roman Catholics and some Anglicans;

though only a small proportion of the Church of England's millions of Easter communicants avail themselves of the privilege of private confession provided for in the Book of Common Prayer.)

There are, however, important differences between standard Catholic (or psychiatric) practice and MRA Sharing-as-confession. In Sharing, however much confidence the sharer may have in the discretion of the lay fellow-Grouper to whom he opens his heart and tells his sins, there is unlikely to be quite the same assurance of secrecy that there is in the Catholic confessional or in consultation with a psychiatrist bound by the Hippocratic oath. To a Catholic, moreover, Sharing would seem an incomplete process because it lacks the element of absolution pronounced by a validly ordained priest. Again, it is a matter of common experience that to 'make a clean breast' of something to a trusted friend does relieve pressure and ease tension; but many Protestants, too, would regard the Buchmanites' apparent reliance on the act of confession alone, with the consequent intimacy between two human beings, however helpful this may be, as inadequately related to the Christian doctrine of Redemption.

The dangers on which Dr Henson and many others have commented arise chiefly from the other sort of Sharing—the semi-public 'witness'. This practice was sometimes carried to absurd lengths: the Changed ones would recite at meeting after meeting the gruesome or, more often, the trifling details of long-past sin ('. . . when I was ten years old, I felt resentment against my sister because she broke one of my toys . . .'), and would reiterate their testimony to the miraculous Change experienced since they had begun to live, under Guidance, in accordance with the Four Absolutes. In a highly charged atmosphere of mass-suggestion, this practice could be psychologically unhealthy, and presented obvious opportunities for self-dramatisation and self-satisfaction. As Dr Henson observed in *The Group Movement*: 'The penitent may feel a strange pride in the sins which he publicly proclaims as once his own. . . . We must add . . . that this danger is never so formidable as when it bears on those in whom the self-confidence of inexperience supplements the unconscious pride of spiritual self-advertisement.' Partly because so many converts later left the Group, disillusioned, there was also a real risk of leakage of private information and even of blackmail.

The Church Assembly report was described by the distinguished theologian, Dr Reinhold Niebuhr, when he reviewed it in the *Observer*, as 'the most authentic and searching description and criticism of the movement which has been produced since its inception'. Dr Niebuhr added: 'The criticisms are devastating, but also so fair that it is difficult to understand the two dissents which are recorded at the end of the document.'

These 'two dissents' were those of Major-General Sir Colin Jardine and Mr Gerald Steel. They differed noticeably in form from the minority reports sometimes appended to the reports of Royal Commissions, Select Committees, and many other official investigating bodies. These minority reports customarily argue their case at some length and even with passion; they reflect substantial differences of principle or detail which have not been resolved during the investigation; and minorities are not often less anxious than majorities to inform the public of their views. It must be supposed that Sir Colin and Mr Steel felt strongly that the report was unfair to MRA. They cannot have been insufficiently articulate to explain why they felt this: Sir Colin was educated at Charterhouse; Mr Steel (Rugby and University College, Oxford) had been a senior civil servant, and was therefore capable of drafting a memorandum. With this background, it is strange that Sir Colin's 'note of dissent' was only four lines long, and Mr Steel's only three, and that both of them, within so small a compass, should have contained identical phrases: the publication of the report, both said, would 'do harm and cause distress'; and each dissenter added that he wished to dissociate himself from it.

These jejune dissents remain inexplicable. Two evident

supporters of MRA could have expressed their views with complete freedom, at whatever length they wished, and these views would have been printed officially for the Church Assembly and circulated with every copy of the report. Such a 'last word', if ably drafted, might have helped to neutralise the criticisms of which the two men disapproved so strongly. More weight might have been given to their objections if they had bothered to write them down.

They were, however, only two out of a Council of eighteen men and women—Anglicans of the highest integrity and considerable and varied scholarship. Sir Wilfrid Garrett, who had been the first Principal of the YMCA College for Adults at Kingsgate, Kent, was their chairman; among them were the Bishops of Sheffield and Birmingham and the Provost of Leicester (now Bishop of Jarrow), none of whom was a sheltered or cloistered cleric. (Their collective experience covered social service on pre-war Tyneside, imprisonment in a Japanese camp, and welfare work among seamen.) With them served such eminent people as Canon C. E. Hudson, sociologist and pastoral theologian; Dame Marian Acton, Comptroller of the Forces Help Society and Lord Roberts Workshops; Mr J. O. Blair-Cunynghame, expert on personnel management; Mr George Goyder, one of the foremost laymen of the Church of England; Mr Basil Sanderson, shipowner and director of the Bank of England; Sir Henry Self, who in 1940-42 had served on some of the highest-powered British air missions in America and Canada; and Sir John Woods, another retired civil servant with a special interest in economic and social research. Moreover, to form a working party, they co-opted a number of specially qualified advisers, at least one of whom, Bishop Geoffrey Allen (now of Derby)[1] was known to be well disposed to MRA. Others were the Bishop of Colchester, Professor Dennis Nineham, Canon Ted Wickham, known for his work in the Sheffield steel industry and now Bishop of Middleton, and two 'rank-and-file' clergy with parochial experience, the Revd John Groser and the Revd Paul Gedge.

[1] See p. 269.

If they had been a jury—as, in a sense, they were—not one of the members of the Council could have been challenged by MRA. Were some of them too 'establishment'-minded, and likely therefore to be out of sympathy with MRA's slangy slogans and unorthodox methods? But MRA itself had relied heavily on the testimony of such pillars of the establishment as Archbishop Lang and Lord Salisbury. This, in any case, would not be true of several notably unstuffy figures among them. Nor could MRA, in its usual manner, denounce them (any more than it had been able to denounce Arthur Deakin) as Communists or Communist dupes.

Long ago, in *Innocent Men*, Peter Howard had written:

> When critics of the Group whose way of life is, on Christian standards, comparable with the standards of the rank-and-file of the Oxford Group step forward, I will pay respectful attention to them. As it is, I disregard them altogether.

I do not know whether Mr Howard was uncharitable enough to assume that, because their report was, on the whole, critical, the 'way of life' of every one of these men and women of the Church Assembly's Social and Industrial Council was incomparably less honest, pure, unselfish, and loving than his own. But he does not seem to have paid 'respectful attention' to them.

Since all of them were convinced and practising churchmen, they were, surely entitled to expect not only attention but the fullest co-operation from the movement which they were charged to investigate. This they did not receive. There is a significant passage in the introduction to their report:

> The present statement has been prepared without much opportunity of discussion of the Movement with those taking part in it. If it is asked how much conference the Council has had with the representatives of the Movement, we are bound to say that we found them unwilling to confer except on terms which would have made free discussion

impossible. We cannot help suspecting that the Movement's neglect of the intellectual factor naturally involves an aversion to argument or even discussion, and that MRA feels sure of itself only when, as at Caux and at the London headquarters, its peculiar technique can operate without check or hindrance.

13

THE CHURCH ASSEMBLY REPORT

MRA's 'blindness to the duty of thinking'—The 'chief aim' approved: the motive questioned—Ends and means—The psychology of the crowd—Sensitiveness to criticism—A four-to-one vote in the Assembly

SINCE THE Church Assembly report is out of print, it may be useful to summarise its contents rather more fully.

Its source and mandate being what they were, it was inevitable, and proper, that the report should begin with theology, 'asking non-theological readers to bear in mind . . . that Theology is . . . the attempt at straight and honest thinking about the data, the content of human experience of God'. This led to the report's most memorable dictum—that one characteristic of MRA is 'a certain blindness to the duty of thinking'; which the *New Statesman* diarist, Flavus, called 'surely the most remarkable example of deadly clerical litotes in the whole history of religious dialogue'.

Many tendencies and phenomena in the history of Christianity have been irrational; yet the historic churches have never dethroned, or ignored, reason. Like their classical forerunners, the medieval philosophers regarded the emotions as subordinate to reason. Or, as the report puts it:

> In its whole tendency . . . the movement seems to leave out of the picture one of man's greatest responsibilities and privileges, namely, the use and development, under God

and with God, of the mind which is one of the greatest of the divine gifts and one essential means of communion with God. We have at times been haunted by a picture of the movement, with its hectic heartiness, its mass gaiety and its reiterated slogans, as a colossal drive of escapism from the full force of the difficulty in detail of responsible living in the world.

For, indeed, the world's problems are *not* simple; and over-simplification of them can be dangerous. It may lead to solutions ultimately seen to be harmful. It may lead to no solution at all, with the consequent disillusionment and despair of those who have accepted the facile over-simplification. It may distract people from the job of grappling practically and thoughtfully with the problems. A classic example of this danger, implicit in all MRA teaching and practice, was Buchman's lighthearted assurance that, if Hitler or any dictator were Changed, 'every last bewildering problem' of his nation would be solved 'overnight'.[1] This is, frankly, nonsense. Quite apart from the implied continuation of dictatorship—perfectly acceptable, it would seem, so long as the dictator personally submitted to 'God-control'—it is simply not the case that every economic, social and political problem would vanish 'overnight' in such a situation. To pretend that it would is, as the Assembly report suggests, escapism.

The report's fundamental theological and Christian comment on MRA is twofold:

(*a*) It approves warmly of MRA's 'chief aim', which is 'to bring belief in God to practical expression'. It acknowledges that 'God is known in MRA not simply as an idea or concept, but as the living God, with whom men can come into a contact which completely changes their lives'.

(*b*) It points out that those Anglican 'social prophets' who have been 'concerned, as MRA is, with the social and economic implications of belief, men like William Temple and Charles Gore and Henry Scott Holland', have started from certain

[1] See p. 68.

concrete historical beliefs about Jesus Christ. 'Their theology, as we say, has been incarnational'. MRA's view and practice of Guidance, 'carried to its logical conclusion, would seem to by-pass the Incarnation altogether'.

This report, it must again be stressed, resulted from a study undertaken by practising Anglicans, within the framework of the Church of England. To those who drafted it, therefore, this point was crucial; and here they go on to refer to that MRA literature, published in India, which 'contains no word to suggest that the acceptance of the principles of MRA would present any difficulty to a convinced Hindu'.[1]

Equally important, theologically, is the *motive* behind MRA. Despite the frequent use of God's name, the report does not find that MRA activities and attitudes are, in the main, theocentric. 'Every human motive, even the strictest sense of duty, contains within itself elements of selfishness which in time will inevitably turn the resultant actions into some form of individual or group self-seeking.' When the priority is that implied in such phrases as 'an idea that will be more than a match for Communism', God becomes merely 'a useful means to desirable ends'.

I may remark, in passing, that in so far as this confusion of ends and means is characteristic of MRA (and I agree with the Assembly report that it is implicit in much MRA propaganda) it is a confusion widespread also among political and ideological campaigners who would not claim any Christian or religious sanction for their activities. Help for the world's hungry peoples has often been recommended *because* it may tend to turn them from Communism, rather than because, by any standard of neighbourly responsibility, Christian or humanist, it is intrinsically right, whether it turns them from Communism or not (though that may be one of its incidental effects).

This part of the report comments penetratingly, too, on MRA's attitude to sin and to the Bible. On sin, MRA seems to ignore

[1] *Cf* p. 163.

the long Christian experience, which began even in New Testament times, of the Christian life as a slow, persevering struggle against recurrent temptation.

Therefore,

> This attitude, combined with the tendency to claim infallibility referred to above, may easily lead to a claim to perfection, to being the elect, and to the over-sensitiveness to criticism which usually accompanies such claims. Perhaps this attitude is connected with the fact that, at any rate in the earlier literature of the Oxford Group, the individual sins most stressed are such 'outward' sins as those of lying and sexual misdemeanour. Less is said about the more subtle sins, such as spiritual pride and exclusiveness, from which it is not so easy to feel certain that one is free.

The word 'one' in the last sentence quoted shows, I think, that the authors of the report were well aware that Anglicans might be at least as prone to these 'more subtle sins' as those whom they were presuming to judge.

On the Bible, a tendency to fundamentalism is alleged:

> The use of Moffatt's translation is encouraged, but no serious account appears to be taken of the results of critical scholarship. . . . Isolated passages are used out of context and with no necessary reference to their original and legitimate meaning. . . . The Bible loses much of the value it might have as an objective source of, and check on, individual guidance. If texts are treated unscientifically . . . a text can be found to support almost any notion, however contrary it may be to the main drift and themes of Biblical religion. (But in fairness let it be added that . . . the ordinary Church member is often in little better case.)

The report's theological chapter is of concern mainly to committed Christians, and specifically to Anglicans. Of wider sociological interest is the chapter on 'The Psychology of Group

Revival'. It distinguishes 'three main factors which constitute the psychological structure of the crowd'. These factors are 'the psychology of transference and detachment, of pride and fear, and of the libido or love energies in the personality'. (The words 'crowd' and 'group' are used in a special sense: in contrast is the 'community', in which 'a society of free, mature, responsible persons use their freedom in service, co-operation and fellowship'.)

In the relations of parents and children, of priest or teacher and disciple, and of psychiatrist and patient, the junior partner must not remain dependent on the senior, or he will not 'grow into the maturity and power of his own free personality'. The senior must help the junior towards this freedom. As Baron von Hügel wrote: 'The golden rule is, to help those we love to escape from us.' The report quotes an example of the opposite impulse—unwise, unconsciously selfish possessiveness—from Charles Williams' play, *The House of the Octopus*. Here an old missionary admits to his converts: 'I do not wish you to live from God alone; I wish always to be your means to God.'

Then the report explains:

> In the psychological structure of the crowd, the crowd by its size assumes the power and authority which the adult world once held in the eyes of the infant . . . and the individuals can find protection and shelter within it. It may be that for some people this is a helpful stage in their spiritual growth. . . . It should however lead on to . . . the detachment of the individual. . . . It is . . . extremely difficult for the group through its leaders to discern the necessity for this later stage of detachment, and to help it forward. . . . There is thus an inevitable danger that the group will hold its members in a dependent relationship. . . . Rather than . . . liberate its members, the group will always tend to regard it as sin in them if they do assert their freedom.

This may remind us of Temple's remark about the 'best folk'

at Oxford[1]—and of the fury with which MRA has sometimes pursued those guilty of the sin of asserting their freedom. I have heard rather less of this particular folly in recent years than in the earlier days of the Oxford Group: perhaps some of the MRA leaders have studied and digested this perceptive passage in the Assembly report.

In its section on 'pride and fear' the report analyses 'the typical adolescent character', compensating for inner insecurity and inferiority by self-assertion:

> In the Oxford Group, and still today in the Moral Re-Armament movement, we cannot help noticing some of the distinctive traits of a repressed and unreleased inferiority, for instance in the rather extreme sensitiveness to criticism and the desire for the approval of great names.

Noted here, too, are those extravagant claims of success in ideological and industrial conflict: the explanation, psychologically, of such claims is a kind of corporate pride—'a vicarious satisfaction in the prestige and power of the group' in which the individual identity has been sunk.

Again, it is not only MRA that inspires this kind of pride in its supporters. To some extent, the psychological hold on its members of any group, religious or political, depends on a combination of fear, focussed inward on to the group, and a compensating pride directed towards the outside world. ('Here we notice a factor', says the report sadly, 'which is common to many forms of religious revival'; it 'tends towards the formation of the exclusive religious sect, and acts as a non-theological influence inhibiting wider Christian co-operation.') Thus, MRA or any religious group may offer a refuge or shelter, at least temporarily, to those unable fully to cope with adult life under the pressures of industrial civilisation. If this is so, it may be a point in MRA's favour: it is providing some sort of psychological ambulance-service or rest-home for a socially inadequate minority.

[1] See p. 191.

No serious group, seeking to achieve a true sense of community (as already defined), and to bring about major practical changes in society, can be content with a membership fixed permanently in a state of emotional adolescence. Yet, precisely to the extent to which a group has attracted such a membership, its leaders will find overwhelming, and will often succumb to, the temptation of clinging to power. There may be less persecution than there used to be of those who shake themselves free from MRA's cloying, cosy *camaraderie*; but the grandiloquent tone of the full-page newspaper advertisements suggests either that the lesson of this chapter in the Assembly report has not been fully learned or that the average level of maturity of the Changed is such that these stimuli of corporate pride are necessary for the Group's coherence.

In MRA, as in other strongly coherent groups, the libido or love-energy of individuals is focussed on the group rather than on other individuals. (Hence, no doubt, the curious subservience of the partners in some marriages within MRA: a marriage having been contracted under Guidance, the Group is sometimes Guided to post the bride and groom to opposite ends of the earth . . . and they go.) The report quotes Freud:

> In a very significant saying he suggests that in any crowd hate tends to heap up round the circumference. The love energies are focussed inward within the group itself; the forces of hatred are focussed outward toward those who do not belong to the group. We do not necessarily mean by this hatred in the ordinary literal sense. . . . The closer the emotional bond within the group, the more will this attitude of exclusiveness and non-co-operation develop towards other rival groups.

A referee suspected of tenderness towards the wrong team by a crowd of supporters on, say, a Glasgow football-ground might not share the report's confidence that the outward-focussed libido of an exclusive emotional group need not express itself as 'hatred in the ordinary literal sense'. Nor would any critic of MRA who had heard a verbatim account of the briefing on him given at Hays Mews.

This chapter of the report contains a good quotation from a book by Professor Gilbert Highet, *The Mind of Man*:

> Throughout the world, most people accept one of these closed systems of belief. And when a critic questions it, they hate him . . . because he is rejecting their revelation, and profaning the charisma of their leader, and attacking the group to which they belong. Usually they do not argue with him. That they leave to the trained expositors. Instead, like the Asiatic Greeks during St Paul's mission to Ephesus, they assemble together and all with one voice for the space of about two hours cry out, 'Great is Diana of the Ephesians!' or else, like the Jews when Paul spoke of preaching to the Gentiles, 'Away with such a fellow from the earth'.

The rationalism of this critique of MRA is balanced by a section on 'necessary lessons', in which the Assembly report, in effect, blames orthodox churchmen for neglecting 'genuine realities' which MRA has rediscovered:

> There is a challenge in the Oxford Group and in MRA to an all-out commitment. There has been a similar challenge in our day in the all-out commitment which Communism asks of its members. While all too many people in the Anglican Church are content tamely to frame and tamely to live by minimum rules of membership, these other movements ask for a total, heroic commitment of the self in every sphere of life. . . .
>
> Corresponding to this all-out commitment, there is in MRA a sense of urgency over racial and international problems, and a freedom of movement wherever there seems to be a call for new Christian service. . . . We need to see by comparison the lack of freedom of movement in much of our present ecclesiastical organisation. . . .
>
> Even if in places we may be critical of the results, we must be ready to ask whether [MRA] has found new

methods of approach toward those who are alienated from the Church. . . .

These self-critical tributes surely show how hard these investigators were trying to be fair, even generous. But MRA —as was foreshadowed in the two notes of dissent—seems always to have treated their report as a hostile document; thus confirming the report's observations on MRA's inability to take even the most balanced and constructive criticism.

The most severe part of the report is, indeed, its third chapter —on 'The Social Thinking of MRA'. The findings in this chapter coincide fairly closely with much that has been said in this book. They may be summarised sufficiently in brief quotations under the five headings of the chapter's subsections:

(1) *MRA fails to take the nature of politics seriously.*

'This is basically because of the movement's strong emphasis on "unselfishness" or "love" as a personal quality, but without any like emphasis on "justice" as a social quality. . . . At best MRA confuses them; at worst, ignores the separate entity of "justice".'

(2) *MRA fails to make a profound enough analysis of the world's social problems.*

'To assume, as MRA apparently does, that "new men" automatically lead to a solution of all the world's problems fails to diagnose the nature of many of the world's social problems. . . . [These] are not directly due to personal immorality, and they are not therefore cured by purely personal morality. This is the predicament of "moral man in immoral society". . . .' Dr Buchman's naïve and shallow appraisal of Hitler and the problems of Germany is given as an instance here, and the report adds:

> One can easily visualise a slave-owner who genuinely sought to observe the 'four absolutes' of MRA—who was a better master for that—and yet who might fail completely to see anything socially evil in slavery.

(3) *MRA is Utopian.*

The report notes MRA's 'ambitious claims'—that, in its own words, it 'does not seek to patch up existing systems, but to create a new type of man, a new society, a new civilisation, a new culture, a new renaissance'. The report suspects that 'a world, or a government, or an industry, or a trade union with MRA leadership would show an astonishing likeness to the old order'. And:

> Christian social thinking does believe in wise patching up of social systems, except . . . where any social change is made impossible by tyranny. Christian social thinking does approve of compromise, negotiation, and concession on almost all issues. Human and social life have to go on, and we always have to start from where we are, furthering the best and most progressive trends. . . . Indeed, as William Temple has written, this is the very essence of what we call 'democracy', which for these very reasons receives a sanction from Christianity. Not because it is perfect, not because it is infallible, not because it is 'inspired', not because a majority is necessarily right—but because it makes possible progressive change, patching up, unpatching and repatching, gives a responsibility to everyone, and denies the capacity of any men, even moral and religious men, to hold unchallenged power.

(4) *The MRA view of change is less than the Christian view of conversion.*

Conversion 'should be a continuing and deepening process. . . . But it is certainly not exhausted in MRA's understanding of the "four absolutes". . . . There is far more emphasis on the moral absolutes than on man's incapacity to observe them.' In any case, 'conversion . . . is not simply to certain moral ideals. It also demands a certain view of reality.'

(5) *MRA makes insufficient appeal to reason.*

'It is clear to anyone who has visited Caux in a spirit of enquiry that the study of facts, teaching, discussion and reasoning together have no pronounced place in the glittering display of fireworks. . . . There is only the opportunity for surrender, and then for witness to one's "change".'

Only a thousand copies of this report were printed. Most of these, no doubt, were used by members of the Church Assembly at the time of the debate on the report. This debate took place in the Assembly on 15th and 16th February, 1955. The Archbishop of Canterbury, Dr Fisher, was in the chair, and—twenty-five members having given notice that they wished to speak—exercised his discretion to rule out an attempt by the Archdeacon of Halifax to prevent any discussion at all by moving next business.

Sir Wilfrid Garrett, chairman of the Social and Industrial Council, moved 'that this Report be received'. After stressing that he had himself 'watched MRA with the greatest sympathy for thirty years', he went on (according to the Assembly *Report of Proceedings*):

> That the movement was inclined to be intolerant of criticism and questioning directed towards it was noted several times in the Report and was amply borne out by the political pressure group tactics which had been used to prevent the publication of the Report and in other ways since it was issued. This attitude had left an unfortunate impression on him and had distinctly altered his attitude towards the movement, because what human institution was beyond criticism? In particular a world-wide movement could not be beyond criticism.

The Dean of Westminster, Dr Alan C. Don, expressed some misgivings:

> He could not help recalling what happened at the beginning of the Wesleyan movement in the eighteenth century. He thought most historians would acknowledge that the hypercritical and unsympathetic attitude of the ordinary orthodox Churchmen of that day was at least in

part responsible for the fact that the early Methodists went into schism and that Methodism hardened into a sect, to the detriment of the Church of England and the cause of Christian unity. They had today to be on their guard lest they said anything that was untrue or uncharitable and thereby alienated from the Church of England a large number of sincere, self-sacrificing, enthusiastic and high-principled people who, whether they liked it or not, had found in MRA something which they failed to find elsewhere.

Those who had drafted the report would have agreed with this warning of the dangers of rigorism. The comparison with early Methodism, however, suggests another and contrary danger—the danger of a seriously misleading error in logic with which I have dealt already.[1]

At the beginning of the second day's debate, the Archbishop of Canterbury observed from the chair:

> If there were faults in the preparation or in the presentation of this Report, then it was clear that there had been faults on the part of the Oxford Group in the way it had reacted to the possibility and then to the fact of a Report. . . .
>
> He did not think any one of them wanted fundamentally to judge by declared resolution of the Assembly either for or against a Movement which, like every other human movement, contained within it good and bad.

The implication of this remark was that it would be best for the Assembly simply to 'receive' the report, since this did not commit them to positive acceptance or rejection. Under the Assembly's standing orders, such a report could only be received or referred back—the latter course implying definite rejection. Mr A. Haigh moved the reference-back. Sir Cyril Atkinson, a former Judge of the High Court, supported him

[1] See pp. 116-18.

strongly, condemning the report as 'unjust and harmful to a movement of great religious value'.

So the issue was clarified. Those who wished to express approval of MRA (or thought the report too severe) would vote for the reference-back of the report. Those who disapproved of MRA and those who, like the Archbishop, wished to refrain from a decisive judgement, would vote against the reference-back. Again and again during the debate, the note of resentment at MRA's pressure tactics was heard. The Archbishop of York, Dr Garbett, put a point that may have weighed with many of his hearers:

> If there was a refusal to receive this Report it would be widely assumed that they had given way to outside pressure. From time to time he had had to speak on controversial subjects, and that he was going to do so had been known beforehand. He had therefore had experience occasionally of what was meant by 'pressure groups'; but he had very rarely experienced such concentrated pressure as during the last few days from those who were associated with the Moral Re-Armament Movement trying to influence him in what he was about to say. Not only had he been inundated with these various papers—beautifully printed on excellent paper, which all of them had had and which could be produced only by a movement with great sums of money behind it—but also he had had a very large number of letters from people, known or unknown, about the value of this Movement. Most of them had been subjected to this kind of pressure. They must not let it be misinterpreted and said that, in view of the pressure which was brought to bear by the Moral Re-Armament Movement, they took the almost unprecedented step of refusing to receive a Report.

It may well be that MRA, by indiscreet and officious importunacy, had helped to defeat its own ends. For, when the vote on the reference-back was taken (in the Assembly's three Houses separately), the result was:

	Ayes	*Noes*
House of Bishops	5	29
House of Clergy	34	218
House of Laity	68	151
	107	398

What may be called the pro-MRA party was thus defeated by four to one, the minority vote being most substantial in the House of Laity—perhaps the least theologically minded of the three Houses. The Assembly then agreed, without divisions, (*a*) that the report be received and (*b*) that it did not 'desire to record any judgements either upon the merits or upon the demerits of this movement'.

This result cannot be regarded as a complete victory either for MRA or for its most convinced opponents, though, in view of the defeat of the reference-back, it must have been rather less satisfactory to MRA.

The report remains an outstandingly valuable document. Many clergymen, college chaplains, and students would welcome its reprinting; but that, in view of its origin and status, seems unlikely. Meanwhile, this short outline—from which I have omitted much that is of interest to the theological specialist rather than to the general reader—may be of some service.

14

RIGHT OF REPLY?

Television disputes—The Bishop of Southwark's half-minute 'onslaught'—Avoiding open discussion—MRA's epistolary habits—A letter from Oxford—Intolerance of questioning 'a sign of weakness'

OTHERS WHO have attempted to engage MRA in open discussion or debate have had experiences similar to those recorded by the Church Assembly's investigators.

In 1961, for instance, Mr Gordon Reece, producer of the Associated TeleVision Sunday evening programme, *About Religion*, arranged to include in an edition of this programme an interview with an MRA spokesman. The spokesman (chosen by MRA) was to be Mr Thornton-Duesbury.[1] Mr Reece intended that the interviewer should be a Member of Parliament, chosen from a short list of four—whichever of the four should turn out to be available for that evening. My name was on the list, but, so far as I know, I was the only one of the four who had ever said or written anything critical about MRA.

A day or two before the programme was due to be recorded, Mr Reece mentioned the four names to the MRA official with whom he had been negotiating. There was an instant unfavourable reaction. Then, on the day of the recording, MRA delivered what was no doubt meant to be a decisive blow: it

[1] See p. 191.

withdrew from the programme altogether—this, be it noted, though the interview was to be conducted under impartial chairmanship, and though it is well-known that any television interviewer who is too obviously hostile only succeeds in creating sympathy with his subject. The producer decided to to ahead with the item as planned—except that the chairman questioned me about my views on MRA and I sat facing an empty chair (the reason for which was explained briefly to the viewers). This set-up naturally obliged me to be as fair as I could be to the absent MRA spokesman, but there was a row afterwards: the producer and senior executives of his company received sharp protests from MRA. Fortunately, his refusal to submit to MRA's attempt at oblique censorship was backed by his employers.

Quite accidentally, because of an unrehearsed passing remark, the same television company was again involved in a dispute with MRA in July, 1963. In the same programme, *About Religion*, the Bishop of Southwark was reminded by an interviewer that—because of developments in his diocese which had been labelled 'South Bank religion'—one of his clergy had written to the press saying that the diocese was 'seething with discontent'. He asked if this were fair. The Bishop replied:

> . . . the man who said that, like another man who wrote to *The Times*, both belong to MRA—you know, Moral Re-Armament, that's the society of Dr Buchman (you know, thank-God-for-Hitler Buchman). Well, I am not concerned with what MRA thinks about my diocese. . . .

Again, there were furious protests from MRA, and a 'right of reply' was claimed. The Deputy Chairman of ATV, Mr Norman Collins, told an MRA spokesman, Mr R. J. K. Rundell, by telephone that he thought it right that MRA 'should be given some means of replying' to the Bishop. He proposed that the Bishop should be 'confronted by, say, two representatives of MRA'; and that the Bishop, too, should be accompanied by 'someone else, of his choice, who could enter into the discussion'. He mentioned that the Bishop had asked that I should be with him. As the Bishop had to leave a few days later to attend the Anglican Congress at Toronto, the discussion would have to be recorded fairly soon. This was on Wednesday, 17th July. The following Monday afternoon was suggested for the recording; and since technical arrangements, such as the reallocation of studio time, would have to be made quickly, Mr Collins asked Mr Rundell to let him know by noon the following day, Thursday, if this would suit MRA. (It was, after all, MRA that wanted this opportunity. . . .)

No message came by noon on Thursday. Mr Collins sent round a note by hand. (It is not far from ATV's headquarters in Great Cumberland Place to MRA's headquarters in Hays Mews.) He asked urgently for a reply later that afternoon. Next morning a letter came from Mr Rundell, asking him to put his proposal in writing—and adding: '. . . I cannot understand why Mr Driberg should be drawn into this matter. This would appear to me only to give a known enemy of MRA a chance for a further onslaught.' ('Enemy' is the translation of 'critic' preferred by those suffering from delusions of persecution; and, since the discussion was to turn on a point of controversy—from MRA's point of view, to correct a misrepresentation—it seems odd that 'a further onslaught' could not be met squarely and answered.)

Mr Collins, who seems to have behaved with exemplary patience, confirmed his proposal in writing: the discussion, he said, would last 'some fifteen minutes', and the chairman might be the well-known television journalist, Kenneth Harris (though he had not yet been approached); Mr Harris had recently interviewed Mr R. A. Butler in *About Religion*, and was thought to be neutral on MRA. Mr Collins added that he was becoming 'acutely anxious about time', and now asked for a reply by noon on the Friday—twenty-four hours later than his original deadline.

Next day came a telephone message: Mr Rundell, with whom Mr Collins had been negotiating throughout, was 'not personally in a position to give a decision'. Mr Collins therefore withdrew his offer.

No one with experience of MRA's talent for wire-pulling will suppose that this was the end of the matter. It was soon evident that Mr Rundell must have been simply stalling for time, keeping Mr Collins's offer open as long as he could, while another approach was explored. This other approach was above Mr Collins's head and behind his back—direct to Lord Hill of Luton, the new Chairman of the Independent Television Authority, which has a statutory duty to see that the programme companies, such as ATV, preserve balance on matters of public controversy. Lord Hill took the view that MRA 'should be invited to nominate one or two spokesmen to be interviewed quite briefly in the same setting of the same programme about what the Bishop of Southwark had chosen to say in reference to MRA'.

This interview took place in *About Religion* on 1st September, 1963, by which time the Bishop was safely out of the country. MRA was represented only by its leading spokesman, Peter Howard. He was interviewed by the programme's regular introducer, Julian Grenfell. Mr Grenfell read out the relevant context of Buchman's Hitler remark. Mr Howard said that to suggest that Buchman or MRA had any affinity with Fascism or Nazism was 'just a low-grade lie'. Mr Grenfell pressed him: had Buchman in fact used the words attributed to him? Mr Howard said that 'forty-three New York pressmen' had met Buchman on his arrival from Germany, and 'only one' had reported this remark. (But surely the 'forty-three' would have been the regular reporters who go on board before passengers land. As we already know, this was a long interview with Buchman 'in his book-lined office in the annex to Calvary Church'.) 'Yes, but did he say it?', asked Mr Grenfell again. Mr Howard referred slightingly to 'one uncorroborated press statement', and rode off on a general diatribe against sin. He also said that 'a lot of people suffered from the illusion that Hitler could be changed', and quoted early statements in praise of Hitler by Winston Churchill and Lloyd George. This was indeed an illusion—but Buchman was not supposed to have illusions: his Guidance was 'always right'. The most fervent admirer of Churchill or Lloyd George would not make that claim for either of them.[1]

One further example may be given of MRA's habit of avoiding free debate except on its own terms. In the autumn of 1961 I was invited to lecture on MRA at the students' clubs of two Scandinavian universities, Oslo and Göteborg. In each case the lecture was followed by a long period of questioning and discussion, which was by no means one-sided. Those who organised the lectures, and I, had only one regret: the spokesmen of MRA, who had been invited to take part, stayed away.

Often, as in the case of the reply to the Bishop of Southwark, this avoidance of open discussion is combined with busily organised private pressure in defence of what are thought to be MRA's interests. This may sometimes be a misjudgement. A few years ago I was invited by the Vicar of the University Church at Cambridge, Canon Joseph Fison,[2] to speak in his church one Sunday evening. When I got to Cambridge he told me that some earnest MRA emissaries had been to see him to rebuke him for asking me to speak in his church—adding some of the scandalous accusations that MRA habitually spreads against anyone regarded as an 'enemy'. (I do not believe that these tales are circulated dishonestly, except by those who invent them: most Buchmanites seem genuinely incapable of imagining that a critic of their movement could be inspired by any but the lowest personal motives.) In this case, Canon Fison—a man of overflowing and humorous charity—seemed to be amused rather than irritated by the impertinence: the only rebuke he permitted himself to administer was to ask me to speak again a year or two later.

I am sorry to refer to so many of my own encounters, direct or, more often, indirect, with MRA, but this is, after all—though I feel no resentment whatever about it—some of the evidence on which I must rely in forming an estimate of MRA. The only other minor incident worth mentioning arose out of a meeting of an Oxford University church society, at which I spoke on Christianity and Politics (emphasising, as my main

[1] *Cf* pp. 74-5. [2] Now Bishop of Salisbury.

theme, the duty of Christians to become involved actively in civic and political life, and referring to MRA only in answer to a question from an undergraduate who was clearly, from the jargon he used, under MRA influence). Some time after the meeting I wrote an article in the *New Statesman* (4th June, 1960), attempting an analysis of MRA's changing strategy rather on the lines on which it has been examined in this book.

The usual letters of protest came in; and, as is also usual, those that were not published were passed on to me in case I wanted to answer them. One of these caught my attention. It was signed by an undergraduate at University College, Oxford, and it read:

> Sir,
>
> Reading Tom Driberg on MRA reminds me of two old ladies who celebrated over-well on a bottle of champagne. 'Jane', said one of them, staring mistily at her companion. 'You are drunk. You've got two noses.'
>
> I have seen both Driberg and Buchman in action with Oxford audiences this year. Driberg used the meeting of a University Christian society for wholly political ends. He stated that no one could be a Christian if he were not of the extreme left and assured a smaller group of us afterwards that 'Communism in some form is inevitable in Britain'. Incidentally he took the opportunity then as now to attack Dr Buchman. I doubt whether anyone left that meeting a better man.
>
> Buchman, on the other hand, brought a film of great beauty and profound content—a film that brings a cure to the bitter racial situation in the world. He introduced to us people whose character change had led to change in conditions around them. Many men were stimulated to rethink their lives, in terms of their responsibility to other classes and races.
>
> Which of the two is using religion for political purposes? Clearly, Driberg. His attempts, by deliberate misrepresentations too numerous to list here, to poison men's minds

against MRA have not gone down well with any of my acquaintances at Oxford.

Yours faithfully,

The content, the style, and the physical form of this letter all interested me.

On content: The statements attributed to me were so wild a distortion of what I had actually said that I found it hard to believe that the writer had really been present on the occasion in question, or that any Oxford undergraduate could be so unintelligent as to be guilty of such inaccuracy.

As an example of the letter's false witness: I did not, of course, say 'that no one could be a Christian if he were not of the extreme left'. What I did say went something like this: 'I happen to be a Socialist, and to me Socialism is the practical, everyday, political expression of the Christian gospel. I have no right whatever to question the sincerity of Christians who support the existing social and economic order. I may find it difficult to understand *how* they can reconcile their politics with their religion, just as *they* can't understand how a Christian can be a Socialist'—and I went on to describe the equal, but different, difficulties that a British Christian Socialist may have *vis-à-vis* some of his European comrades whose tradition is strongly anti-clerical and, in philosophic ancestry, Marxist. It would be wearisome to detail the letter's other misrepresentations: I showed it to the college chaplain who had chaired the meeting, and he assured me that these were as extreme as I thought them.

On style: Whoever wrote this letter had certainly got right inside the mind of MRA. *Le style est l'homme même*. It was a remarkable achievement for a relatively inexperienced youth, reading history at Oxford (and therefore soaked in the rather more 'mandarin' and sonorous English of Trevelyan and Stubbs), to be able to model his language so closely on the jerky, snappy, 'vivid' journalese of the master propagandist of Buchmanism. Also, the moral fable with which the letter opened, uproariously funny though it might seem at a

Buchmanite beanfeast, did not strike me as altogether original. After a time, I recalled where I had seen it before. Chapter VI of Peter Howard's *Innocent Men*—published nearly twenty years before this letter was written—opens:

> Did you ever hear the story of the two ladies who for the first time in their lives drank champagne? After half the bottle had gone, one leaned across the table and said solemnly to the other: 'My dear, you must be drunk. *You've got two noses.*'[1]

It is disappointing to find a convert to Absolute Honesty indulging in unacknowledged plagiarism.

On physical form: This letter was typed—not only its text, but the address 'University College, Oxford', at the head of it. Several other letters from university addresses arrived simultaneously. All attacked the *New Statesman* article in rather similar terms. All except one were typed (including the addresses).

This is puzzling. Members of Parliament and editors of weekly reviews receive a great many letters from Oxford and other university students, mostly from the secretaries of undergraduate political societies inviting them to address these societies. Except when the letters are sent during vacations, from the writers' home addresses (and sometimes even then), it is my experience, and that of the colleagues whom I have consulted on the point, that letters from undergraduates are almost invariably written, not typed, and that they are written on college writing-paper with engraved letter-head (and, often, crest); or, now and then, on Union Society paper.

Can it be that MRA, like the organisers of some secular pressure campaigns, keeps a list of people willing to sign letters to the press, and on appropriate occasions circulates such letters, pre-typed and ready for signing and posting? If so, the letters would be rather more convincing if a stock of properly headed writing-paper of the various colleges could

[1] Mr Howard is loyal to little old jokes. He uses this one again on p. 119 of *Britain and the Beast* (1963).

be kept at Hays Mews. I hope this friendly hint will not be taken amiss.

A similar postal pressure campaign was launched against the Bishop of Southwark after the television incident already described. Some letters came from the 'big names' of the movement (an actress, a PhD, a Major-General, a Conservative MP); some writers boasted of having served in the forces during the war against Hitler; some were abusive, some more restrained and courteously puzzled; some refused to believe that Buchman had, in fact, ever made the remark about Hitler . . . and there was one, ostensibly from an undergraduate at Keble College, Oxford, on which text and address were type-written.

If the young man who sent me the letter from University College did indulge in any such mild deception, it seems better that I should not print his name. He was a son of a Congregational minister in Sussex, was described by those who knew him as 'a nice, simple lad', and may now have grown out of his adolescent Buchmanism. If the deception was partly his, it was, as I say, mild. If he was persuaded to sign the letter by older supporters of MRA, their conduct seems (like so many other actions already mentioned) wanting in Absolute Honesty. But perhaps that Absolute is now practised only within the fellowship of the Changed? Perhaps it can be shelved while an attempt is made to scotch an 'enemy'. If so, MRA will merely be following the ancient tradition of human governments and other organisations concerned with power, and taking the end to justify the means.

One thought has often occurred to outside students of MRA: if the Buchmanites are so anxious to avoid open public debate, and yet so active in epistolary controversy and backstairs pressure, they must either have a very poor case or feel extremely unsure of their ability to state and defend it orally. Yet this seems inconsistent with their known and observed confidence—their exuberant over-confidence, indeed.

One answer to this problem is suggested in the introduction to the Church Assembly report:

We have encountered many signs that the movement is inclined to be intolerant of criticism or questioning directed towards it. Such resentment is always a sign of weakness. In this particular movement the sense of being God-controlled or even divinely dictated perhaps produces a feeling of infallibility. . . .

Such a feeling is surely bad for any human being—not least for young men and women not out of their 'teens.

15

TRUTH IN ADVERTISING

Absolute Honesty: possible and desirable?—Doubtful devices in an 'ideological offensive'—Sportsmen embarrassed—Exaggerated claims—The 'miracle' of Cyprus—Disguising failure—A Governor-General's testimony

THERE IS only one point at which I would venture to make stronger and more explicit the Assembly report's general critique of MRA; and this is at a central and crucial point—the doctrine of the Four Absolutes. The report, indeed, mistrusts MRA's 'perfectionist thinking', and remarks that 'a really literal observance of the absolutes (if that is in fact what MRA does want) would lead to complete anarchy'. But it does not directly challenge the formulation and content of the Four Absolutes—absolute honesty, purity, unselfishness, and love.

At first glance, it is difficult for any Christian, or anyone who tries to lead a decent life, to do so. Most people would vaguely agree that it would be a good thing if all of us were honest, pure, unselfish and loving. So it would—but one essential word is missing from the previous sentence: the word 'absolute'.

The absolutism of MRA seems vulnerable in several ways. It may be true, as has been claimed in some recent MRA propaganda, that 'a standard is not a standard unless it is absolute,' and that the Four Absolutes are simply ideals to be aimed at, and tests by which every action or intention is daily to be judged. But if this is all that they are, it is difficult to see why the new formula had to be devised at all: Christianity and other world religions already had ethical codes, laws and precepts for the guidance of believers. Christians know that they are called to perfection, and that they constantly fall short of it; but MRA, despite this recent concession to human frailty, has often in the past given the impression that, once a man is Changed, he does *in fact* 'live by' the Four Absolutes. 'Live by' is a loose phrase, but it seems to imply 'live up to': the frequency of failure is ignored or understressed—and the twofold result may be, on the one hand, a spiritual arrogance in those who deceive themselves or others into thinking that they are actually living up to these impossible standards, and, on the other hand, frustration, a morbidly excessive sense of guilt, and, ultimately, blank despair in those whose self-examination is more thorough.

Moreover, the Four Absolutes, when compared with any of the classical codes of ethics, do not form a well-balanced or comprehensive rule of life. They read as if they were framed on the spur of the moment, in a flash of Guidance, by Dr Buchman; and as if, since 'Frank's guidance was always right', nobody ventured to question his authority and to suggest that other Absolutes, too, might be required. As has already been noted,[1] there is in this code no mention of the social virtue of justice or of the personal virtue of humility. When MRA spokesmen defend the Four Absolutes as simply a summary of the Sermon on the Mount, they show that they have not read that Sermon recently, or have forgotten some of its teachings—on the Law and justice, for instance, on humility,[2] and, most of all, on the avoidance of ostentation in well-doing. It is hard to square the success-stories detailed so brashly in some of MRA's newspaper advertisements—indeed, the publication of such advertisements at all—with Matthew vi, 1-4.

In any case, is *absolute* honesty or purity (in the MRA sense of the word) really desirable? To quote the usual examples of the justified 'white lie': if a violent psychopath is looking for a

[1] See pp. 213, 179.

[2] 'Blessed are the meek' (or, in the *New English Bible*, '. . . those of a gentle spirit').

gun, the honest citizen is not obliged, when asked, to tell him where it is; and it is not sinful dishonesty, but common courtesy, to let a worthy bore think that you are glad to see him. Similarly, one can imagine many cases in which Absolute Honesty might dictate the reporting to parents or teachers of a minor delinquency by some boy or girl: in a few cases it might be right and necessary for a neighbour or stranger to do this; in far more cases it would be an intolerable impertinence and intrusion—and a symptom of pharisaical self-satisfaction and priggishness, rightly condemned by sensible people who dislike prying busybodies or 'nosey Parkers'. This is not to say that 'minding one's own business' is an adequate rule of social conduct: it may be an excuse for cowardice, laziness, and failure to help where help is needed. But there is a reasonable middle course between not caring at all about one's neighbour and forcing unwanted information or advice upon him; and, as with the strange teaching on the breaking of engagements under Guidance,[1] the ordinary amenities of social life would become impossible if Absolute Honesty were universally practised.

An advocate of MRA has no right to shrug off such examples as absurdly extreme cases in which common sense would obviously come into play: 'of course we wouldn't behave so extravagantly'. For extravagant behaviour is exactly what the Absolutes require. If you tell the psychopath that you don't know where the gun is, when you do, you are not being absolutely honest. This is the cleft stick into which MRA's absolutism forces its disciples: either they must behave extravagantly or they fall into dishonesty—minor dishonesty which they are debarred from calling, as others would call it, excusable. So, by deliberate training, they must come to lack that most precious of civilised human attributes, a sense of proportion.

In fact, however, what is not allowed to the individual rank-and-file Buchmanite appears to be allowed, or to pass without comment or self-criticism, in the movement as a whole.

[1] See p. 195.

A number of instances in which MRA propaganda and practice fall short of Absolute Honesty have already been cited in this book, in relevant contexts; a few more deserve to be recorded.

First-hand evidence of the methods used in a specific MRA campaign is given in an article by Russell Barbour in an American review, *The Christian Century*, for 17th January, 1962. It seems fair to take this campaign as typical of similar campaigns in many countries, since it was not conducted primarily by local people but by visiting MRA representatives. One may suppose that these were among the most responsible agents of MRA, since the campaign took place on Dr Buchman's home ground, in Pennsylvania, shortly after his death in 1961: clearly this campaign had to be a success.

Mr Barbour was a member of the local human relations commission on which sat 'leaders in business, labor unions, journalism, churches, education, and community agencies' from two towns, Easton and Phillipsburg, not far from Allentown. Four MRA agents appeared before it to seek endorsement for local showing of the MRA film, *The Crowning Experience*.

> They began by indicating that the mayor of Easton had received them with open arms and was a devotee of their cause—a claim which, we later discovered, did not square with the facts.

Since this commission is 'concerned with advancing the welfare and rights of minority groups' and 'the film seemed to lie within that area of concern', the commission endorsed its local showing. Mr Barbour says:

> In the light of what has happened since, the general opinion is that we let ourselves be taken in.

As soon as this endorsement had been given, the members of the commission were 'exposed to continued harassment by MRA teams seeking to convert us to "the ideology that alone can save the world from Communism" '. These teams seem to have behaved with a gracelessness hardly calculated to advance their cause:

> With something less than good manners they insinuated themselves into our homes and managed to obtain from us meals and lodging. They used the commission's name far beyond the purpose implied in our simple endorsement of a film for local showing. They advertised—erroneously and to our embarrassment—that we had sponsored and paid for the dinner that preceded the showing of the film. Without authorisation they sent out invitations to the dinner over our chairman's name. Certain businessmen did agree to pay for some of the luncheons and dinners that multiplied in the days and weeks following the film's presentation, but after reflection and consultation with others they came to realise that they too had been used.

This was only the start of the trouble that the commission had so innocently let itself in for:

> In MRA publications and in regular news media there appeared statements reputedly made by local community leaders, all in support of the movement. The catch: those leaders had never made such statements.

Typical of the extraordinary tactics of these missionaries was a report in *MRA Information Service* for 16th October, 1961:

> The ideological offensive of MRA in the Lehigh Valley industrial area of Pennsylvania concentrated last week in the cities of Easton and Phillipsburg. . . . The Commission on Human Relations of the Easton-Phillipsburg area invited *The Crowning Experience* to spearhead the move. . . . [Its chairman said] 'This film is the most moving experience in motion pictures I have thus far encountered. . .'. The Commission commended *The Crowning Experience* by sending an invitation and information on Frank Buchman's life to the 24,000 homes in the area.

Of this report Mr Barbour remarks:

> None of those statements was true: we did not 'invite' the film to the area, our chairman does not hold the opinion credited to him, we sent out no invitations or

> Buchman biographies nor did we know it was being done. When MRA people were confronted by proof of the misrepresentations, they acknowledged that some 'misconstruction' could be placed on the release.

That was big of them. But, to readers of *MRA Information Service*, the false information had been impressively conveyed. Despite MRA's 'highly developed skill in public relations' and 'a network of meetings, visits, dinners', this campaign does not seem to have been an unqualified success. According to Mr Barbour:

> The small attendance the film drew in this area would bring into question the publicity blurbs' claims. Few of the people who saw it were able to discern in it the dynamic quality it is said to possess; most found its theme vague, the acting amateurish. Some acknowledge, however, that while the production is too naive and illogical to convince audiences in the least sophisticated, its story might appeal to the people of undeveloped areas.
>
> Despite the fact that the film gains its title from an episode in the life of a prominent Negro leader . . ., members of the local Negro community were not enthusiastic. Some found it difficult to get the point of the story, and Negro leaders were suspicious of the techniques used to put the showing over.

Moreover, Trade Union officials 'were amazed at the devices used to win them over'. Their opinions were misrepresented publicly; one said that 'never before had he met with such dishonest practices'. Mr Barbour asks, pertinently, if MRA elsewhere is 'quoting as enthusiasts those of us who gave a simple endorsement to a film only to be embarrassed ever since because of it'. And: 'Could it be that those quoted endorsements by world leaders are simply enlargements in like manner from casual remarks?'

It could indeed. If MRA has often embarrassed others by pushful methods such as those described by Mr Barbour, it has itself sometimes been embarrassed by the carelessness—attributable, of course, merely to excess of zeal—of its own supporters. One such embarrassment arose out of a full-page advertisement in *The Times* of 16th February, 1961—one of a series, headed 'FOR GOD'S SAKE WAKE UP!', that preceded the London *première* of *The Crowning Experience*. As *MRA Pictorial* put it, 'pages followed each other in quick succession, bearing the signatures of nationally known sportsmen, leaders of labour, educators, and people from all parts of the Commonwealth'.

The 'nationally known sportsmen' whose names appeared in *The Times*, with vigorous action-photographs, were Herb Elliott, T. C. Dodds, Bryn Meredith, Joe Mercer, Brian Boobbyer, and Eddie Stuart. The signature of a seventh, Ossie Wheatley, also appeared at the foot of a statement displayed between the six photographs. Beneath each photograph was the name of the sportsman shown in it, followed by a colon, followed by a testimonial to MRA or to the film in quotation-marks. The readers were entitled—and, clearly, expected—to assume that these testimonials were actual quotations from original statements by these six sportsmen.

Within a few days two of the six had repudiated their own testimonials. Olympic athlete Herb Elliott (to whom the advertisement had attributed the sentiment 'The spirit of *The Crowning Experience* is the spirit that Britain needs to match the challenge of our times') said to a *Sunday Express* reporter: 'When I signed the letter I did not realise that it would be used as an advertisement. I was embarrassed when I saw it published.' He went on to describe more than one MRA party that he had attended, and said that the Roman Catholic chaplain at Cambridge, Mgr Alfred Gilbey, had advised him 'not to get involved in MRA any more'. In another interview he said: 'Because they are enthusiasts they are apt to push people about a bit.'

Next day there was another shock. Welsh Rugby International Bryn Meredith ('Everybody in the whole world must see this film') wrote to *The Times* saying that he had nothing to do with MRA—and adding: 'Neither did I give written or verbal consent to my name or photograph being connected with the advertisement. . . .'

MRA put out a slightly huffy statement about one defector: 'As far as we know, Elliott was told his letter would be appearing and he was delighted to sign it. . . .' T. C. Dodds wrote to *The Times* apologising to Mr Meredith: 'I thought that he understood exactly what was intended . . . I am the one to blame.'

Why should these tiresome misunderstandings occur? I wonder if it could be because MRA is, for some reason, reluctant to use the word 'advertisement'. Mr Elliott and Mr Meredith were asked to sign a 'letter' or a 'statement': these words do not immediately convey, to those unfamiliar with MRA's methods, the idea of a full-page advertisement with pictures and headlines in large type. After all, *The Times* does also publish letters as letters.

The description of this campaign in *MRA Pictorial* also managed to avoid mentioning that it was an advertising campaign, in America and in Britain: beside a montage of sketches of the front pages of eighteen newspapers—*Le Monde* and *Die Welt* as well as *The Times* and the *New York Times*—ran a text beginning 'An estimated 110 million people read a call to the American people . . .'. They did so because 'the great American newspapers carried a full page under the banner headline: "The hour is late. Here is the answer. For God's sake wake up." '

'Carried a full page': no word to identify it as an advertisement. Innocent readers might have supposed this lavish space entirely editorial: how newsworthy, how important a movement must be that could command such attention! The fact that the pages were 'carried' because they were paid for was, however, hinted at in a delicate circumlocution: 'Backing this initiative was the conviction of thousands of ordinary citizens. . . . Their money . . . made the pages possible'—and this, I suppose, does just, by a hair's-breadth, free *MRA Pictorial* from the suspicion of a lapse, on this occasion, from Absolute Honesty.

A similar coyness was responsible for some unfavourable

reactions to another full-page advertisement in *The Times*, on 9th June, 1960 (and in many other papers). This contained the text of Dr Buchman's 82nd birthday broadcast. It started:

> There is a hurricane of common sense sweeping through the world. 'A Hurricane of Common Sense'—that was the headline in a newspaper read by the leaders of Washington. It refers to the manifesto *Ideology and Co-existence*, which in the last six months has gone to 73,000,000 homes. . . . It puts squarely to the modern world the choice—Moral Re-Armament or Communism.

Unless there was a streak of almost incredible naïvety running through his shrewdness, it is strange that Buchman should have felt Guided to open his broadcast with these words; for they certainly did not 'measure up to the test' of Absolute Honesty. As in instances noted earlier in this book, they were, just possibly, literally true, in that such a headline was printed in a paper sent to, if not read by, 'the leaders of Washington'; but they were misleading in that they suggested that the paper in question was one that would automatically be on the White House breakfast-table and eagerly turned to by 'the leaders'. It was, in fact, a small local sheet, the *Bethesda-Chevy Chase Advertiser*. In its issue of 31st March, 1960, a columnist whose regular feature, 'I Cover Suburbia', was signed with the whimsical pseudonym, 'Tar' Paulin, had indeed used, and headlined, the phrase that had caught Dr Buchman's fancy. After saying that he had once been a cynic, 'Tar' Paulin reviewed the *Ideology and Co-existence* booklet. He wrote:

> . . . As I progressed through its thirty-one pages of text, something almost wonderous [*sic*] and magical happened to me. My cynicism gave way to a deeper, greater emotion —moral re-armament. . . . Read it and re-read it. It's powerful. It takes the offensive against Communism.
>
> I'm a dedicated anticommie. I cheer Moral Re-Armament. Its little pamphlet is like a hurricane of common-sense sweeping away the fog of confusion.

Confusion is not dispelled, however, by ambiguities such as those repeatedly used by Buchman in his references to these advertisements. Later in the same broadcast (and in the advertisements in which it was printed) he said:

> When Chou En-lai arrived in India for his conferences with Prime Minister Nehru, the *Times of India* and the *Hindustan Times* carried full pages with the double-banner headline, 'Moral Re-Armament—the next step for Communists and non-Communists alike'.

This provoked a letter of protest to *The Times* from the editor of *The Times of India*, Mr N. J. Nanporia. The effect of Buchman's statement, he wrote, would be 'to suggest that *The Times of India* published an article or news story of the kind to which Dr Buchman refers':

> To remove any misunderstanding may I emphasise that Dr Buchman's reference is to an advertisement inserted by Moral Re-Armament and the sentiments expressed therein have nothing whatsoever to do with *The Times of India* policy. At no time have we expressed any approval in our editorial columns of the role and objectives of moral rearmament. It is remarkable . . . that the contents of a paid advertisement should by implication be ascribed to a newspaper as its considered opinion.

No blame attaches to the newspapers that have published these advertisements. Almost invariably, they print 'Advertisement' or 'Advertiser's Announcement' at the head of the page. Sometimes they simultaneously publish editorials criticising MRA: on 7th March, 1961, the *Daily Herald* published an MRA advertisement signed by a number of Trade Unionists, whose organisations were given after their names (though not the usual intimation that they had signed in their personal capacity only); on another page was an editorial expressing 'the belief that the alert readers of the *Herald* will not be beguiled by this kind of soft soap'. So the readers of these newspapers are not deceived: the misunderstanding creeps in later, when MRA, glorying retrospectively in its bought publicity, uses phrases as vague as Buchman's in the 'Hurricane' broadcast. The Revd E. C. E. Bourne, Rector of Hedgerley, Buckinghamshire, summed the matter up in a letter to *The Times*. The publication of such a full page *as news*, he pointed out, would imply that it was 'the considered opinion of the newspaper' that MRA was 'of sufficient importance to warrant such exceptional treatment':

> If Dr Buchman did not mean his readers to infer that *The Times of India* attached such exceptional importance to MRA, it is difficult to see the point of his statement.

When the 'dedicated anticommie' of 'I Cover Suburbia' was experiencing 'something almost wonderous and magical' on reading *Ideology and Co-existence*, he probably did not know that his reflexes were being set working by stimuli that were, in part, bogus. This booklet contains a number of statements alleged to have been made by Lenin and other Soviet leaders. Several of these have been used repeatedly, in the course of the Cold War, by anti-Soviet propagandists. This does not in itself prove that they are not genuine; but both internal evidence and the testimony of scholars, in Britain and in Russia, who are intimately acquainted with Lenin's works suggest that some of them were invented at 'factories' of the kind maintained at various times by great powers for the production of convenient forgeries. Several, at any rate, cannot be traced in any of Lenin's copious published writings and speeches.

One Lenin quotation in the booklet is not actually false, but doctored so that its context and real meaning are obscured:

> It is necessary . . . to resort to all sorts of stratagems, manœuvres, illegal methods, to evasion and subterfuge, only so as to get into trade unions, to remain in them and to carry on Communist work within them at all costs.

At least the three dots in the first line of this quotation are, if not absolutely, relatively honest. The quotation is from a booklet written by Lenin in 1920, *Left-wing Communism, an*

Infantile Disorder. In this he dealt, among other things, with the argument of the 'revolutionary' extremists in some countries that it was unbecoming to work in 'reactionary trade unions'—i.e., in trade unions led, for the time being, by 'reactionaries'. He explained that, on the contrary, it was 'these opportunist leaders' who 'will have recourse to all the tricks of bourgeois diplomacy, will appeal for the help of bourgeois governments, of priests, police, and courts, in order to prevent Communists from entering trade unions, by all and every means to put them out, to make their work inside these organisations as unpleasant as possible, to insult, hound, and persecute them.'

To illustrate the kind of situation he had in mind, Lenin cited the example of the illegal underground resistance in pre-1917 Russia, under the Tsars: in those days the Bolsheviks, in order to have some access to the workers, had joined even the sham 'unions' created by the police. In such a situation as that, Lenin said (and I italicise the words omitted in the booklet):

> It is necessary *to be able to withstand all this, to go the whole length of any sacrifice, if need be* to resort to all sorts of stratagems . . .

And so on. Impartial historians may consider such advice no more shocking than the 'stratagems' and 'manœuvres' necessarily resorted to by those resisting any tyranny, whether that of the Nazis in wartime France or that of Franco in Spain today. It has nothing to do with conditions in Britain, where (though some unions debar Communists from office) membership of unions is open to people of all parties or of none.

The most entertaining—and the most dishonest—Lenin 'quotation' in *Ideology and Co-existence* is intended, quaintly enough, to expose the dishonesty of Communists:

> 'Promises', he said, 'are like pie-crusts—made to be broken.'

Now, Lenin did in fact use this old English saying—but he used it in October, 1913, in the course of an article entitled 'The Liberals and the Land Question in Britain', in which he attacked Lloyd George and his 'land campaign'. Towards the end of the article he wrote:

> As for the promises of reforms, . . . doesn't the English proverb say that promises are like pie-crusts, made in order to be broken?

So Lenin was not laying down a principle of Communist conduct: he was quoting an English saying in order to cast doubt on the sincerity of a British politician! The remark does not appear again anywhere in his published works. The flavour of this extreme misuse of a quotation would be most fully appreciated, perhaps, by the writer to whom the *Oxford Dictionary of Quotations* attributes the origin of the 'pie-crust' saying—the great ironist, Dean Swift.

Since it is the agreeable habit of MRA to attribute Communist sympathies to its critics, I may point out that I am not saying here that no Communist politician has ever told a lie. I am trying simply to check MRA's professions of Absolute Honesty. It may be that the American authors of *Ideology and Co-existence* included these dubious texts in good faith, and that the British leaders of the movement did not bother to examine them critically and to verify the references; but it seems almost certain that the texts came to them, indirectly, from one of the official or semi-official, but secret, lie-factories to which I have referred. In the interests of Absolute Honesty, they ought to be more careful in future.

In the same connection, I have already commented more than once on MRA's habit of overstating what it has done towards the solving of industrial, interracial and international disputes.[1] Here I must make one exception. MRA propaganda has frequently cited the case of Eudocio Ravines, whom *Ideology and Co-existence* describes as 'a former Communist of great distinction and authority'. Mr Ravines was trained in Moscow, and became the leading Communist in Peru; and it seems that, in this instance, the description in the booklet is correct. At any rate, when I met an old friend from Peru at the

[1] *Cf* pp. 119-38.

Amsterdam congress of the Socialist International in September, 1963—Victor Haya de la Torre, chairman of the Aprista party of Peru and one of the leading democratic Socialists in Latin America—I asked him about Ravines and MRA; and he confirmed that Ravines was indeed a man of outstanding ability and intelligence, with a long record of militant Communist activity (and, consequently, of opposition to the Aprista party); and that he had, a few years ago, gone over to MRA. De la Torre found this change, in so solidly grounded a Marxist, inexplicable. He added that, after the change, Ravines had identified himself with and defended 'capitalist forces of the extreme Right'; but that, more recently, he had seemed to be moving slightly more towards the Aprista party.

Apart from this substantiation of one claim, I find only scepticism about MRA in the Labour movements of most democratic countries, though MRA can always produce an 'endorsement' signed by some fairly reputable politician—all these endorsements being worded in remarkably similar language, familiar to all students of MRA literature.

A case in point is that of Cyprus. In a *New Statesman* article in June, 1960, and in a lecture published as a pamphlet in 1962, I mentioned the surprise expressed by Archbishop Makarios when I showed him an *MRA Pictorial*, embellished with his photograph, claiming for MRA the main credit for the 'miracle' of the Cyprus settlement. One MRA full-page advertisement (*Daily Express*, 4th June, 1962) quotes the Turkish-Cypriot Vice-President, Dr Kutchuk, as saying:

> The principles of MRA constitute the basis of the Cyprus constitution. They have enabled Greeks and Turks to forget the antagonism which existed. . . . Greeks and Turks will stay united.

Recent events in Cyprus have shown that this forecast was too optimistic. The miraculous solution has not, in practice, been working out at all well: it has broken down. But the prophecy may be excused as a laudable aspiration; and MRA did, I believe, try to bring Greeks and Turks together. The apparently factual statement about 'the basis of the Cyprus constitution' is, however, nonsense. A Briton who knows as much about Cyprus settlement as anyone—but whose name, because of his official position, I cannot disclose—summarises thus the factors leading to the settlement:

1 The declaration of the Macmillan Plan in mid-1958 under which it was proposed that each community should run its own affairs and both come together over a period of years to run the island.
2 The Turkish acceptance of that Plan.
3 Archbishop Makarios' declaration in the autumn of 1958 in favour of Independence rather than Enosis.
4 The Zürich Agreement made by Averoff and Zorlu.
5 The acceptance of that Agreement by all concerned, including (most reluctantly) Makarios.

He adds that it was not Archbishop Makarios who made the settlement, but Averoff and Zorlu, the Greek and Turkish Foreign Ministers—'and I don't think that MRA had the slightest influence on any of them (or on Macmillan or Selwyn Lloyd[1]).' Nor, one may add, did it have any influence on Mr Julian Amery, then Colonial Under-Secretary, who conducted on behalf of the British Government the long-drawn-out negotiations on the British military bases in Cyprus.

One senior Cypriot diplomat, Mr Zenon Rossides, is a supporter of MRA. On 2nd February, 1959, through the good offices of Sir Hamilton Kerr, Conservative MP for Cambridge and one of MRA's few convinced supporters in Parliament, Mr Rossides, who was then Secretary of the Ethnarchy Council in Cyprus, was received by the then Prime Minister, Mr Macmillan. It is unlikely that anything said at that stage would have contributed to the settlement; and in any case this meeting was confidential (though MRA later exploited it, attributing to the Prime Minister, without permission, remarks which he may or may not have made to Mr Rossides). Even more surprisingly, in view of MRA's claim, the British official

[1] Then Foreign Secretary.

whom I have quoted writes to me, of Mr Rossides' attitude to the settlement:

> He tried to prevent it in London, and subsequently he did what he could to stop it being put into effect.

So much for the MRA-inspired 'miracle of Cyprus'. Yet MRA is able, truthfully, to quote a number of messages of general goodwill signed by Archbishop Makarios, and to boast that, on the day of Independence, he sent to Caux a flag of the new Republic of which he was now President. No doubt His Beatitude, who has his own domestic political difficulties, finds it desirable occasionally to oblige, in this relatively painless way, so staunch an old supporter as Mr Rossides. As Mr Ivan Yates wrote in the *Observer* on 26th March, 1961 (when Dr Buchman was still alive): 'Most of these messages are clearly put before him to sign. It is difficult to believe that each year, when Dr Buchman's birthday comes round, the Archbishop reaches for his pen and scribbles a note.'

With equally exact information in each case, MRA claims in many other territories could be punctured similarly. To take only one further example: Nigeria. MRA's official obituary hand-out on Dr Buchman said that his influence 'saved bloodshed in Nigeria, and hastened the day of peaceful self-government'. One of the names most often cited by MRA is that of the present President, Dr Nnamdi Azikiwe ('Zik'), who is reported to have said that MRA was 'the secret of independence for Nigeria'.

Another distinguished Briton, Sir James Robertson (whose name I can quote, since he has now retired from the Service), gives a rather less glowing account of MRA activities in Nigeria. He is in a position to do so, for he was Governor-General in the years immediately before Independence, from 1955 to 1960. He writes:

> MRA was very lavish with its invitations to film shows, parties and other gatherings, and if one accepted such an invitation out of mere politeness or interest in the film to

be shown, one ran the risk of being included among MRA's supporters. More than one of my African Ministers mentioned to me that they had had their names quoted as sponsors of an MRA function when they had never agreed to do so.

I presume that earlier Zik had perhaps shown some interest in MRA but had wearied of it, and certainly in my time in Nigeria he was not an active MRA fan.

I feel sure that, like all such movements, they do a lot of good, but their emotionalism, publicity, and what for want of a better word I might call 'snobbishness' rather put one off. They want to know the top people, to show that they are in with Government House etc. I know that they used to try to get hold of notepaper marked 'Government House' as a proof they were staying there!

It does not sound from this as if Buchman's influence really 'saved bloodshed . . . and hastened the day of peaceful self-government'. Perhaps it did so: a single punch on the nose causes bloodshed; it is worth dissuading even a few human beings from violence. But, in view of MRA's constant attempts to disguise its failures as successes, and to take credit for the results of others' efforts, it seems a pity that Buchman and his followers abandoned so soon the discipline that he imposed on himself after what may have been a disappointing visit to the Republican Party Convention in 1936: asked by the *New York Times* what he had accomplished there, he said that he had 'made it a rule not to evaluate results'.

We have no right to expect easy miracles—and those who profess to work them are deluding humanity and making just that much more difficult its slow, patient, uphill progress, and the hard thinking and hard work which are the real solvent of our ills.

16

PREOCCUPATION WITH VENUS

Peter Howard's 'Beast'—Mr Macmillan compared unfavourably with Mr Khrushchov —The BBC's 'flow of filth'—An MRA Assembly in London—Dr Claxton on the 'new morality'—Statistical uncertainty on VD

In the past year or so, especially since the Profumo affair, MRA advertisements have concentrated more intensively on sexual vice in high places. If the Buchmanites can fairly be said, on the evidence in the previous chapter, to fall rather too far short of Absolute Honesty, they may also be said to go too far towards Absolute Purity.

In *Britain and the Beast*, Peter Howard quotes from an article by the Archbishop of Canterbury: 'Today there is in our society an immense outbreak of preoccupation with Venus.' What Mr Howard fails to see is that MRA's tremendous emphasis on 'impurity' (with its relative disregard, noted in the Church Assembly report, of other, more subtle, possibly more serious sins) is itself part of the 'preoccupation with Venus' deplored by the Archbishop. In MRA this is not merely a preoccupation: it is an obsession. Mr Howard's own book, with its lurid anecdotes of wild parties, horrific warnings of international homosexual conspiracies, and slick, alliterative chapter-headings ('Sods and Squares', 'Queens and Queers', 'Bedding and Wedding'), might well be found in the windows of certain shops in Soho or Villiers Street: it was written, of course, with the highest intentions—but it is a truism that those sensational revelations by call-girls or aristocratic divorcees, published by some Sunday newspapers 'in the public interest', are often read for less exalted motives.

This topical theme has been appearing also in the once-cheery full-page advertisements. One of these (*Daily Express*, 31st July, 1963) solemnly rebuked the then Prime Minister, Mr Macmillan, for being less 'moral' than Mr Khrushchov! Mr K. dislikes non-figurative art and 'improper' dances and thus earns a pat on the back from MRA—a gesture which may have disturbed some of MRA's wealthier American supporters: it would not, I think, have been made in Dr Buchman's lifetime. But Mr Macmillan? Who would dare to smear that impeccable character? MRA has the evidence:

> Last month, as Chancellor of Oxford University, Mr Macmillan gave an honorary degree to the publisher praised by the Public Orator for his unswerving determination to make the story of *Lady Chatterley's Lover* available to the British people.

Another example of MRA's total lack of a sense of proportion is its attack on the BBC. The same advertisement says that 'a startling failure of Government and Opposition is their refusal to check the flow of filth from the BBC (and ITV) into British homes'; which 'is like the broken sewer of Zermatt that infected a community'. This, be it noted, is a straight demand for state censorship of broadcasting—censorship, in detail, of both television and sound programmes. Though people often complain of programmes that they dislike, and MPs sometimes ask the Postmaster-General to intervene, successive Governments have taken the view that this would be a retrograde and potentially dangerous step. It would certainly be a step more characteristic of a dictatorship than of a democracy: while shrilly disclaiming any such tendencies, MRA has always had its totalitarian affinities.

The intemperate violence of the language used here is also characteristic. Whether or not Mr Howard approved of this advertisement, he was himself, at about the same time, hurling the same cloacal metaphor at the BBC. In a speech at the MRA Assembly in London, in August, 1963, he said:

> From some programmes of the BBC a spiritual sewer flows out into the homes of the nation. . . . It is time that decent men and women resigned from the Governorships of the BBC in protest if this sort of diet of dung continues to be served to the people.

To the *Spectator* columnist, Strix, this 'inelegant tirade' seemed 'merely Goebbels-esque'. Mr Howard, stung (as always) by any mention of a Nazi leader, complained that Strix wanted to 'throw mud' at him (a sensitiveness curious in one who had been throwing not mud but dung); and insisted that he did not 'advocate censorship of radio and TV programmes, as Nazis did and Communists do'. He did not explain how action by 'Government and Opposition' to 'check' certain broadcast programmes, as demanded by the MRA advertisement, would differ from censorship; but, defending 'fuller liberty of public expression', he seemed to be saying, in effect, that this could be secured by diminishing liberty of public expression—or, as he put it, ending 'censorship' by 'faceless' men and women and others 'who hate traditional morality'. Strix retorted that while Mr Howard continued 'to use imagery on which Dr Goebbels, alone of the orators of our time, extensively relied', he had 'only himself to blame' if 'a stylistic affinity' were noted.

The *Daily Herald* columist, Henry Fielding, seeing that Mr Howard had also said that 'Parliament should deal with the corrupting influence of the BBC' (apparently in special reference to a single programme in which Dr Alex Comfort had been allowed to put a non-Christian view of sexual morality), analysed the programmes listed in that week's *Radio Times*. He 'reckoned up a total of eight hours twenty-two minutes devoted to the Christian case'. Despite such factual rebuttals, MRA's quaint misconception about the BBC persisted. Four months after Mr Howard's attack, on 7th-8th December, 1963, another MRA Assembly was held, this time in Sheffield. According to *The Times*, which did not mention any connection with MRA, this was called an Assembly for National Character; and Mr Roland Wilson, national secretary of MRA, took the opportunity of expanding considerably Mr Howard's strictures on 'some' programmes of the BBC. There was no qualifying 'some' in Mr Wilson's diatribe, as reported by the *Yorkshire Post*:

> It seems to me that the aim of the BBC is to foster and increase a taste for sex so that the more leisure people will have that is all they will want. If you soften the people of a nation limitlessly by feeding them with sex, you may so reduce their power to say 'no' that there are certain other things to which they will be unable to say 'no', such as dictatorship and tyranny.

This Sheffield Assembly was a week-end event. The London Assembly in August, 1963, had attracted more publicity, for two reasons: it lasted throughout the month and August is a time when papers are short of 'hard' news; and, since it gave a good airing to MRA's obsession with sex, it helped, in a traditional circulation-building way, to meet the needs of news-editors waiting for the Denning report and still greedy, in the post-Profumo and post-Argyll lull, for such titbits. These dedicated journalists were catered for handsomely by Dr Ernest Claxton, Assistant Secretary of the British Medical Association. He got into the news twice—once by reading to the assembled Buchmanites a paper on 'The New Morality and National Health', once by attacking Sir Edward Boyle, Minister of Education, for refusing to 'disown or deal with' his principal medical officer, Dr Peter Henderson, who had expressed a personal opinion on pre-marital intercourse by engaged couples at a meeting (which he had understood to be private) of teachers and other professional people.

The 'New Morality' paper is a remarkable document. Dr Claxton uses statistics and percentages in a loose and alarmist way: thus, while recording the admittedly serious increase in venereal disease among the young, he does not set the figures in proportion by giving the percentage of those infected *in relation to the total numbers in their age-group* (which would be, roughly, 0·18%) but prefers to give the more frightening percentage of 68. (This is the percentage *increase*, in 1957-61, in the number of patients aged 15-24 undergoing treatment for gonorrhoea: the actual increase, in figures, is from 7,315 in 1957 to 12,265 in 1961—bad, indeed . . . but the number of persons in that age-group, in 1961, was 6,802,000). From this increase Dr Claxton argues an increase in sexual promiscuity. There may be such an increase; but Dr Claxton does not compare the evidence of promiscuity today with such evidence as there is of promiscuity at various periods in history; and—strangely, in view of his medical knowledge—he does not mention other possible factors in the statistical increase, such as improvements in diagnosis, a greater readiness to come forward for treatment, and the growing resistance of these diseases to penicillin, treatment with which was dramatically successful fifteen or twenty years ago. This may be a factor because the figures are of patients undergoing treatment; because, due to the growing resistance to penicillin, treatment is apt to take longer; and the number of patients undergoing treatment at one time can, therefore, be larger. So the net increase—when population increase also is taken into account—may be considerably smaller than Dr Claxton suggests. A report on the venereal diseases issued on 16th December, 1963, by the Office of Health Economics (a body set up by the British pharmaceutical industry) associates the increase in these diseases with increased promiscuity, but states that, in 1962, the number of patients (of all ages) suffering from syphilis and seen for the first time at clinics—4,120—was 'less than half the pre-war figure'. Similarly, cases of gonorrhoea in 1962, while more numerous than in 1954, were still fewer than in the early 1930s.

Dr Claxton also says that an increase in convictions for homosexual offences is 'another pointer to the problem'. (He admits that these were fewer in 1961 than in 1954, though there were still more than in 1946.) He does not mention the highly relevant point that different chief constables and different police forces have different policies on these offences: at some times and places—e.g., in Manchester in 1963—the law is enforced with greater strictness, at others with less. On this matter, therefore, official statistics mean little.

Dr Claxton then broadly attacks the 'new morality':

> You can find this in the Cambridge school of theology, the Quaker report on sex, the Bishop of Woolwich's book, *Honest to God*, and in the so-called South Bank religion . . .

Having lumped together these often quite dissimilar elements, Dr Claxton proceeds, a few sentences later, to say of 'this new morality' that it—and presumably, therefore, the group of persons just listed—'in the name of compassion . . . condones adultery, fornication, and sodomy. . . . It certainly opens the door to even more widespread promiscuity.'

Set against this grave charge an actual passage from *Honest to God*, on the precise subject of extra-marital intercourse:

> To the young man asking in his relations with a girl, 'Why shouldn't I?' it is relatively easy to say 'Because it's wrong' or 'Because it's a sin'—and then to condemn him when he, or his whole generation, takes no notice. It makes much greater demands to ask, and to answer, the question 'Do you love her?' or '*How much* do you love her?', and then to help him to accept *for himself* the decision that, if he doesn't, or doesn't very deeply, then his action is immoral, or, if he does, then he will respect her far too much to use her or take liberties with her. Chastity is the expression of charity—of caring, enough. And this is the criterion for every form of behaviour, inside marriage or out of it, in sexual ethics or in any other field. For *nothing else* makes a thing right or wrong.
>
> This 'new morality' is, of course, none other than the old morality, just as the new commandment is the old, yet ever fresh, commandment of love. . . . Such an ethic cannot but rely, in deep humility, upon guiding rules, upon the

> cumulative experience of one's own and other people's obedience. It is this bank of experience which gives us our working rules of 'right' and 'wrong', and without them we could not but flounder. . . . But love is the end of law precisely because it *does* respect persons—the unique, individual person—unconditionally. 'The absoluteness of love is its power to go into the concrete situation, to discover what is demanded by the predicament of the concrete to which it turns.'

Here the Bishop of Woolwich is quoting from Paul Tillich's *Systematic Theology*. It might have been expected that a movement one of whose Four Absolutes is Absolute Love would have responded sympathetically to this insistence on the unconditional 'absoluteness of love'. Many churchmen do not agree with all that the Bishop of Woolwich has written (though some condemn without having actually read it); and it is arguable that the South Bank theologians overstress the tension which is bound to exist between love and law, and fail to see that the real antithesis is between love and legalism. But this quotation, in its depth of thought and tenderness, is enough to dispose of Dr Claxton's suggestion that the Bishop, with others, 'condones adultery, fornication and sodomy'.

An even more controversial passage in his paper is that in which he recommends chastity as a prophylactic against interracial unions:

> Chastity . . . removes fear of mixed liaisons, mixed marriages and of children of mixed blood that are becoming an increasing problem.

The *Tribune* columnist, Francis Flavius, drew attention to this statement, remarking: 'It seems that Dr Claxton implies that MRA also believes in *apartheid*. Can this be true?' I do not think that it is—but MRA has neither clarified nor repudiated Dr Claxton's statement, with its overtones of 'racial purity' and white supremacy.

Dr Claxton's second reported intervention at the MRA

Assembly was, in a way, even more serious; for on this occasion, condemning Dr Henderson and Sir Edward Boyle, he said:

> As a doctor and official of the BMA, I can tell you that extra- and pre-marital intercourse is medically dangerous, morally degrading and nationally destructive.

On moral degradation and national destruction, Dr Claxton has no more and no less right than any other citizen to express his views, and is perhaps rather less qualified to do so than a theologian, a historian or a sociologist. 'As a doctor', he should be qualified to speak on what is 'medically dangerous' (though many doctors would not agree with his views, and he is not in practice). But what right had he to say these things as an official of the BMA? And if the Council of the Association allows him to express his personal and controversial views on such a platform, why does he blame Sir Edward Boyle for extending a similar tolerance to Dr Henderson?

Despite its professions of Absolute Love, intolerance is one of the marks of MRA's collective character—no doubt for the psychological reasons indicated in the Church Assembly report. A minor example of this intolerance was in a letter to the *Daily Herald* signed by eleven trade unionists attending the MRA Assembly, who gave an address in New Road, Rotherhithe:

> . . . we are deeply incensed at the Voice of the Herald defending the right of Dr Henderson . . . to air opinions on morals offensive to the vast majority of trade unionists.

This letter was doubly intolerant: it denied Dr Henderson's right to 'air opinions' that the writers disagreed with; it denied an editor's freedom even to defend that right. It was also fantastically presumptuous in daring to speak for 'the vast majority of trade unionists'. The 'vast majority' *may* agree with the writers (or signatories) of the letter, but they can have no proof of this. It is much more likely that 'the vast majority of trade unionists' regard MRA with bored disapproval or active suspicion.

A letter to the *Herald* from James Hemming, of Teddington, put another view, in reply to an assertion by Dr Paul Campbell (who used to travel with Dr Buchman as his personal physician) that the *Herald* editorial supporting Boyle 'did a serious disservice to Britain':

> The claim that sexually repressed societies have more cultural energy than sexually uninhibited ones is just not true. Sexually robust Elizabethan England was highly creative. And in time of war, when the rigid rules of sexual deportment invariably slacken, cultural energy becomes intensified.

Be that as it might, MRA continued on its repressive, intolerant, censorious course, undeterred by sensible remarks by Archbishop Heenan[1] and others, always equating 'morality' almost exclusively with sexual morality, apparently abandoning Absolute Love altogether in the pursuit of the mirage of Absolute Purity. This was no new pursuit: throughout its history, Buchmanism has suffered from this obsession with sex (which seems, in MRA's catalogue of sins, to have replaced pride as the root of all evil). In an article in the *Guardian* of 22nd May, 1962, Mr Wayland Young (himself, it had better be said, happily married and the father of five children) commented on this 'deep preoccupation with sex, and especially masturbation'. Mr Young had been reading *Frank Buchman's Secret*, by Mr Howard, where he had come on such choice items as this:

> They tell you in some factories impurity is so common it is organised among the workers and especially among the subversive groups, who use it as a weapon.

He also put his finger on one of those all-too-common Buchmanite leaps in logic:

> There is a paragraph which at once roundly and insinuatingly—the combination *is* possible in MRA language—accuses all those who testified to the Wolfenden com-

[1] Who denied, on the eve of his enthronement in Westminster Cathedral, that the moral state of our society was worse than in the past.

mission in favour of a relaxation of the homosexuality laws of being homosexuals.

He added:

> Everything else in the MRA world is shifting, but the emphasis on sexual guilt is constant. Jesus is preached to Christians, avoided when dealing with non-Christians. Thus, though you must always change, it need not always be towards more or better Christianity, but it must always be towards greater sexual abstinence. . . .

Mr Young also wondered, as many others have, *why* 'a fair number of people are running around the world in favour of this nonexistent "ideology" and its illiterate and arrogant trimmings, and a few people are evidently paying them a great deal to enable them to do so'. He attempted to explain the phenomenon thus:

> This book suggests one possible answer; it is the curious relation of subserviency and dependence into which a sexual puritan falls towards the person to whom he has confessed his 'sins'. Buchman said: 'Verse I Chapter I of changing men is when somebody tells you something he has never told anyone else before about himself', and quoted a man who said to him: 'Buchman, I'd have cursed you tonight if you hadn't got at my real need.'

If Buchman did indeed get at this man's 'real need', this would seem to me to be to his credit; but I would agree with Mr Young, and with the Church Assembly report, that the consequent relationship of clinging dependency was less to his, and his movement's, credit. Baron von Hügel's aphorism[1] is much to the point here. This art of 'soul-surgery', as Buchman's admirers called it, is an art requiring tact and delicacy as well as skill; it may take a lifetime to learn it fully. In his earlier years Buchman may sometimes have attempted his spiritual probing rather too abruptly and clumsily. A Harvard

[1] See p. 209.

law-student, describing a 'house-party' in the *American* on 30th October, 1926, quoted a graduate who was also present as having said to him, of Buchman: 'He started asking me intimate questions about sex before I'd been alone with him for five minutes. I left in a hurry.'

The last paragraph of Mr Young's article sums up his reactions to MRA with a wit, both light-hearted and a trifle cruel, which may contain a grain of truth about some at least of the Buchmanites:

> It seems from this book that the main reason why some people are ready to go crusading against Communism in the name of no mistresses or masturbation is that they are mortally scared of mistresses and masturbation. If it were one single millionaire paying for MRA, the bash he is paying off must be about the most expensive anyone ever had. Even if it is a credible number of the guilt-ridden affluent, they are inflating the amortisation rate of pleasure fairly sharply.

Such ridicule is not altogether unfair: the Buchmanite pursuit of purity is sometimes carried to lengths which invite a gust of healthy laughter to blow away the cobwebs of fanatical puritanism. Some of MRA's most ardent supporters in Holland are members of the Philips family—owners of the famous electrical business whose headquarters are at Eindhoven. One of these is Mr Fritz Philips, who succeeded to the Presidency of the firm in 1961. He, or one of MRA's other supporters in the firm, was able, a few years ago, to register one triumph for Absolute Purity: the Philips radio advertisements, some of which had shown a girl with slightly too much cleavage leaning over a set, were de-sexed.

Equally absurd, and more unbalanced, were some of the phenomena noted at Caux by an enquiring American correspondent. At a session for Guidance and Sharing, he was startled and embarrassed by one contribution—from a man who said: 'Here's something I want to share. . . . This morning my wife tried to seduce me.' A youthful neophyte told him that he had had Guidance always to go to sleep with his hands outside the blankets. (This seems, incidentally, a testimony to the adequacy of the central heating at Caux.) He also met a family from California. At dinner one day one of their female MRA helpers was lecturing them on the wickedness of their state, and in particular of Hollywood. Turning to the son of the family, who had been mechanically answering 'Yes' (or, more probably, 'Mm') while munching his food, she said, with the utmost intensity: 'If you know about California, Peter, set it as your task *now* to *change California*.' Peter was four years old.

It may occur to some orthodox Christians that, since Christianity has always regarded chastity as a virtue, there can't be much wrong, from a Christian point of view, in this aspect of MRA. This, I think, is to misunderstand the MRA doctrine of Absolute Purity, and to underestimate its extravagance. Historic Christianity has recommended complete chastity, or celibacy, for a few—for monks and nuns and, in the Roman Catholic Church, for most of the clergy. For most of the laity, the vocation is normally to married life. Marriage, according to the Book of Common Prayer (as revised in 1928), is not only for 'the increase of mankind', though that is given as its first purpose. The priest's address to the congregation, at the beginning of the marriage service, continues:

> Secondly, It was ordained in order that the natural instincts and affections, implanted by God, should be hallowed and directed aright; that those who are called of God to this holy estate, should continue therein in pureness of living.
>
> Thirdly, It was ordained for the mutual society, help, and comfort, that the one ought to have of the other.

Though this is an extract from an Anglican formulary, I believe that it expresses principles accepted by the majority of Christians. But MRA's teaching, not only on chastity but on marriage itself, is quite different from this and, from a Christian point of view, eccentric. MRA professes to stick to 'the old morality'; but its attitude on these matters is nearer to that of those early heretics—the Manichees, for instance—who were condemned by the Church for teaching that the flesh was intrinsically evil and thus contradicting the basic Christian doctrine of the Incarnation. Manichaean deviations might be detected in the subconscious of many Buchmanites. The first Oxford convert, Mr Loudon Hamilton, has said of his 'strict Scots' upbringing: 'That didn't prevent me from committing sin. It only prevented me from enjoying it.' Of the numerous Buchmanite publications, the most authoritative handbook of MRA is *Remaking Men*, by Dr Paul Campbell and Peter Howard: it has been reprinted many times in ten languages, and is given or recommended to the newly Changed. *Remaking Men* has this startling and significant passage on sexual intercourse within marriage:

> Indulgence by the married, while having the cloak of legitimacy, may nevertheless be the source of irritable tempers and of inability to answer the real needs of the children. *Parents indulgent inside marriage need not be surprised if their children are indulgent outside marriage.* A union which could otherwise be powerful for remaking the nation thus remains a soft and uninspired association.

Mr Bamber Gascoigne, in the *Spectator* article already referred to,[1] comments thus:

> I took this amazing passage to be advocating sexual abstinence between married people except for the purposes of procreation, but when I asked an MRA worker about this he said that I must have misread it. I still cannot see that I did; but in any case a majority of readers would probably not ask; and some of them, in their new fervour, might actually accept the terrible advice which the passage certainly appears to offer.

It is clear—for the words italicised are, otherwise, meaningless—that Mr Gascoigne's interpretation of the passage is correct. I also asked a married man who had been in MRA for some years if this were not what the passage meant. He

[1] See p. 153.

confirmed that it was—adding 'We have intercourse when we are Guided to'. There was, too, a member of an MRA task-force in India who testified that he had 'conquered impurity' because he had not been to bed with his wife for a year.

Remaking Men is also a rich mine of the sort of extravagant nonsense of which I have already given some examples. The most purely comic pages are those which pretend to enable the inexperienced to identify at sight various kinds of 'defeated men'—i.e., people who haven't fallen for MRA. From the section headed 'Signs of the sexually-driven', the reader may learn how to recognise homosexuals, promiscuous heterosexual men, and sexually-driven women. Thus:

> There are many who wear suède shoes who are not homosexual, but in Europe and America the majority of homosexuals do. They favour green as a colour in clothes and decorations. Men are given to an excessive display and use of the handkerchief.

When I first read this, I recalled the array of suède shoes in the shops of that ardent Buchmanite, the late Mr Austin Reed, and wondered if even Dr Campbell and Mr Howard could mean this 'diagnosis' to be taken seriously. I am afraid they do. It is really most unfortunate, therefore, that the photograph selected for the wrapper of *Frank Buchman's Secret* shows a handkerchief protruding from Dr Buchman's breast-pocket with exceptional lavishness; and the same vain touch may be noted in many other photographs of him. What *are* the newly-Changed to think?

Next class:

> The heterosexual, promiscuous person ordinarily has an aggressive spirit, and not infrequently is possessed by a short volatile temper. The man who is unfaithful to his wife is apt to talk too much and maintains an unconvincing false buoyancy. A most reliable sign of sexual defeat is piosity. Men who are unctuous and unreal are licked by impurity.

Women adherents of MRA are usually Guided not to use any make-up at all. They had better not—for, says *Remaking Men*:

> A woman can be diagnosed by the way she uses her eyes, by her use of make-up and clothes. Lipstick and provocative dress reveal a dominating desire to be noticed and sought after. They are signals to the predatory male that any attention will be appreciated.

Among the 'sexually-driven' also lurk some rather less dangerous types than these. Even shy people 'are often living in defeat'; and shyness is said, unkindly, to be due to 'lack of conviction on issues of right and wrong'.

Mr Gascoigne was given an example of 'how accepting MRA would bring comfort to a man':

> A businessman . . . had for some time been sleeping with his daughters (yes, plural). Each time, after the event, he felt somehow 'tainted', but, after changing to a new life of the Four Absolutes, he felt himself a new person entirely. When I suggested that multiple incest was hardly the norm for a businessman, my informant's smile implied that my idea of the normal was remarkably innocent.
>
> This is partly the familiar Puritan conviction that the devil is never far off; and it is also, of course, in the interests of MRA to emphasise the viciousness of their members' lives before they changed.

MRA's real horror and fear of sex, even in its most harmless, normal, and universal manifestations, comes out in passages of which Mr Gascoigne observes that 'the mere idea of "flirtation" makes the authors wince': ordinary flirtation is condemned as 'lust' and (shockingly, it would seem) 'is seen at the party where the men gravitate towards the attractive girl'. If MRA people are denied even this elementary love-play, it is hard to guess how any of them ever manage to get engaged or married, except under the compulsion of the grimmest Guidance. Moreover, the strain of their abstinence must be considerable—one explanation, perhaps, of their puritanical intolerance of even the mildest indulgence by others.

Though MRA disapproves of marriage in its fullest consummation, it also disapproves of divorce, or at least of 'divorce by consent, whether legalised or wangled'; this was listed, together with 'pacifism, which seems to make war certain', 'pressmen who abuse their liberty by distorting or suppressing news of Moral Re-Armament', 'producers and critics who uplift grime as genius', and many other items that MRA is 'AGAINST', in a full-page advertisement in the *Daily Express* of 23rd April, 1963. There seems recently to have been something of a *rapprochement* between MRA and the *Express*. MRA advertises most frequently in the *Express*: the *Express* responds with editorial support. This is not a case of *post hoc, propter hoc*—of an advertiser's influence on editorial policy, such as Mr Austin Reed once, unwisely, tried to apply, on MRA's behalf, to the *Evening Standard*: from internal evidence—from, for instance, the enthusiastic support given by the *Express* to Mr Patrick Wolrige-Gordon, the young Conservative MP whose adherence to MRA led to trouble with his party in East Aberdeenshire—it is apparent that MRA has friends inside the *Express* office. Lord Beaverbrook himself, in the closing years of his life, may well have felt a renewed affection for his brilliant former employee, Peter Howard; and he, in turn, must long have recovered from any disappointment that he may have felt when Beaverbrook did not pick him as one of those to accompany him in 1940 to the Ministry for Aircraft Production—a disappointment soon followed by his conversion to Buchmanism.

Beaverbrook, however, always took what he believed to be the correct Presbyterian view of marriage and divorce—that marriage is a terminable contract, not a sacrament. By a happy chance, no Guidance contrary to this view seems to have come through lately, for, apart from the one instance quoted, the evil of divorce by consent has not been emphasised in recent MRA advertisements. One of these, incidentally—a fable roughly in the manner of Kipling (*Daily Express*, 1st January, 1963)—identified two of MRA's 'allies' in high places: these were Lord Beaverbrook and Lord Hailsham.[1]

A formidable onslaught on those who are said to reject 'traditional Christian values' in teaching about sex is in a booklet published by the Blandford Press in January, 1964—*The New Morality*, by Arnold Lunn and Garth Lean. Possibly because it is partly by Sir Arnold, who was in the early 1930s a skilful controversialist, this is better-balanced, better-argued and better-written than much MRA propaganda; and it has an occasional glimmer of humour. It avoids the excesses and absurdities of *Remaking Men*: these are as far from 'traditional Christian values' at one extreme as the views of Dr Alex Comfort, which are strongly attacked, are at the other.

One aspect of their booklet is so peculiar that it deserves special comment. Sir Arnold, as I have recorded, has defended MRA (without being himself fully committed to it). Mr Lean is one of the best-known members of MRA's 'hard core'. Their booklet overlaps at many points with current MRA propaganda. The 'traditional' clerics whom they quote include several—such as Mr Thornton-Duesbury and the late Canon Streeter—known for their staunch support of Buchmanism. Yet there is, in the 154 pages of the booklet, no mention of MRA, the Oxford Group, or Dr Buchman. The blurb gives their religious affiliations thus: 'Sir Arnold Lunn is a Catholic and Mr Lean is an Anglican.' Some reference to Mr Lean's attachment to MRA might surely have been of interest to potential readers. Indeed, Sir Arnold in his introduction goes out of his way to avoid mentioning Buchman. He writes:

> 'When I was young,' said that great Hellenist, Sir Richard Livingstone, to a friend of mine, 'there were still moral fences. . . . Since then, most of the fences have gone.'

The words 'a friend of mine' are not so informative as they might be. They conceal the identity of Dr Buchman. Connoisseurs of MRA full-page advertisements may recall that one of them opened with this quotation from Sir Richard Livingstone, and that in quoting it Buchman said plainly that the

[1] Now Mr Quintin Hogg.

words had been spoken to him. It seems ungrateful posthumously to deprive him of his credit.

The omission must be deliberate. The reason for it is a matter for speculation. Perhaps Sir Arnold did not want to be labelled too definitely as an MRA propagandist; or possibly he and Mr Lean both realise that the image of MRA is not universally attractive and that mention of it might set up a certain sales-resistance.

This may also be why MRA has often seemed coyly reluctant to take credit for activities which it certainly approves of and may have helped to promote, such as the plays at the Westminster Theatre. Except for a passing mention in a biographical sketch of Peter Howard, there is no reference to MRA in a lavish brochure, publicising this theatre. Mr Howard's play, *The Diplomats*, is described as 'hilarious and moving . . . shrewd . . . heart-warming.' The *Daily Telegraph* critic said: 'His characters are puppets, his dialogue . . . amateurish. . . . He can only hope to convince an audience of wishful-thinkers. That . . . is just the kind of audience he has got.' *The Times* said that, with two exceptions 'the playing outdoes the text in stilted mannerism'. The *Spectator* called it 'soft and mushy, intellectually non-existent'.

Alas for Absolute Honesty! The posters outside the theatre quoted only a few favourable words, from the *Daily Express*, the *Scotsman*, and a Pimlico paper.

Typical of the methods by which the Westminster audiences are packed is a letter received in March, 1964, by an Australian pressman in London. It was signed by Colonel the Hon C. M. Hore-Ruthven. It began: Dear Mr ——, Through my own stay of six years and through my brother, Lord Gowrie, who was Governor-General, I am privileged to have the most intimate links with Australia. . . .' Then followed an invitation to supper at 41 Charles St, to hear a talk on India and China, and to go on to a performance of *The Diplomats* ('penetrating and hilarious'). Again, no mention of MRA. The pressman replied thanking the Colonel and asking if the invitation were personal or was some organisation behind it? He heard no more.

Propaganda issued by the 'Women of Britain Clean-up TV Campaign' not only does not mention MRA: it states explicitly, 'We are not sponsored by any particular body. . . .' A Campaign meeting in Birmingham Town Hall on 5th May, 1964, was reported on the main news-page of *The Times*, whose Midland Correspondent apparently accepted the assurance that 2,000 women had been brought from all over Britain, to fill this large hall, without any substantial organisation or backing. This feat, which would seem almost miraculous to many organisers, was achieved, ostensibly without outside assistance (or so *The Times* suggested), by two women who claimed to have received 120,000 signatures in support of their campaign: this must have involved them in a deal of letter writing.

Since their demands are strikingly similar to MRA pronouncements on this subject, since a strong MRA 'presence' in the Birmingham audience was reported, and since at least one of the two is a known MRA activist, this exercise may be described as a triumph of dissociation.

Our last reflection on Absolute Purity may be that of one of the intellectuals of Buchmanism, Philip Leon, whose *Philosophy of Courage* appeared in 1939. In it he wrote that the subject of sex was 'a closed book to the mere psychologist', and 'opens itself gradually only to the surrendered man'—i.e., to the Changed. The surrendered man, he said,

> . . . learns that sex impurity goes far beyond the sex experience and can coexist not only with continence but also with total abstinence, that it can obsess most those who have the least desire or need for the physical experience, and that it can work in all sorts of sentimentalities and in peculiarities of the imagination, will and intellect which most people never dream of associating with sex.

Abstruse and mystifying as this must seem to many rank-and-file Buchmanites, it is in line with much that psychologists, both before and since 1939, have learned about human nature. But it is a hard saying for MRA to take.

17

PERSONAL ENCOUNTERS

The 'hard-core' Buchmanites, and those who leave—When Sam Shoemaker fell out with MRA—Beverley Nichols shocked—James Coltart's apologia—Trouble in Aberdeenshire—A tragic breakdown—A school taken over

PEOPLE WITH direct personal experience of MRA fall into several categories.

There are those who have become, and remain, unshakeably attached to the movement; and it must be conceded that some of the earliest pioneers—some of the 'inner ring' around Frank Buchman—have remained faithful through four decades of pretty tough controversy. They would themselves, no doubt, point to this fact as, in itself, proof of divine inspiration and Guidance: it does not really prove any such thing, since those driven by strong emotion to commit themselves totally to an idea—whether the idea is later seen to have been sound or wrong-headed—are apt to cling all the more tenaciously to it the more fiercely, or the more logically, it is attacked.

How many of these hard-core Buchmanites there are cannot readily be estimated. In 1961, in his *Observer* series, Mr Ivan Yates stated that MRA had 3,000 full-time workers throughout the world, 300 of them in Britain—all unpaid but living, comfortably enough, on Guided charity. Round these is a much larger floating population of the Changed, with a number of not totally committed 'fellow-travellers'. At their heart is the 'inner ring', such as those who form the Council of Management in Britain.

There is not much point in even guessing at the movement's total following, for here indeed it is at its most nebulous. Tens of thousands of enquirers must have been put off, or welcomed in, with the stock explanation that this is a 'way of life' without formal membership.

The second category of those with first-hand knowledge of the movement consists of people who have at some time been drawn into it and have then either gradually drifted out of it or been sharply disillusioned and broken with it. Again, obviously, there are no figures; but I have met so many people in this category—mostly middle-aged men and women who were young in the '30s and were involved in the Oxford Group—that I cannot resist the impression that the 'turnover', so to speak, is exceptionally high in MRA. We have all met lapsed Roman Catholics and people who were brought up as Anglicans or Methodists or Baptists but no longer attend any place of worship or practise their religion; but, bearing in mind what must be the relatively small total number of MRA's supporters, I doubt whether any other religious body in Britain suffers so drastic and steady a wastage of active members.

Among ex-Groupers, however, there are at least two kinds. Some, if they will speak of their experiences at all, do so with bitterness and even with horror; others, though they have 'outgrown' MRA and are in many respects critical of it, also say that they gained much good from it and feel that they cannot now publicly attack it.

There are plenty of the former kind—and one sometimes feels that their emotional reaction *against* Buchmanism is as unbalanced as their conversion to it must have been. However, what the more sensible of them record is of value as eyewitness evidence—such as the description of a Guidance session by Bishop Henson's informant quoted on pages 196-8 of this book.

Those who have fallen out with the movement, after years of intimate association, but are reluctant to state publicly their revised opinion of it, include a few Anglican clerics on both sides of the Atlantic. One such in America was the Revd Samuel Shoemaker (possibly the 'Sam' who led the Guidance session in Dr Henson's quotation).

For some years Mr Shoemaker was the most prominent of the American clergy and ministers identified with the Buchman Group. He was Rector of Calvary Church in New York, and his parochial mission house was used as MRA's national headquarters. As such, it was frequently the scene of characteristic Buchmanite gatherings. At one of these (described in the *New York Herald Tribune* of 26th February, 1933) there seems to have been what may be called an orgy of Sharing. A business man (whose name was printed) testified that the Group had helped him to get rid of 'impurity of thought and act, fear, a critical cast of mind, an inferiority complex'. A clergyman (whose name and parish were also printed) confessed that 'sins men don't boast of' had 'brought him near jail once and disgrace another time', but that he had been saved with the help of Mr Shoemaker and the Group.

Then, on 1st November, 1941, came a sudden and surprising break. Mr Shoemaker addressed to his parishioners a letter informing them that he was evicting the Buchmanites at once from their national headquarters. He wrote:

> Certain policies and points of view . . . have arisen in the development of MRA about which we have had increasing misgivings.
>
> With this in mind, and also because it has become increasingly difficult to function as a parish church when the facilities of Calvary House were largely taken up by its use as a national headquarters for Moral Re-Armament, it has seemed advisable to us, after careful thought and prayer, that this house should cease to be used in this way, as of this date.

This letter was signed by Mr Shoemaker and his assistant. They included in it an expression of 'deep gratitude to Dr Buchman' and a tribute to 'the spiritual truths enunciated by the Oxford Group'; but these hardly serve to conceal the mistrust and mounting irritation hinted at between the lines of the letter. (The Buchmanites, for their part, must have found the words 'after careful thought and prayer' particularly galling: Sam's Guidance can't have been properly cross-checked that time.) It is indeed clear that something had gone very wrong in the relations between Calvary Church and the Group: hearing a rumour of this breach when I was in New York some time later, I telephoned Mr Shoemaker to ask if Dr Buchman were still working with him. 'No, he is not,' he answered tersely, 'I had to ask him to leave'—a strong phrase to use of one to whom one has formally expressed 'deep gratitude'.

I did not speak to Mr Shoemaker again until 17th January, 1962, when I was again in New York and he—now retired—was on holiday in Arizona. He told me by telephone something of his considered views of the Group: he no longer spoke so sharply of it, and would not talk at length about the separation of twenty years before. Some day, he said, he hoped to 'evaluate the Group fully'. Meanwhile, his judgement, though an interim one, was fairly balanced. He spoke of 'the tremendous good we all found in it', but also of 'the thing that finally began to change in the movement'. He went on:

> If the Church had been willing to listen to the Group in its earlier and better days, and if the Group had been willing to listen to historic Christianity, things might have worked out differently. . . . I and many people owe it a great deal—it has vitally and radically transformed many people—but there comes a time when a man's soul is his own. . . .
>
> The Group has got to learn to say 'Yes, but . . .'; it has got to listen to the voice of other people. . . .

There is a whole series of contradictions and paradoxes here. This Group 'has vitally and radically transformed many people': yet it had to be expelled from the parish of the clergyman who says this of it; and in the same sentence he implies that it was so totalitarian in its ways that it allowed these 'transformed' people no independence of spirit, no freedom of conscience. Was Dr Buchman Dr Jekyll, and is there a Hyde lurking somewhere in a schizophrenic set-up? Are these vital and radical transformations valid and lasting—or is it a case of *corruptio optimi pessima*?

Unfortunately, Mr Shoemaker's full evaluation of the Group is unlikely to have been completed, and these problems, therefore, must remain obscure; he died in 1963.

A fairly close English parallel to the case of Mr Shoemaker is that of the Bishop of Derby, Dr Geoffrey Allen, whose ardent support of the Oxford Group has been noted.[1] When I asked the Bishop about his present attitude to MRA, he was good enough to write to me:

> I have had no active association with the Oxford Group or Moral Re-Armament for many years. I would still say that I learnt many things through my time with the Oxford Group in the early thirties; but I became dissatisfied with some of the later developments in the Oxford Group. My book *He that Cometh*, was written at the time of my association with the Oxford Group; but my later books, *Christ the Victorious* and *The Courage to be Real*, published a year or two later, marked my break as I was feeling my way more deeply through some of the issues raised at that time by the Oxford Group.

One prominent pre-war convert to the Oxford Group—Mr Beverley Nichols, the writer—found himself, as a result of his experiences with the Group, obliged to take a less favourable view. The story of his encounter with Buchmanism was told, in part, in his autobiographical essay, *All I Could Never Be*.[2] As he told it to me, more fully and more recently, I found it so revealing (though also so saddening) that I asked him to write it down for me—which he did, as follows:

> In order that there may be no misunderstanding, I

[1] See p. 202. [2] Jonathan Cape, 1949.

think I had best set down my impressions of the Oxford Group in the form of a letter, from which you could quote, either in part or in whole. And I should like to begin by observing that a large proportion of the rank and file of its followers are sincere, well-meaning people, whose adherence to the Group can do them no harm and may possibly do them quite a lot of good. I hope you will mention this opinion.

However, my own reactions to the Group and to its wider influences are somewhat more complicated. I cannot remember the precise date of my first contact with them; I am almost certain that it was in the year 1936. However, I do recall that it came about as the result of an extremely private conversation, in the course of which I poured out my heart to one of its members, whom I prefer to leave anonymous. Like many of us, I was in a pretty distracted state at the time, because of the increasing danger of war. This is not merely a personal meandering, it is apposite to the story. After all, I was the author of *Cry Havoc!*, which, as you may recall, was a passionate plea for unadulterated pacifism. I was prepared to go to any lengths to prevent war, even maybe to blind myself to the essential evil in the figure of Hitler. Anyway, as a result of this conversation I attended my first meeting, and was so deeply impressed that I wrote an article about it in the *Sunday Chronicle*. A long telegram from Frank Buchman, congratulating me, arrived on the following morning. Odd as it may seem, I had not run into him at the meeting; indeed, I only met him once in my life, when I found him strangely antipathetic. After that, for the next few weeks—or was it months?—members of the Group were constantly calling and ringing up and writing letters, and I am bound to admit that by and large they were kind and helpful. They were aware of the tensions through which I was passing, because, at my very first meeting, I had got up and confessed that part of my hatred of war was based on simple personal physical cowardice. It was not a very sensational confession, and I hope you know me well enough to realise that this was not the sole reason for my pacifism. But though these young men did their best, I was not greatly impressed by their mental calibre. One of them, I remember, was quite shocked when I suggested that it might be a good idea if there was some moral rearmament in the actual armament industry itself: in the vast firm of Schneider-Creuzot, in Krupp's, and, of course, in our own Vickers. In *Cry Havoc!* I had stressed the appalling fact that there were secret agreements between these great firms of which the ultimate outcome must be war. For the weapons of war were their trade. But no member of the Oxford Group, as far as I am aware, ever thought it worth while to call on the Merchants of Death, a phrase of my own which was later attached to a best-seller in America.

Somewhere around June, 1936, I was at the end of my tether, and I suddenly decided to motor up to Oxford to see if these kindly people could give me any personal assistance. And there I had a most bitter experience. For my original sponsor, assuming that I was now irrevocably 'one of them', blandly informed me that the first meeting which I had ever attended had been 'staged' entirely for my benefit. They had a shrewd idea of what was wrong with me, and how I could best be 'got at', and so all those first confessions had been rigged. In other words, they had put on an act for my especial benefit, hoping that I would give them good publicity, as of course I did. Perhaps there was nothing so reprehensible about this procedure, but the effect on myself at the time was devastating. It seemed to me to go completely counter to their first fundamental principle of Absolute Honesty. Feeling as I did, I decided to be absolutely honest myself, and I got up on to the platform in order to tell them how I felt about it. But I could not speak, and I left the platform with the tears streaming down my face. I left the hall by a side door, and went out to sit in my car. Nobody followed me. It was two o'clock in the afternoon, and I stayed in the car for about half an hour, trying to pull myself together. The next ten hours were a complete blank, but shortly after midnight my servant returned to my small house in Hampstead, to find me standing in the hall, staring at nothing and saying 'I can't stop crying.' . . .

This little episode marked the beginning of a total nervous breakdown.

Probably the most interesting aspect of my relationship with the Oxford Group—and certainly, to me, the most disturbing—was revealed in the early days of the war. Like most other writers of military age, I was not at all sure what I should be called upon to do, nor how I could best employ such talents as I had. And so, for the first few months or so, I carried on as before, writing my column, and feeling as miserable and thwarted as everybody else. Then I suddenly received a mysterious message from—I think—a branch of the War Office, asking me to go and see a certain Major X. I call him Major X for the simple reason that I cannot remember his name. And the reason I say that I *think* it was the War Office, or a branch of it, is because I am sure it was not the Ministry of Information and because I imagine that in every other department I should not have been dealing with an officer in uniform. The one thing of which I *am* sure is that the appointment was in the neighbourhood of Whitehall Court. . . .

The gist of the interview remains clearly with me. After cross-examining me on my relationship with the Oxford Group and after having assured himself that I no longer had any connection with it, Major X asked me if I would be prepared to go to America in order to start a counter-movement. The suggestion was so fantastic that at first I could not take it seriously. However, Major X persisted. He gave me to understand that Dr Buchman—whom he did *not* label as an 'enemy agent'—was nevertheless exerting an influence which was detrimental to our war effort.

At a distance of twenty years I cannot give you 'quotes'

of this conversation. Nor can I recall any suggestion that he [Buchman] was actually in contact with any prominent members of the German government. But I am quite emphatic in asserting that Major X told me that our own people were concerned enough about his activities to consider the possibility of counter-action. Which was why they had sent for me. Was it conceivable, he asked, that if I were sent to America, and given adequate funds, I might organise a sort of counter-group which would take the sting out of the Oxford Group? If I had been a different sort of person, or if I had thought that any such effort had the remotest chance of success, I might have said 'Yes'. Playing the role of an affluent evangelist in New York might have been very much more comfortable than writing a newspaper column in London during the blitz. However, the whole idea seemed to me totally impractical, and I declined the offer. And that was the last I heard of Major X.

Mr Nichols' recollection of his interview with 'Major X' is obviously genuine—the more obviously because he does not try to embellish it with direct 'quotes' that could not, after this lapse of time, be relied on. (This is apart from the fact that I know him as a truthful and candid person.) Some comment is, however, needed, if only in fairness to MRA.

As a result of Buchman's 'Hitler interview' and of known pre-war contacts between Oxford Groupers and leading Nazis, there was inevitably some doubt at the beginning of the war—especially in 1940—where the Group's real sympathies lay. The security and intelligence services, therefore, might have been failing in their duty if they had not included the Group or some of its adherents among their potential suspects. Moreover, there was conflicting evidence from America about the Group's activities there: I have written at length about the curious episode of the 'world broadcast' that Buchman tried to induce President Roosevelt to take part in, in December, 1939; on the other hand, some prominent Americans were found to testify to the patriotic worth of the Buchmanites' efforts. It was natural that some such project as that outlined to Mr Nichols should be mooted secretly in Whitehall.

The fact that the project was mooted does not, however, mean that it was a necessary or desirable project, or that official suspicions of the Buchmanites' *bona fides* were well-founded: the British secret services have not been shown on every occasion to be infallible. And whatever some of the leaders had been up to before the war, it was certainly true by now, as we have seen, that large numbers of rank-and-file Groupers or ex-Groupers were serving loyally in the armed forces. I therefore conclude that Mr Nichols' recollection is correct; that 'Major X' was only doing his job; but that, interesting and significant as this incident is, for the light that it throws on some official reactions to Buchman, it cannot be taken as conclusive proof that he was, during the war, actively hostile to the Allied cause.

A more stalwart and, at the present time, more influential friend of MRA is Mr James Milne Coltart, sixty-year-old right-hand-man to the redoubtable Lord Thomson and managing director of his chain of newspapers, which include the *Sunday Times*, the *Scotsman*, and a number of important provincial newspapers. Mr Coltart is also a director of firms with press and television interests in Africa, and was from 1957 to 1961 managing director of Scottish Television, a commercial programme-company which forms part of the Independent Television Authority's network. (On being awarded this concession, Lord Thomson[1] made his often-quoted observation that it was 'a licence to print money'.)

Mr Coltart has been known for some years as an MRA supporter. It was naturally thought, by critics and, no doubt, by some supporters of MRA, that he would use his powerful position in the press and television to promote the interests of a movement which demands, after all, total commitment to its ideals. Many people (including myself) assumed that he would not hesitate, if Guided to do so, to interfere with what would be regarded on most serious newspapers as the normal

[1] Then, and until 1964, Mr Roy Thomson.

discretion of the editorial and advertising staff. There seemed, indeed, no other interpretation of a speech made by him at Caux on 17th April, 1960, as reported in the *Scotsman* (and therefore, it may be supposed, accurately):

> Mr Coltart pledged himself to re-orientate the thinking of Great Britain and to root out evil ruthlessly in every quarter. He said that he had determined to reach every member of the Cabinet, every trade unionist, the directors of television, radio and the press in his country.
>
> Mr Coltart . . . told how last October he had received a full-page advertisement from East Germany undermining the forthcoming visit of Chancellor Adenauer to Great Britain.
>
> 'I could not stand for it', Mr Coltart said. 'I went to the Foreign Office. I went to the editors of the largest newspapers in Britain. They unanimously agreed not to run the advertisement. I believe all of us must take up the task to outmatch Krushchev regardless of profits or prestige.'

Quite apart from his full-time work for Lord Thomson, Mr Coltart seemed here to be taking on a second full-time job, if he was really going to 'reach' all the people he was 'determined' to reach, including 'every trade unionist' (all nine million of them). But it says much for his energy and persuasiveness that he was able to induce a number of editors to depart from the accepted newspaper practice of not imposing political censorship on advertisements.

At that time it was not known whether Lord Thomson shared Mr Coltart's view that MRA must be campaigned for 'regardless of profits'; this did not seem to be entirely in harmony with Lord Thomson's general approach to newspaper publishing. In television interviews since then, however, Lord Thomson has expressed reasonable satisfaction with this aspect of his publishing business.

In one such interview—in the BBC programme *Tonight*, on 11th February, 1963—Lord Thomson was quite explicit on the subject. He said:

> Our papers are not at all inclined towards Moral Re-Armament. *One* of our executives had some association with them. He had—he doesn't now. It never affected our business in any way.

Since Lord Thomson stressed the word 'one', and since Mr Coltart is his principal executive, this remark was generally taken to refer to him. If this assumption was correct, Lord Thomson was announcing a breach between Mr Coltart and MRA. As I had heard rumours to the same effect from other sources, I thought it best to check the facts with Mr Coltart himself. I had once met him briefly at Geneva airport, when he was on his way to Caux and I on mine to Lausanne; we were introduced by Peter Howard, who was meeting him off the 'plane from London. Circumstances prevented our meeting again, but I wrote to Mr Coltart, asking him a number of questions—among them, whether it was true that he was no longer closely attached to MRA; what his 'principal function' in the movement was or had been (I had heard that he had provided useful contacts with various influential people); whether he still thought wise his action in preventing the publication of advertisements critical of Dr Adenauer; to what extent he had 'thought it right to encourage Thomson newspapers, Scottish Television etc to publicise MRA values and activities'; and whether, in his opinion, Buchman's talents had included the ability to delegate responsibility.

I also said that if he wanted to make 'a balanced statement, expressing both praise and criticism', I would include it in full in this book. Despite the immense pressure of his work, Mr Coltart was courteous enough to reply to me at length. I found this reply of great interest. It contains no word of criticism of MRA; and it is evident that, if Mr Thomson was referring to Mr Coltart in his *Tonight* interview, he was wrong in thinking that he no longer had any association with the movement (even though Mr Coltart does indicate that he gives a certain priority to his business affairs). At least, it does not seem from Mr Coltart's letter that he broke off this association temporarily at about the time of the television interview. Although this letter is not, therefore, the 'balanced statement' that I undertook to print in full, it seems right that I should fulfil this undertaking. The letter reads:

Office of the Managing Director

THOMSON HOUSE,
200 GRAY'S INN ROAD,
LONDON, WC1.

Wednesday, 11th September, '63.

Dear Tom,

Thank you for your note. Unfortunately I am fixed to go to Africa for the week commencing 22nd September, but we could meet sometime after your return. I wasn't thinking that we would confine our whole conversation to MRA, as there must be many other things we have to chat about.

Yes, as you say, I have noticed that you have been fairly persistently critical of the Movement, and while it never distressed me, it sometimes puzzled me.

I have known MRA for many years, and during that time have had very close association with Frank Buchman and his associates. My loyalty to him and to them has never wavered because I was only too conscious that they lived a quality of life which was deeply sacrificial, and while I have a certain personal faith, I could never see myself giving up the adventure of industry and giving my whole time so selflessly. To be factual, I should add that I was never asked: I think the truth is that I simply love being in this business of publishing and printing, and to this must be added a strong touch of materialism which I must have got from my Scottish forefathers.

As to my involvement in MRA, naturally this has varied from time to time, and since taking over the running of this expanding business of Thomsons, and all its divisions, I think it is fair to say that I have not been so available.

You ask—what attracted me to it. I had to reflect on

this for a moment, then I remembered saying to my late wife about 1938 when we were agnostics, yet seeking some kind of faith: 'This Oxford Group Movement seems interesting, although I don't agree with all I hear about it, but let's go and see the men around Frank Buchman who are carrying the load.' We did, and although for many weeks we indulged in much critical and rather scathing argument with them, I realised that these men were neither pious or pompous, but they had qualities that I lacked. Thereafter I moved closer. Don't think that I was down the drain, or distressed either by women or men—far from it. I was just restless to do something. For two years I had been working with my brother-in-law with the ILP in Glasgow, very much inspired by Jimmy Maxton, John Wheatley and David Kirkwood, who were always seeking to do something to improve mankind's lot.

So far as function is concerned, I don't think I've ever had a function. It is true that I have met many dignitaries in many countries, but I've also met many working men—you obviously just meet many people who are interested in the progress of the movement. I have had conversations on MRA with men like Adenauer, Kishi, Makarios etc, but also with Johnnie Byrne, ETU, John Boyd of the AEU, etc, and even with Tom Driberg at Geneva! I am afraid the latter was not very much impressed. I don't quite see the point of your question, because you must realise that in my everyday life I speak to men like Julius Nyerere, Jomo Kenyatta, Bustamante, Eric Williams, Diefenbaker etc, also Willis, Bradley and Briginshaw.

I don't think anyone ever got the full story about the advertisement which was offered to a few newspapers, prior to Adenauer's visit. I would hardly trust my own memory at this date, but I know the original approach regarding the attitude in dishing out this type of advertisement was made by another newspaper to me, but I never was the initiator of the action. I agreed and encouraged the decision of the publishers involved, including ourselves.

It would be impossible to answer the second part of your question,[1] because like circumstances could never recur. Time changes climates and attitudes, but if there is anything I can ever do to strengthen the unity in Europe, I hope I have the courage to do it.

Never have I used my influence to insist that Thomson Newspapers and Scottish Television publicise MRA. In the first place the ITA would never allow any MRA publicity on any station, but Editors and Producers are at liberty to assess News Value of any MRA activity, and publish as they think fit. I think many of my colleagues in MRA must feel disappointed and may be surprised that the *Scotsman* has given less than average space to MRA over the years, and I know of no instance where MRA has been mentioned in Scottish Television over many years. If my memory serves me well, this doesn't reflect an article once written by your goodself.

Now to your next question about Frank Buchman during the closing years of his life. During all the years I have known him, I considered that one of his great strengths was his ability to delegate. You must have realised through the years that he was fairly constantly in the background and always building the team around him. He was seldom on a platform, and only once a year did he make a regular statement to the public, usually on his birthday. I don't think he delegated to any particular person or persons, but to many men and women from many countries. Certainly not to me, as I only saw him about twice a year. No, Tom, whatever your book may say or whatever your personal impressions may be, of the activities of MRA, make no mistake—this was a truly great man. In every sense he was a man of God, a man of great humility and the evidence of this to me was the quality of the people around him. Most of them whom I knew in 1938 were working with him when he died. You seldom see this kind of dedication these days.

[1] 'On reflection, do you still consider that this action was correct?'

The last question[1] is not difficult to answer, but it would take a long time and a lot of space. My impressions have never varied, and I still believe that MRA is a sound ideology. It gives men faith and it gives men purpose. It aims at the acceptance of the beliefs in which you and I believe or should believe. Its acceptance as a world ideology could change the character of nations, but this is a mighty task, and it is around the development of the strategy to accomplish this that much criticism will arise. Apart from anything else, it sets up the task of keeping informed and inspired hundreds of thousands of people across the world. There is also the task of developing and using vast manpower in all fields. Much that I have done must seem a bit balmy to others, but the same can apply to my business. I have made mistakes, but most times I have tried to correct them.

People talk about where the money comes from, but if they are in doubt they can see the audited accounts. I was always more interested in how it was spent, and this to me was effective. People have talked a lot of baloney about them being pacifists, but they could not refer to one conscientious objector. I know of none. But of course MRA endeavoured to get deferment for a small nucleus of administrators. I think it was 12, and much was made of this. And all this tosh about Hitler, which is brought from the grave several times a year, 25 years after it was supposed to have been said. If there was some real criticism of some real weakness, the faithful band of critics would quickly put Hitler in his grave and get on to current affairs.

I think I am a fairly critical type, but I always get a little suspicious of my validity when I keep repeating old chestnuts.

Tom, you have asked my frank opinion. Well it is this. MRA as an ideology is soundly based, and if lived it will be effective. I can never be sufficiently grateful for the way

[1] 'In general, can you sum up your impressions of MRA (*pro* and *con*)?'

it has helped me to face daily issues which were always a problem with me. But it is a world family of many kinds of people who may interpret differently the part they should play. Mistakes will be made, mistakes in strategy and tactics, but they will be quickly exposed and corrected.

Now may I be frank with you, because I am sure you would expect no less from me. When I said earlier on that your constant criticism didn't disturb me, what did concern me was that a man like yourself would persist in criticism year after year, yet after twenty years you had not to my knowledge been able to discover and expose any real weakness in the beliefs of MRA. I know the repeated stories about Hess and Hitler. I have even seen the little bit of extra colour that is added to them as the years go by. I have heard of people who didn't like some of their moments with MRA, and all I can say is that I felt many of them very uncomfortable myself; but I know of men and so do you, who didn't feel comfortable with John Wesley or Martin Luther, men who attributed to them all kinds of statements and behaviour. They know the truth now.

I hope to heaven that this doesn't sound like preaching. I don't mean it to be.

All I ask is that you have a good look at the men at the centre, and at the life they live.

Personal greetings,

Yours sincerely,

James M. Coltart.

In printing the text of this letter, I have corrected only a few minor slips of spelling and punctuation. There are several comments to be made on its content:

Mr Coltart says that he 'was never asked' to give his 'whole time' to MRA—i.e., to become one of the full-time MRA workers. It seems probable that, rightly or wrongly, the MRA leaders were Guided to think that he would be much more useful to them where he was.

It is just possible that Lord Thomson's statement in the

Tonight interview is consistent with the fourth paragraph of Mr Coltart's letter.

Mr Coltart refers to my 'conversation' with him at Geneva. This rather dignifies a superficial chat that lasted, perhaps, two or three minutes. He was kind enough to ask me to lunch with him in London (an invitation which, through the fault of neither of us, did not lead to a further meeting). I am sorry that he thought that I was 'not very much impressed'. This must have been my natural shyness! Actually, I found him most likeable.

I accept, of course, Mr Coltart's assurance that he has never used his influence 'to insist that Thomson newspapers and Scottish Television publicise MRA'. In any newspaper office, however, the views of the men at the top—in this case, Coltart as well as Thomson—are known; and it is only natural that, with some exceptions, news-editors and sub-editors should take account of their views when selecting material for publication. I am sure that Mr Coltart did not ask that his speech at Caux, for instance, should be reported in the *Scotsman*; but an intuition that publication of the report would not displease him may have been one factor—together with an objective estimate of its news-value—in the decision to publish it.

Probably Mr Coltart was writing away from his *Scotsman* files. When he says that this paper 'has given less than average space to MRA over the years', it is not clear whether he means an average of the space given to MRA in the press generally, or an average of the space given by the *Scotsman* to comparable religious or political movements. It would be shocking indeed if the *Scotsman* had actually been discriminating unfairly against MRA: had it been, I almost feel that Mr Coltart might have done something, gently, about it. I do not think that he need worry, however; I have a sheaf of *Scotsman* cuttings about MRA, some of which do not seem to me to have a very high news-value. (One boosts rapturously an MRA musical which other Scottish critics found 'trite', 'boring', and 'embarrassing'.) As for STV, of which Mr Coltart says 'I know of no instance where MRA has been mentioned . . . over many years': I am afraid that his memory does *not* serve him well. To give one instance: on 25th April, 1960, the TV column in the Glasgow *Evening Times* contained this item:

> And at 10.30 STV's John Watson has a half-hour interview about Moral Re-Armament with Roger Hicks. This is the second time in a few weeks that the MRA ideology has been discussed on Scottish Television and I must say I felt it had been adequately covered in the *Here and Now* spot.

I have heard a recording of the interview with Roger Hicks referred to here. It seemed to me that Mr Watson (who had been invited to Caux before the broadcast) was putting the least awkward questions in the mildest way: they were what may be called 'feed' questions. The interview ended with an invitation to Mr Hicks to recommend one book on MRA to enquirers. 'The standard work', he said, 'is the collected speeches of Dr Frank Buchman.' 'I must read that,' said the interviewer, meekly.

The 'audited accounts' of the company registered in London do not, of course, indicate the total wealth of the movement throughout the world; nor do they show the source of the donations, large or small.

I can well understand MRA's impatience with 'all this tosh about Hitler'; I have dealt with this argument in Chapter 4; I do not think that this matter is irrelevant to an assessment of the movement as a whole. As for 'old chestnuts', almost every MRA book repeats, *ad nauseam*, the same anecdotes from Buchman's early years; and it may be agreed that this book deals with 'current affairs' also. Elsewhere in it I have examined the logical flaw in the comparison with Wesley and Luther.[1]

These qualifying comments do not diminish my gratitude to Mr Coltart for taking the trouble, in his busy life, to write me so long a letter—and a letter so obviously and so movingly sincere. His tributes to Frank Buchman personally and MRA in general must be weighed fairly against the criticisms that I and others have made. I have never denied that MRA has

[1] See pp. 177-8.

done some good to some individuals, of varying ages, backgrounds and temperaments: it is evident that Mr Coltart is one of these. Since he challenges me personally, I can only say that I am not; but I do not doubt for a moment that the 'quality of life' of many in MRA is far higher than my own (though an equally high quality of life may be found in many others to whom MRA is repugnant). This need not, surely, inhibit me from the critical attention that Mr Coltart rightly invites to the *beliefs* (or the 'strategy and tactics') of MRA; and it is these that I have been analysing and illustrating in the preceding chapters.

Another Scottish supporter of MRA is Mr Patrick Wolrige-Gordon, MP for East Aberdeenshire. Compared with Mr Coltart (or with his predecessor in East Aberdeenshire, now Lord Boothby), he is a lightweight; and he cannot be said to have made a deep impression on Parliament, though he is well-liked by those who know him and plays a good game of cricket (always an asset in British politics). His ardent and open support of MRA led to a serious dispute in his constituency Conservative Association: the chairman of the Association and the Conservative agent were both among those opposed to their MP; and both ultimately felt obliged to resign their offices when it became clear that a majority of the Association were prepared to support him.

So far as a long and complicated quarrel of this kind can be disentangled from outside, there were two main reasons for this opposition: it was alleged that Mr Wolrige-Gordon had devoted too much time to MRA and, consequently, insufficient time to his parliamentary duties; and it was felt that he was too apt to 'plug' his MRA views in the constituency on all sorts of occasions, however unsuitable (for instance, at a Burns Night dinner at which he was reported to have suggested—courageously enough!—how much more valuable and wholesome Burns's poems would have been if he had not lived before the age of Buchman).

As for Mr Wolrige-Gordon's industry as an MP, this, judged

by his division record and by the Hansard index (which are not the only tests), has fluctuated. When he was first elected, in November, 1958, he had the newcomer's ardour: between then and 31st March, 1959, he missed only eight out of 68 divisions. Then his zeal waned or he had important outside duties: in the next few months he missed 46 out of 98.

After another poorish patch in 1961—which perhaps led to his showdown with his Association—he was much more assiduous in his attendance (as he would have to be, having become a Parliamentary Private Secretary); and asked a good many questions of interest to his constituents. It was reported that, as part of the agreement that he had reached with his local Association, he had moved out of MRA's 'VIP hostel' in Mayfair, where he had been living when in London.

This fairly straightforward dispute was confused by two issues which should never have arisen between an MP and his constituents but were played up sensationally in the popular press, especially the *Scottish Daily Express*. Mr Wolrige-Gordon married Mr Peter Howard's daughter, who was, like her father, a supporter of MRA; and the *Express* and other agencies favourable to Mr Wolrige-Gordon were able to picture the dispute as a dramatic duel between a romantic young hero and a clique of crusty bigots trying to prevent him from exercising his undoubted right to marry whom he pleased ('the girl I love', as he called her, almost in Duke of Windsor vein). It was suggested, further, that he was being persecuted for his religious convictions; and Mr Wolrige-Gordon, pursuing this useful side-track, hinted solemnly that similar persecution might befall some MP who happened to be an Episcopalian or a Jew.

No question of religious freedom really arose at all. For one thing, as we have seen and as its adherents are careful to emphasise in other contexts, MRA is now much less a religion, in the ordinary sense of the word, than an ideology. In any case, if an Episcopalian or, say, a Roman Catholic MP suddenly had a vocation to the monastic life, joined a religious community and absented himself from Parliament, without resigning his seat, his constituents would be entitled to call him to order, without being accused of religious intolerance.

This distortion of the basic issues, leading as it did to Mr Wolrige-Gordon's victory, may have been largely due to defective public relations on the part of his opponents (these Highland lairds having probably never heard of this alien magic) and skilled public relations on his own side. Mr Wolrige-Gordon had not been a particularly articulate MP. It was surprising to read his eloquent handouts, couched in prose almost as muscular as that of his father-in-law—from whom, perhaps, he had a few tips (in addition, of course, to Guidance).

Only one conventional ornament seemed for a time to be lacking: a touch of magnanimity in victory. Not much Absolute Love could be discerned in this MP's references to some of his constituents as 'limpets' and 'negative elements' (a curiously Stalinist-sounding phrase).

Lord Boothby did not allow himself to be drawn too closely into this dispute in his old constituency; but it saddened him, and he made it clear privately, and on at least one occasion publicly, that he regretted Mr Wolrige-Gordon's infatuation with MRA and the dissension it had caused. He had himself suffered a good deal from the earnest importunities of his youthful successor—who on one occasion startled him by announcing that he had a message for him, embodying some of Dr Buchman's own Guidance, to the effect that he, Boothby, had a great part to play in the future leadership of MRA.

Some idea of Mr Wolrige-Gordon's intellectual stature may be derived from a series of three articles which he wrote for the *Aberdeen Press and Journal* (by a coincidence, one of the newspapers of which Mr Coltart is managing director). In these articles he explains 'how the ideological battle is being fought' by the Communists. 'In one vast college in Czechoslovakia, 36,500 agents are trained every year, particularly Asians and Africans.' (Vast, indeed!) Khrushchov 'has been known to say [when and to whom?] that the Bolshoi Ballet is worth more to him than two divisions . . .'. The Communists win men's minds more subtly than the West does: 'in Asia everyone knows about the rape of Tibet. The country has been

FRANK BUCHMAN IN OLD AGE

desecrated, the men have been transported or castrated' (an ingenious new way of winning minds). The trouble at Little Rock was caused by 'over a hundred Communist agents, white and black', who got there just before it started (or so a friend of Mr Wolrige-Gordon's was told by Governor Faubus, himself cited, rather surprisingly, as having been changed by MRA, together with a leading coloured woman—'and that solved the problem for Little Rock'). As for Britain: 'one man in every four approximately . . . is reckoned [by whom?] to be homosexual', and 'when you find the national church of a country prepared to countenance homosexuality if it is done privately, you find the final hope of moral leadership dissipated'.

I do not know whether to describe this stuff as ingenuous or disingenuous. It is at about the propaganda level of *Ideology and Co-existence*, or even *The Pentagon Case*; Mr Wolrige-Gordon cannot have acquired all the material for these articles by the light of nature or of Guidance. He must have had sources. Someone presumably did the necessary research—not, I fear, too accurately. In the hope that he might throw some light on the provenance of his articles, I wrote to Mr Wolrige-Gordon asking, politely, if he would let me know the evidence for some of his assertions—particularly for his statement that a 'national church' (of England or of Scotland?) was 'prepared to countenance homosexuality if it is done privately'. The *gauche* phrase 'done privately' suggests that by 'homosexuality' Mr Wolrige-Gordon meant 'male homosexual intercourse'. Leading dignitaries of the Church of England had taken the view that, although such intercourse was certainly a sin, it was not best dealt with by penal action by the State. They therefore supported the Wolfenden proposal on the subject. If Mr Wolrige-Gordon could see no difference between this attitude and the positive encouragement of vice implied in his words, he was not fit to write what purported to be a serious article on the moral state of the nation. He was, in any case—as even he might have realised, or could have ascertained—bearing grievously false witness against a church and its ministers, many of them at least as God-fearing and clean-living as himself.

I did not, of course, include all this argument, which might have been too elaborate for him, in my letter to Mr Wolrige-Gordon: it was a simple request for information and evidence. Unfortunately, he never replied to it; and when I saw him a few weeks later and asked—in the friendly way customary between MPs even if they differ profoundly in their views—when I might expect an answer, he merely smiled weakly and 'passed by on the other side' (of the lobby).

Not all personal encounters with MRA are so happy throughout their whole course as Mr Wolrige-Gordon's has been so far and, I trust (since he seems the ideal MRA subject), always will be. One distressing case of mental disturbance attributable—in part, at least—to Buchmanism is that of a young man whom I will call W. He was a twenty-five-year-old librarian when he first wrote to me on 24th July, 1960. His letter was literate, neatly typed, and apparently rational, and it contained enough about his family and background to show that he was a phenomenon that I had not encountered before—a second-generation Buchmanite.

If all that W. wrote was true, it was clear that he had been right inside MRA, at the highest level. Relatives of his had responsible jobs at MRA headquarters, he himself had lived for a time at the 'VIP hostel' in Mayfair and had toured Britain and the world in MRA campaigns.

During one of the assemblies at Caux, a job was arranged for him at a public library in Ohio. Since that was ostensibly the main purpose of his going to America, his fare was paid by the civic authority employing him—but he understood well enough that, once there, he was to devote all his spare time to MRA. On his way to Ohio he spent ten days at Mackinac, where he took part in the making of *The Crowning Experience*. No doubt the pressure was too intense. In Ohio he had a breakdown and tried to commit suicide; after a recovery that can only have been partial, he returned to England.

When he wrote to me, it was nine days since W. had broken with a movement that he had, in effect, been in all his life; and he was still living with two Buchmanite aunts (and therefore asked me not to send my reply in a House of Commons envelope). Whatever his state of mind, I thought that I had better see him.

He came to the House of Commons one afternoon, and we talked for an hour or more. He spoke collectedly, but his face was pale and tense. He attributed his breakdown in America to the relentless pressure put upon him, day after day, to get up at MRA meetings and give false testimony—to say, for instance, that he had been sacked from a job through Communist influence because he was a Christian; a statement which was, he said, quite untrue. It was difficult to know what to make of all this: one must exercise some reserve in these cases, but he spoke with such assurance—and such obviously detailed knowledge of the whole MRA set-up—that I could not disbelieve all that he said. Possibly it was a mixture of fact and fantasy.

A day or two later he wrote again, enclosing an interesting note on the row that there had been with Mr Adam Black, publisher of *Who's Who*, when Dr Buchman's falsification of his *Who's Who* entry was exposed,[1] and saying that he had been invited to Aston Bury, 'an important MRA centre near Stevenage'.

The next letter I had from W. was a short one—and the address on it was that of a mental hospital. Soon after that, his father came to see me—primarily to collect some private letters which W. had sent me. Naturally I gave them to him: I had no right to keep them. I did not, however, feel obliged to let him have a tape-recording which W. had also sent me, having made it specially for my information (stealthily, he said, at night when his aunts were asleep). It is a macabre, disjointed, often rather sordid account of what goes on inside a Kafkaesque semi-religious oligarchy—some of it corresponding, no doubt, to the facts of life in MRA, some of it merely trivial gossip, some perhaps the imaginings of a disordered personality. I could not possibly rely on it for unchallengeably authentic data, any more than I could accept without question

[1] See pp. 50-4.

W.'s account of his experiences in Ohio. Yet I know that it was not all false—for one surprising personal reason.

W. had included in this recording a full report of the 'briefing' about myself (as an old 'enemy' of the Group) allegedly given to enquirers at Hays Mews. Now there was one detail in this that startled me, for it concerned an incident that I had long forgotten, an incident in which my own brother had been involved. The account of the incident was much distorted, but there was just enough truth in it to make it quite certain that something of the kind was being said at Hays Mews; for W. could not have known about it otherwise, and he could not have made it up or imagined it.

One of the most disconcerting personal encounters with MRA was that experienced collectively, within the last few years, by the staff and pupils of a grammar school in south-west England attended by some 420 boys and girls. I refrain from naming the school, and the persons involved, only because I am reliably informed that after much painful controversy, publicised in the local press, 'things have now settled down' and 'only the school would suffer if old troubles were to be stirred into life again'. Nevertheless, the campaign which caused these 'troubles' deserves to be recorded as an example of MRA in action. The school will be identified by many people in its neighbourhood; and I would provide data for those with a serious reason for verifying the facts.

It was in the summer of 1959 that the Headmaster of this grammar school first became actively interested in MRA. He and his wife (a part-time piano teacher), went to Caux during that summer holiday, taking with them a senior member of the staff; and two teachers (of mathematics and English) went to MRA headquarters in London. All five adults, when they returned, were committed Buchmanite converts.

Early in the autumn term the Headmaster called a full staff meeting, which was also attended by the whole of the Upper VIth form. The Headmaster proclaimed the Four Absolutes, and announced that, from then on, the school was to be run with 'moral training' as the first priority. He read from a typescript: there was no discussion, and comments by the staff were not invited. The staff were then dismissed, but the pupils in the Upper VIth were kept back for a further meeting; later the staff learned (not from him) that the Headmaster had discussed with the pupils certain disciplinary weaknesses of some of the staff.

A few days later the Headmaster called another staff meeting. Here, in the traditional Buchmanite manner, he confessed at some length his own shortcomings as a man and as a teacher. The English Teacher did the same. The rest of the staff sat silent and embarrassed.

Shortly after this the Headmaster sent for the Head of the Languages Department and informed her that the part-time teacher of Russian could no longer be employed, as Russian was being dropped from the curriculum.

A few days later the Mathematics Teacher and the English Teacher (two MRA converts) almost simultaneously approached the girls' Physical Education Teacher and invited her and her husband (not a member of the staff) to supper at their homes. As she had never before received such an invitation from them, she accepted on behalf of her husband and herself—stipulating, however, that they were not prepared to discuss MRA. The invitations were dropped and not renewed. Instead, the English Teacher sought more directly to interest the Girls' PE Teacher in MRA, telling her that the converts had come back from Caux and Berkeley Square with a plan, and that the two PE Teachers—the Boys' and the Girls'—were their 'first targets': they had been selected for this honour because all the pupils passed through their hands and, by the nature of their jobs, their influence was considerable. Once they were Changed, the Changing of the senior boys and girls would be easier.

At the end of the previous term—before the visit to Caux—the Headmaster, in consultation with the staff, had picked the Head Boy, the Head Girl, their deputies, and the prefects for the new school year. Now, without consultation with most of the staff, he decided that the post of Deputy Head Boy should be filled by a different boy from the one already chosen. Certain members of the staff protested, unavailingly. Later they were to be confirmed in their judgement: the new Deputy Head Boy—though his initial interest in MRA did coincide, for a time, with an improvement in his appearance and attitude to work—proved unsatisfactory.

Throughout the years that followed, an intensive drive to popularise MRA persisted. It must not be supposed that the Headmaster and his MRA colleagues neglected their ordinary duties: no doubt they carried them out as keenly as ever, though always with the new emphasis in their approach that they had derived from MRA. Thus, much of the Headmaster's time was spent in correspondence and telephone calls concerned with MRA rather than exclusively with the school, and in interviewing senior pupils in an effort to interest them in the new ideology. As he explained when questioned about this, he saw the development of character, especially among senior pupils, as his primary obligation: he clearly held this view with passionate sincerity, and it is a tenable view—though many who might share it would deplore the insistence on MRA as the principal means of character-development.

Many examples could be quoted to show how completely the Headmaster's mind was filled with MRA's special doctrines. He began, for instance, to collect newspaper cuttings that seemed to support his contention that 'morals' (i.e., sexual morals) were deteriorating, especially among the young. Once he showed a non-MRA teacher a Sunday newspaper article describing an experiment at a secondary modern school whose senior girls were being instructed in the art of make-up. The teacher's reaction, being one of qualified approval, earned her a tedious lecture and the loan of a sheaf of cuttings relating to sexual misdemeanours.

In the summer of 1960—the school's first MRA summer—a new rule was made, in order to promote Absolute Purity: boys and girls were not to stand or sit in mixed groups on the school fields; mixed groups must keep moving. One unwanted, but not unnatural, reaction to this unbalanced puritanism was an outbreak of deliberate and ostentatious flirting among some of the less impressionable senior boys and girls. Some time later, Vth form girls were forbidden to wear nylons. This time protests came from parents. The Headmaster made a concession: nylons could be worn if they were thick enough to 'veil the flesh'.

The more tractable pupils were invited to free showings of MRA films. The case for MRA was put to them on every possible occasion (including one speech day, when the guest of honour was a leading MRA spokesman). Each December, as in many schools, a play was produced for public performance. In 1960 the English Teacher chose the MRA play, *The Forgotten Factor*, for that year's production. One by one, members of the cast asked to be released—no easy gesture, for it involved an uncomfortable interview with the English Teacher. In the end he had to choose another play.

Most embarrassing of all, however, seem to have been the interviews with the Headmaster himself. A member of the staff who was considered a desirable convert found at one time that she was being waylaid by him almost daily—so frequently that she devised routes on which she would be unlikely to meet him. Then he would send for her—sometimes while she was taking a class, once when she was invigilating an examination. On each occasion there was a school matter to be discussed; but the conversation invariably came round to MRA. Some of those who were exposed to these interviews say that the Headmaster's attitude and demeanour during them were variable. Generally he was full of sympathy, understanding and patience, but sometimes he became angry and aggressive—and this was, on the whole, a rather less agreeable mood to encounter, since it was usually followed by abject penitence and overflowing pleas for forgiveness, far harder to take than the outbursts of wrath. Some of the staff wondered whether the interviews with senior pupils followed similar patterns, and, if so, what the psychological effect on sensitive adolescents would be.

Equally distasteful were the Headmaster's attempts to persuade members of the staff to report to him on the attitude and conduct of their colleagues. He seemed to be obsessed by the notion that some of them were 'disloyal' to him—finding grounds for this fear in scraps of unguarded staff-room gossip about MRA that had come to his ears. Naturally, there was much of this: during these years, MRA had become a central topic of divisive argument in what had hitherto been a singularly happy and united group of people. Children, too, were encouraged to report on each other and on the staff.

Year after year the tension became more acute. Inevitably, the incessant concentration on MRA provoked discord and resistance among staff, parents, and pupils alike—especially when it became apparent that those pupils who succumbed to the propaganda were, on the whole, more likely to become prefects than those who resisted. There is no doubt that the Headmaster did not deliberately exercise favouritism, or promote those totally unworthy of promotion: equally, it is obvious that, in such a situation, boys and girls who were acquiescent and responsive—i.e., 'loyal'—would seem more promising candidates for leadership than those who were obstinately rebellious.

Matters seem to have come to a head in the winter of 1961-62. There was a controversy in the local press, reflecting the deep anxiety of parents and local clergymen. By seven votes to three, with five abstentions, the Borough Council passed a resolution requesting the Headmaster to place less emphasis on MRA. Serious concern was felt by some of the school governors and the Local Education Authority; and HM Inspector of Schools became aware of a potentially dangerous situation. Eventually the Governors and the Authority took action. While recognising that the Headmaster had many good qualities and had, in various ways, served the school well, they made it clear to him that the incessant 'plugging' of MRA must stop. Early in 1964 it became known that he was retiring from the teaching service at the end of the summer term. In fact, he resigned his post some months earlier, after an incident which attracted unpleasant publicity. Press reports stated that two senior girls had been flirting with senior boys on the school premises and the Headmaster had punished them, in the presence of the Senior Mistress, by 'spanking' their 'bare bottoms'. He was charged with assault: on 2nd July, 1964, he pleaded guilty and was fined £50.

There have been other MRA essays in academic infiltration. Ever since the first days of the Oxford Group, the Buchmanites have concentrated on the universities. In recent years there has also been evidence of considerable activity among boys and girls still at school. In February, 1961, there was controversy in the correspondence columns of the *Guardian* about a sharp whiff of MRA propaganda to which senior pupils at the Howardian High School for Boys, Pen-y-Lan, Cardiff, had been exposed. One of the MRA agents who visited the school, Mr H. S. Addison, of Penarth, wrote to say that they had gone there 'at the invitation of the headmaster, who himself introduced his guests and was present throughout the brief talks that were given'—adding: 'To judge by the applause with which they were greeted, the boys responded to them warmly.' Thereupon, 'Five Sixth-Formers'—whose names the *Guardian*, with altruistic prudence, withheld—retorted:

> ... Many of the sixth-formers feel that this type of political indoctrination is totally undesirable, especially in schools. Would similar Communist propaganda visits be viewed in the same light and be welcomed in the same way?
>
> Mr H. S. Addison, in his letter, states that we were encouraged to chant 'Men must choose to be governed by God or they condemn themselves to be ruled by tyrants'; this we agree was correct, but combined with all the speeches it was obviously intended to mean, 'Men must choose between MRA and Communism'. . . . Surely Mr Addison also noted that a high percentage of sixth-formers remained mute when called upon to chant William Penn's famous phrase? The applause at the end was merely a formality which is observed on all occasions when visitors address the pupils. . . .

Another letter, published on the same day as Mr Addison's,

was also from the head of a Welsh school—Miss Constance Smith, Headmistress of Penrhos College, Colwyn Bay. She stated that the Headmaster of the Howardian High School had not himself been connected with MRA; but she expressed her own point of view thus:

> I feel profoundly thankful for Moral Re-Armament which by its insistence on absolute moral standards is making us look at the alternatives—a new moral climate or collapse. And from the former who would wish to exclude the schools?

Clearly the doctrines of MRA would not be excluded from Penrhos College. Nor, we can assume, would they be excluded from another reputable seat of learning—the Royal Grammar School at Guildford; for on 7th December, 1963, the Headmaster of this school, Mr Michael Hallowes, spoke at the 'Assembly for National Character' already referred to. Here he permitted himself invective of a kind not often heard in public from responsible teachers, and treated the Assembly to a gripping, if bizarre, account of the awful consequences of a hypothetical triumph of the 'new morality'—or, as he called it, 'Baalism':

> If it succeeds in taking root, homosexual practices will be accepted as normal and a state of moral anarchy will develop which will be succeeded by a dictatorship in which the people who engineered the moral collapse will take over positions of power.

Many other examples of MRA activity in schools could be quoted; but I know of no 'take-over bid' for a whole school so thorough and so persistent as the one I have described in detail. The Headmaster was a prominent speaker at the MRA Assembly in London in August, 1963. It must be hoped that, wherever he may in future be propagating his beliefs, he will learn to encourage that freedom of choice and of thought which is a prerequisite of spiritual growth.

18

BUT WHAT *ARE* THEY REALLY AFTER?

WHEN ALL the facts, speculations, and arguments about MRA have been considered, a certain element of mystery remains. This factor is sometimes defined, crudely enough, in the question most often asked by sceptical outsiders (or next most often, perhaps, after 'Where does all the money come from?'). This question is: 'What are they really *after*?'

It is not a question that can, ultimately, be answered with certainty. It is not even a very thoughtful question—though the answer to it would be important if one could be sure of it. For MRA, despite its public manifestations, is at its highest level a semi-secret society; and, even if the processes by which its leadership is evolved were less obscure than they are, no one, in or out of MRA, could analyse with confidence all the motives which impel the leaders—or, for that matter, the rank-and-file—to adhere to such a movement. Nor is it any fairer to generalise about all Buchmanites than to generalise about Jews or policemen or teenagers or any other minority group (though Buchmanites themselves are by no means free from this failing). What are the members of any unconventional religious, social, or political movement 'after'? What are Mormons after? What are Freemasons after?

MRA itself states its main objective clearly enough: to change the world, to establish 'God-control' everywhere. The fallacy in this notion has already been examined; but the objective sounds impressive. Every such organisation, of course, has a grand aim, a super-programme to which its policies are geared. But human motives are rarely pure, and the tendency to rationalise is incurable: it seems safe to risk one general statement—that, as in politics, as in much of academic and ecclesiastical life, the motives of many Buchmanites are a mixture of zeal for a cause and personal ambition.

'Personal ambition'? We shall at once be told of the immense sacrifices that so many of them have made—giving all their time and money to the movement, maintained only by the Guided charity of sympathisers, ready at a moment's notice to go with a task-force to India or Brazil, living by the Four Absolutes. . . . Yes, but they *like* doing it; they *believe* in it; they have achieved the emotional satisfaction and fulfilment that come from complete surrender of self to a movement with total claims—this satisfaction and fulfilment, enjoyable as they are for the individuals concerned, providing neither proof nor disproof of the validity of those claims. The satisfaction, incidentally, shows: converts—especially recent converts—to any such movement are often 'nicer' than they were before; and they glow with a special radiance.

'Personal ambition'? Serious political movements are concerned with power, its transfer and its use. Occasionally one meets a politician of whom it can be said that he is completely selfless. Most politicians would admit to a mixture of motives and would hope, in their moments of self-examination, that they can gradually learn to think less of self and more of the cause which—quite sincerely—they are trying to serve. Similarly, MRA, at least since its transformation from Christian evangelistic mission into global ideology, is, frankly, concerned with power: spiritual power, yes—to some temperaments, the most thrilling kind of power—but temporal power also; for God-control of the world means control by God's instruments, his Changed and Guided men. It can be an intoxicating vision; and it would be surprising if MRA's leaders were so superhuman, so immune from the common frailty of our race, that they could always resist indulging in the Utopian dream of a world run from Caux and Mackinac and Odawara and Berkeley Square. Others may find the vision less entrancing.

That this is not too fanciful or unjust a suggestion is shown by many of their public announcements—some of which have been quoted in this book—and in particular by the public pomp and circumstance of the closing years of Frank Buchman's life. As I have already noted, every order and decoration that he received had to be proclaimed with the most fulsome deference; his last 'birthday speech' (published as the advertisement headed 'BRAVE MEN CHOOSE') was said to have 'reached by press and radio an estimated thousand million people'—a slight stretching of Absolute Honesty, since this must have been an approximate totting-up of the entire readership of the newspapers in which the advertisement appeared and the maximum *potential* audiences for the stations that transmitted the broadcast. He even once, coolly, offered his teaching as 'a programme upon which there can be ecumenical . . . reunion of all Christians'. Always there was, and is, this sweeping exaggeration, this preoccupation with quantity; with its kindred besetting fault of over-simplification of infinitely complex problems.

Although MRA has helped people temporarily or permanently, even after they have left the movement, I would guess, so far as one has any right to judge, that the harm done by the movement has outweighed the good. In particular, while claiming to be a movement dedicated to revolutionary change, it seems to me to be, in essence, counter-revolutionary—a philosophy not of change but of no real change, at any rate in the economic basis of Western society. Hence its sometimes rabid anti-Communism (modified slightly, in recent advertising, to an ideology that can 'overarch' Communism and anti-Communism alike).

The change in the movement's character and 'image', which is one of the main points emphasised in this book, was clearly illustrated on a solemn occasion—the funeral of the founder, on 18th August, 1961, at St John's Lutheran Church, Allentown (where Frank Buchman had been ordained nearly sixty years before). To this small Pennsylvania town flew hundreds of Buchmanite 'notables' from all over the world. Certain tensions arose before the funeral. When the MRA leaders arrived in Allentown, they seem to have expected that the conduct of the funeral would be left entirely to them. The pastor of the church, the Revd Arnold F. Keller, firmly explained that this was a Christian church and that he would be responsible for conducting a Christian funeral service.

A compromise was reached, and the service began with tributes by supporters of MRA, of many races and creeds, compèred by an 'educator' from Richmond, Virginia. Princess Adalbert of Prussia said: 'He is now in heaven looking on all of us as his children.' Rajmohan Gandhi quoted his grandfather, the Mahatma, as having said that MRA was 'the greatest thing to come from the West to the East'—no doubt an authentic testimonial, but not to be found in any of the many biographies of Gandhi, and collections of his sayings, that I have consulted; indeed, none of these mentions Dr Buchman, who often claimed to have been a close friend of Gandhi's. The young Gandhi also said: 'Frank Buchman has given us the one and only answer to Communism, corruption and war.' General Ho Ying-chin, formerly (for a couple of months in 1949) Prime Minister of China, said, through an interpreter: 'If we had had Moral Re-Armament, we would not have lost the Chinese mainland to the Communists.' Nahashon Ngare, described as 'a former Mau-Mau leader', who, according to local press reports, 'wore an animal skin robe over his western suit', testified: 'Moral Re-Armament is not a question of personal conduct.' This was a surprising statement: unless Mr Ngare was misheard and misreported, he must have misunderstood everything that he had been told. He added, however: 'But it is a matter of survival in Africa'—not, apparently, explaining whose survival, in what circumstances, he had in mind.

Another speaker was Colonel Alan Knight, who had commanded the Kenya camp in which Mr Ngare had been detained for four years. If, as is claimed, MRA has brought about genuine reconciliation and mutual respect between these two men and others who were on opposite sides during the Mau-Mau conflict, this is an achievement, at the personal level, that is greatly to MRA's credit.

So the tributes went on—a representative from Iran, the French Deputy Mme Irène Laure[1] ('In uniting France and Germany, Frank Buchman gave backbone to Europe'), a Brazilian General, an American naval officer ('Frank Buchman was an all-out personality who took God seriously') . . . and then, last of all, Peter Howard. Mr Howard quoted a message from Buchman's physician, Dr Paul Campbell, which restated the familiar theocratic doctrine: 'Men and women who now will fight his fight with God's strategy will see a world run by men governed by God.' Mr Howard concluded: '. . . Shoulder to shoulder with him, we take up the task. We will begin our service.'

At once—slightly, but significantly, modifying the close of this peroration—Mr Keller, the pastor, announced: 'We will now begin the service.' The local newspaper, the *Morning Call*, reported:

> The liturgical service and Rev Keller's sermon were in sharp contrast to the previous ceremony. The first dealt almost exclusively with the achievements of Dr Buchman and MRA. The Lutheran service was devoted to the meaning of death and salvation to the Christian.

During this latter part of the ceremony, scripture lessons were read by Bishop Bengt Johnzon, of the Lutheran Church of Sweden, Anglican Bishop Charles West (formerly of Rangoon), and Archbishop Andrey, Metropolitan of the Bulgarian Orthodox Church—i.e., of that part of it established among immigrant Bulgars in the United States, where it is one of about twenty Eastern Orthodox bodies. (Altogether, the Orthodox churches have about $2\frac{3}{4}$ million members in the United States; in 1961, Archbishop Andrey claimed 25,000 of these and had ten churches in his jurisdiction.)

[1] See pp. 122-5.

Some 1,200 people packed the church for the funeral. The *Morning Call* report observed that, as they poured out after the service, 'it was almost impossible to find someone smoking', and that 'if there were a person or two around smoking a cigarette, he was a curiosity-seeker, not an MRA follower'.

Among the mourners were the Revd J. P. Thornton-Duesbery, Chief Walking Buffalo, and Joel McCrea, with other Hollywood actors. (After the service Mr McCrea 'paused from autographing a shower of papers and cards to call Dr Buchman "a great American patriot" . . .') A number of Lutheran ministers were present, 'but no official representative of the Synod'.

The MRA leaders and old friends of Frank Buchman who had acted as pall-bearers[1] also lined the graveside in Fairview Cemetery. Mr Keller conducted the committal. The casket was 'a simple Black Forest pine box . . . of European style', with a pyramidal top. There was a profuse array of flowers, including a large wreath sent on behalf of Dr Adenauer. Muriel Smith, the coloured actress who had starred in *The Crowning Experience*, sang a solo; and the ceremony ended with the singing of the Hallelujah Chorus by an international MRA choir.

For some days, naturally, the local press was full of funeral news and obituary tributes. Many of the visitors stayed on and toured the countryside, calling at places associated with Buchman—the white farmhouse in which his father was born, the graves of his mother's ancestors, the house in Allentown which, like all his modest estate, he had left to 'the Oxford Group, Moral Re-Armament, MRA, Inc, a New York corporation'. According to the local press, 'a caravan of four buses and about twenty-five automobiles made the tour a genuinely impressive pilgrimage'. Among the pious tributes, however,

[1] Michael Barrett (Scotland), General Hugo Bethlem (Brazil), Attorney Nimson Eckert (Allentown), Barclay Farr (West Orange, New Jersey), Rajmohan Gandhi (India), Loudon Hamilton (Scotland), Willard Hunter (California), Archie Mackenzie (Foreign Office, London), James McLaughry (New Wilmington, Pennsylvania), Takasumi Mitsui (Japan), Nahashon Ngare (Kenya), and Kenaston Twitchell (Princeton, New Jersey).

there was a more disobliging comment by no less a person than the President of the United Lutheran Church in America, Dr Franklin Clark Fry, who criticised the movement as 'not Christ-centred' and said of Buchman that his connection with the United Lutheran Church had been 'only nominal'. By accident, this comment was printed in a local paper in black type, as if it were specially important. Despite the many pages of entirely favourable comment, this one slip earned the paper a cold rebuke from an MRA tycoon.

Memorial services were held at Mount Kisco, New York; at Lima, Peru; at Gelsenkirchen, in Germany (where those present included the West German Minister of Labour and 'a group of forty-three Chinese from Caux'); in the Westminster Theatre, London; and no doubt in many other centres of MRA activity.

MRA Information Service for 28th August, 1961, was mainly an obituary issue. Messages from many parts of the world were headlined 'TWENTY CHIEFS OF STATE PAY TRIBUTE'. Some of these personages were correctly so described—for instance, 'His Imperial Majesty the Shahenshah of Iran' (who headed the list), President Tubman of Liberia, and (technically, at least) Generalissimo Chiang Kai-shek, still officially, to the United Nations as to MRA, 'President of the Republic of China'. The status of others, such as 'Their Majesties King Michael and Queen Anne of Rumania' (second in the list), seemed more questionable; and there were a good many 'former' and lesser dignitaries, among them Saburo Chiba, 'Chairman of the Japanese Government Party Security Committee' (who, despite the onerous duties of this post, wrote that he would give the rest of his life to making MRA 'the policy of all nations'), and Chao Sopsaisana, Foreign Secretary of Laos.

It may well be that Frank Buchman was mourned most sincerely among the anti-Communist puppet rulers of South-East Asia, so many of whom had been honoured with his friendship and had honoured him, in turn, with their orders and decorations. One of the most eloquent of these tributes (sent 'with deep emotion') came from one who is, unfortunately, no longer in a position to promote the cause of MRA—Ngo Dinh Diem, President of Viet-Nam and brother-in-law of the celebrated Madame Nhu.

Diem died violently, by suicide or assassination, on the 1st or the 2nd November, 1963, a military coup having brought his rule to an end. This was the last act in an extraordinary and gruesome drama. Not surprisingly, the United States—as the *New York Times* noted—had made 'studied attempts to dissociate itself from the Diem régime's repressive policies'; for these policies included religious persecution so savage that—to the shocked horror of the world—a number of Buddhist monks had been driven, in desperation, publicly to burn themselves to death. Madame Nhu made jokes, in almost incredibly poor taste, about 'barbecued monks', and raged at American perfidy. Diem and his family were Roman Catholics: the Vatican's disapproval of their cruelty and intolerance was made public.

As for MRA, so much admired by Diem: Frank Buchman had enjoyed good relations with many Buddhist monks; but if his followers ever uttered a word of criticism of Diem's tyranny, they did so with unwonted unobtrusiveness.

What will happen to MRA, now that Frank Buchman is dead? Will it follow the pattern that sociologists discern in the evolution of most movements of this kind—that is, with the removal of the charismatic leader, will the organisation men take over and the process of sectarian crystallisation be intensified? It is not for us to probe these mysteries—but we are entitled, since MRA makes such comprehensive claims, to continue to watch its development with care and to hope that it will fail in its apparent main task of perpetuating the Cold War and the tragic division of mankind. For—to sum up the main criticisms—MRA is irrational in its mystique and authoritarian in its methods; it rejects free discussion; it practises with insufficient discrimination the dangerous, and often deadly, doctrine that the end justifies the means; and, by seeming to proclaim the possibility of instant perfection, it raises hopes that cannot be fulfilled. In short, it is essentially non-Christian and anti-democratic.

Finally, however—since I dislike writing only in negative and polemical terms—I must add this, especially to those who are Christians. Every heresy magnifies, often disproportionately, some aspect of Christian belief which Christians have neglected: Christian Science arose because the Church had largely forgotten its healing vocation, Spiritualism because many Protestants had, for centuries, ceased to be aware of the Communion of Saints and to remember in prayer their dead.

It is the primary job of the Church to help in the creation of the Kingdom of God—the just society—here on earth. I am afraid that Frank Buchman had only faint intimations of this duty. Despite his evident powers of mass-hypnosis, he was in some ways essentially in the nineteenth-century individualist tradition. But MRA is there, and it may be largely our fault that it is there, because we have undervalued the Christian teachings that it has diluted or exaggerated—teachings about the reality of guidance and the necessity of repentance in fellowship; and it is at least partly our fault that so many of our churches and our democratic political parties have failed to offer a sufficiently dynamic leadership, especially to the young. So, just as Communism is seen as a challenge and, by sensible Christians, as a true judgement on the evils of Western society, MRA may be taken as a challenge to our minds and hearts and a judgement on our imperfections and vices. We can learn something from the ardent self-dedication of the best of those who accept MRA, just as we can learn from the icy self-dedication of convinced Communists; for, though I believe that our reasonableness, our sense of proportion, our realism, and our refusal to see everything in simple black-and-white are good, the defect of these liberal virtues is a certain lukewarmness, a hesitation to be committed, and an emotional rather than an intellectual laziness. If, then, we can learn from them, perhaps it is not too arrogant to wish that they in turn might, now and then, feel disposed to learn something from us.

INDEX